Venial Sins:
An Autobiography

By
Thomas J. DuVall

ISBN: 0615844588

ISBN 13: 9780615844589

SkyStar Press

To my mother, CONSTANCE LUMPKINS,

and

my grandmother, JENNIE BUCHANAN.

Acknowledgments

I would like to thank the following:

Hortense (Bunnie), my loving wife and talented copy editor of my book, who is my best friend: you are solely responsible for my being alive to tell this true story, and we've shown how love and marriage can conquer all evil;

Nubia DuVall Wilson, my gifted writer-daughter, who contributed her editing skills;

Michael Babatunde Olatunji, the Nigerian drummer, who inspired me;

Artist catalysts Rudy Irvin, Theo Gleaves, and Gabriel Majorga; and

Former Maryland Governor William Donald Schaefer, whose awarding of the State of Maryland Governor's Citation has been the driving force behind my artistic endeavors.

Contents

Part I   **1**
Chapter 1: Thunder and Lightning   1
Chapter 2: Life with the Catholics   9
Chapter 3: Summer Vacation   27
Chapter 4: Second Grade   33
Chapter 5: Summer Vacation (1939)   45
Chapter 6: He Made Me Hate My Name or
        Thomas, the Cat Killer   49
Chapter 7: Third Grade   53
Chapter 8: The Spelling Bee   65
Chapter 9: The Booker T. Washington Banner   75
Chapter 10: The Meatloaf Sandwich   83
Chapter 11: My Setback   89
Chapter 12: Five Pennies   95
Chapter 13: Keep That Hat On   97
Chapter 14: The Cardboard Boxes   101
Chapter 15: Fourth Grade   107
Chapter 16: Officer Cowan's Boxing Team   119
Chapter 17: Purple and Yellow and Cowboys and Indians   125
Chapter 18: Horse Racing and the Haunted House   131
Chapter 19: Fifth Grade   139
Chapter 20: The Monument Grounds' Big Art Show
        and Contest   155
Chapter 21: The Hustling Blues   159
Chapter 22: Sixth Grade   173
Chapter 23: The Summer of 1947: The New Neighborhood   199
Chapter 24: The Piper Cub Contest and Other Fun and Games   221
Chapter 25: St. Cyprians: 1947 to 1948   229
Chapter 26: The Winter Overnight Hike   241
Chapter 27: Life after the Hike   257
Chapter 28: Back on the Block   271

Part II   **277**
Chapter 1: Got t' Git a Job   277
Chapter 2: The Red Ball (Circa Summer 1950)   281
Chapter 3: Headed for Jump School   287
Chapter 4: Jump School   291
Chapter 5: The Boxing Team   305
Chapter 6: Driving While Black (1951)   309
Chapter 7: Willie B. (Circa 1951)   315
Chapter 8: The "General-Purpose" Bag   321
Chapter 9: Nicodemus, the Black Paratrooper (1950 to 1952)   325
Chapter 10: The Black Paratrooper   329
Chapter 11: The Second Year with the
            Eighty-Second (Early 1952)   337
Chapter 12: Integration in the Ranks (Mid-1952)   341
Chapter 13: Having Fun on Route 301
            (Circa Late Summer 1952)   343
Chapter 14: From Being Ski Trooper to Being Discharged
            (Circa 1952 to 1953)   345
Chapter 15: Back on the Block and Hangin' Out
            (May 9, 1953)   351

Part III   **357**
Chapter 1: The Office Boy (Circa 1955 to 1956)   357
Chapter 2: The Guadalupean   363
Chapter 3: Michael Babatunde Olatunji   367
Chapter 4: My First Art Job   379
Chapter 5: Purple and Yellow: Phase 2   383
Chapter 6: Art on the Move in Harlem
            (Circa 1957 to 1959)   387
Chapter 7: The Black Art Movement in Harlem   393
Chapter 8: The Winter of 1964 and the Weusi Artists   397
Chapter 9: Cooperate or Perish   407
Chapter 10: The River Niger   411
Chapter 11: The Lingua Franca   413

Chapter 12: The Mural (Circa 1968)   417
Chapter 13: The Big Mistake (Circa 1973 to 1974)   433
Chapter 14: The End of My Life as a New York City Artist   437
Chapter 15: Li, Chung, and Hsai   443
Chapter 16: Long Live My Eighty-Second Airborne
          Buddies and My Wife, Hortense DuVall   447

Grandma Jennie.

PART I

CHAPTER I

Thunder and Lightning

It was around midnight, April 24, 1934, in the midst of the worst thunderstorm the Washington, DC, metropolitan area had ever seen. It rained and thundered until I "popped out of the womb" at five thirty that morning. "The storm stopped immediately," Mama said. I weighed in at eleven pounds, six ounces. (Mama was only about five feet tall and about ninety-eight pounds.) She also said the hospital told her that she had set a new record for birth weights in the DC area.

"Wow!" I said. "That must have been painful, Ma!"

She said, "Yeah, and you have been a 'pain in the butt' ever since!" We both laughed. (I was in my early forties when she told me this story and then shortly after that she died.)

I seem to be able to remember only as far back as when I was three and my household consisted of Grandma Jennie (Jennifer Elizabeth Buchanan), my sister (all of us called her Sister), my cousin Thelma, and Walter Johnson (I called him Mr. Wal'er). Mr. Wal'er worked and lived in the woodshed in our backyard.

One thing I remember was that Sister had bought me this army truck that I *slept* with! I loved this truck! It was made of metal and had real rubber wheels. The back of the truck, where the soldiers rode, had a real canvas cover that could be removed if needed. *Maaan,* I loved that truck!

One day I decided I would take my truck out into the front yard to play with it. I remember looking up and seeing a boy about my age with a very dark brown face watching me through the fence. He wanted to know if he could come in the yard and play with me. He also had a truck—a little truck, much smaller than mine—and it had no removable parts. He wanted to know if he could play with my truck a little. "OK…" I said reluctantly because he had a peculiar look in his eye.

While we were playing, it began to rain, and Sister called me to come inside out of the rain. I did so, but then remembered that I had left my truck out in the yard. I ran to the window to look outside. It was raining hard, so I figured it was pretty safe there because the rain would keep everybody off the street. All of a sudden, I saw that same little boy sneak into the yard in the driving rain, grab my truck, and take off down the block. The truck was under his arm, and he was soaking wet. I ran to tell Sister what I had just seen. "Thomas, in the driving rain? Are you sure?" she asked. She also asked me if I had seen what house he went to. I said yes, so she said we would go to the house when the rain stopped.

The rain stopped, and we proceeded to the house of the boy who had taken my truck. We knocked on the door, and the boy's mother opened the door. We began to tell her that her son had taken my truck from the front yard and that we wished she would have him return it. She looked at Sister and said, "How do you know that it is your truck? Is his name on it?"

I said, "I know it's mine because I saw him take it." I also said that I knew there was a scratch on the side door of the truck and asked her to check it out. I could see the boy in the living room sheltering my truck. The mother replied that she was not going to check anything! She also said that she had bought that truck herself and that if my name was not on the truck, it was not my truck.

WOW! I was in shock. I could not believe a mother would lie like that for her child. All she had to do was look at the scratch or ask the child if I was telling the truth. Then Sister disappointed me by turning to me and saying, "Maybe the woman is right." I was crushed. I thought to myself, *But why would I lie to you?* Sister could have *at least* looked for a scratch! What does a child, three years of age, know about scratching his name on a toy he had just received to protect himself from a grown woman who would lie for her child, with the child sitting there knowing she was lying? He looked up at me and smiled as he played with my truck. He had the smile of a winner!

(*Wow,* I said to myself, *I wonder what my daddy would say if he were here. He would have handled it differently, I bet! But I have no daddy to talk to. And where was* his *daddy?*)

I was not yet four and had to learn that there are mothers who would do such dastardly things. I was not a prophet, but I could see the ruination of a child who knew his mother would lie for him. To this day, I often wonder what else that mother would have done to destroy her child's concept of what life was really about. There is no way you could tell me that he could have turned out to be an "OK" adult. That was a heart-wrenching experience for any three-year-old child to have. Plus Sister never did buy me another truck. I never took anything else of mine outside after that! I did not trust any mother's son. From then on the toys I cherished I played with only in the house.

Shortly after that experience, I was introduced to my just-born little brother, Roland. I was confused and amazed about having a new brother now but still no mommy or daddy! Sister put Roland into a crib across the room from me and took care of him as a mommy would. He did a lot of crying in the beginning but toughened up as the days zoomed by. There was a lot of activity in the kitchen now that Roland was here and a lot of water boiling all the time. In those days, all of the baby's things had to be boiled before being used, especially the bottles and the diapers. I remember how the house used to smell all the time, it seemed. I also began to wonder, *When will we see our mommy and daddy?*

So now I was keener than ever to find out about our mother and father and their whereabouts. But that got pushed to the side when a big argument came about between Grandma and Sister. Sister ran up the stairs, and Grandma ran up the stairs behind her with my baseball bat in her hand! I was frozen to the spot, waiting for the worst. Suddenly Grandma's bedroom door opened, and Grandma stepped out without the bat. She passed by me as if I was not even there. I was still glued to my spot. Grandma was visibly upset about *something*.

Sister came out of the room dressed up and said she was going to Church to make the Stations of the Cross (a Friday night Catholic service reenacting the Crucifixion), and from there, she was meeting a friend and going out. "Grandma will tell you what time you are to go to bed," she said to me and left the house. Grandma was still visibly *upset*! On Monday nights Sister went to the Novena services and saw her friend afterward, and on Friday nights she went to the Stations of the Cross and saw her friend afterward. Grandma was not a happy camper! When I went downstairs, I saw Grandma sitting in the kitchen and gazing out the window. She had her elbows on the table and her hands folded in front of her face. She looked different to me somehow. She did not talk much and rarely moved from room to room. I felt sorry for Grandma but did not know why. I just knew I loved my grandma, and she hardly knew I was around now.

I was now four years old, and there was talk around the house of me going to school. I had heard Grandma say I would have to get my hair cut. So Grandma yelled out the window to call Mr. Wal'er. He also sold scrap iron and old papers for money. I thought he was dark-complexioned and assumed he was someone in need of a family until I saw him one day without his shirt on. I was surprised to find he was light-skinned like me and began to assume we were related. *Maybe he is my grandfather,* I thought. Grandma asked Mr. Wal'er to take me to the barbershop to get my first haircut. Pictures were taken of me in my little navy blue sailor suit, which everybody seemed to love (the suit, that is). I didn't know why there were so many sailor suit pictures around town—everybody had one. I asked Sister if Mr. Wal'er was my grandfather. "Heavens no, child, he is just a friend and handyman of your grandmother," she said.

Then I asked her, "Do I have a grandfather?"

She said, "Yes, but he is *always* at sea, and when he is in port, he stays in Baltimore, so you may never meet him. I am sorry about that!" Sister still had not said *anything* to me about my *father. Wow!* I thought to myself. *Will I ever get to meet my father and my grandfather or either one of them?*

Sister had taught me how to read and write, so I was "ready for school," she said. She was a little concerned about my age, though. They started kids at five, but Grandma didn't want to wait another whole year, and neither did I.

One day, just before summer's end, I was standing outside in front of the house when an elderly, dark-skinned man walked up to me and said, "Hi, young man, can you tell me where 1218 Half Street is?"

I said, "Sure, it's right here!"

He said, "Is this where Jennie Lumpkins lives?"

I said, "Yes, sir, she is my grandmother!"

He said, "Then you must be little Thomas! Little Thomas, I am your grandfather!" Then he grabbed me and gave me this big hug and handed me a quarter. He also gave my two-year-old brother Roland a quarter and two of Uncle Willie's daughters a quarter, I later learned, and that was ALL he gave, too. Next he went right into how he was going to buy me everything I wanted, starting with a new bicycle, electric trains, and anything else I could dream up.

All I could say was, "WOW, Grandpa!"

I went to fetch Grandma and tell her the good news. When I told her who was out on the front porch asking for her, Grandma jumped up and said, "What does he want around here? Thomas, you don't have to tell me anything; I bet he told you he was going to buy you bicycles and toys and everything, right?"

I said, "Right!"

Grandma grabbed me and said, "Don't believe a word he says, do you hear me?"

"Yes, Grandma."

Grandma went on to say that he was the biggest liar in all the world. Then she said, "You wait here." Grandma went to the front door and invited him in. They talked for a little while, and he asked if he could stay for a couple of days because he wanted to see Constance and William before setting sail again. William (called Willie) was Grandma and Grandpa's son. Uncle Willie had three daughters— Jeanne, Joyce, and Maria. Uncle Willie was married to Elizabeth Herbert, nicknamed "Sis Herbert," which is all I ever knew her by. My grandmother and Sister did not like Sis Herbert. Sis Herbert was upset because Grandma and Sister did not tell us children to call her "Aunt" Elizabeth. I never asked why.

Grandma was angry with Grandpa but agreed to let him stay there for a week. I asked her why she was so mad at him. She said, "Because he is such a fanatic. All he did the whole time we were married was primp, talk about Marcus Garvey and his Navy, and brag about how proud he was to be a merchant seaman on one of his back-to-Africa ships. That's why you never saw him, and you won't be seeing him again, I betcha! So I'm sorry he got your hopes up. But at least you know now that he is a cheapskate and a liar."

"Yes, Ma'am," I said.

A week later, Grandpa Lumpkins was on his way back to Jamaica, his native island. And Grandma was right—I never saw him again or got any of the promised gifts. So be it!

"Little Jimmy," Oil Painting. © Taiwo DuVall

This painting is dedicated to James Skinner.

CHAPTER 2

Life with the Catholics

When Christopher Columbus reached the New World, he landed in the area that he decided would be called Mary's Land and renamed Grandma's birthplace St. Mary's County. The first Catholic Church was built in St. Mary's County in Mary's Land, now known as the State of Maryland. Then the missionaries went about "saving" the natives.

Grandma Jennie, a descendant of the indigenous people of that area of Maryland, was a product of this transitional period. It would stand to reason then that her children would be Catholics. So we were Catholics from the cradle, and it was not unusual to come into the house to find the Reverend O. J. Assing, Pastor of St. Vincent de Paul Catholic Church, sitting in the kitchen, drinking from a fifth of Scotch at the kitchen table. Grandma Jennie did *all* the talking. The Rev.

Pastor did all the listening, as Grandma was always *"telling it like it is"* about something! I was too young to understand all that was being said but knew it was about me. I also knew I was destined to go to Catholic school—no ifs, ands, or buts about it!

Sure enough, I was off to St. Vincent de Paul, a Catholic school located at Third and I Streets SW in Washington, DC. It was called a mission school and was dedicated to teaching Black and Indian children, who were not allowed to attend the all-White Catholic schools. I also found out that the White students attended school tuition-free but that the Blacks and Indians had to pay because we were from a "poor" neighborhood. This made no sense to me! The White Priest told us that the White parishioners put more money in Church on Sundays, so they were entitled to free tuition and new books. What he said made no sense to me. How could the poor pay more?

Our school had five classrooms: kindergarten in one room, first and second grades in a room, third and fourth grades in a room, fifth and sixth grades in a room, and seventh and eighth grades in the last room. Each teacher had to teach two grades simultaneously. The school was very overcrowded and did not have enough seats. If you missed a day, you would miss your seat. I unfortunately missed a day once and had to sit on the floor the next day, all day. It was a drag, but it kept absenteeism down to a minimum because nobody wanted to lose his or her seat. This was especially true for girls but did not seem to bother the boys so much.

The Oblate Sisters of Mary, a Black Order of Nuns based in Baltimore, Maryland, operated the school. We arrived at the school, and Grandma talked to the Nun who registered the new students. Grandma told her that I could read and write and wanted to know if she could start me in the first grade. The Nun told her that because I was only four, I would have to be placed in kindergarten. I could see Grandma was disappointed. Nonetheless, she allowed them to place me in kindergarten. Grandma said good-bye, and I was escorted up the boys' stairway and into kindergarten. The boys and girls had separate stairways so that never the twain would meet.

I was stunned and amazed by what I saw in kindergarten: sand-boxes, building blocks, and GAMES and TOYS galore! Oh boy! I just knew I was going to enjoy this school. I immediately headed for the building blocks. I was going to build myself some of the biggest and mightiest castles that my imagination could conceive of!

I had been in kindergarten for only a few weeks when Mr. Wal'er showed up just before lunchtime. I saw him talking to the Nun and pointing to me. The Nun came over to me and said, "Thomas, your grandmother has just died, and Mr. Johnson is here to take you home." She said she was very sorry and that she would pray for us.

I was out of school for the rest of the week. Grandma was not there; I kept looking around for her. A few days later, there was a knock at the front door, and it was the man from the funeral parlor. He said Mrs. Buchanan was ready to be laid in state. I did not understand a thing he was talking about. I watched as they wheeled a casket into the living room, put this purplish drapery behind it, and opened up the casket for viewing.

Grandma, looking as if she were only asleep with her hands laid across her chest, did not move. She lay there for a week in the living room. People signed a book on a stand in the living room as they came and went. Every day, Sister and Cousin Thelma combed and restyled Grandma's hair, readjusted her clothes, freshened her makeup, and watered the flowers. Sister had asked Thelma to come over and stay with us because she had to work and we could not be left alone.

About a week later, the undertaker came, closed the casket, and delivered it to St. Vincent's Church, where they held this grand funeral service. I was then taken back home. Children did not go to the grave site. I was glad I was spared that scene.

A few hours later, Sister and Cousin Thelma returned from the cemetery. They went straight to work clearing the table and bringing out big dishes of food. As the people trickled into the house, the music got louder and louder. The front door was constantly opening and closing. Relatives like our Cousins Mary and Adolphus Clark, Ernestine, Winona, and Sammy Cresswell, and other people were filling the house, and we kids had to take to the steps to keep from being stepped on. Everybody was dancing, eating, drinking, and singing until way after sundown.

On Monday morning Sister took me back to school. I went *straight* for the kindergarten, gathering my blocks for the next great castle. Before I could get a good start, the teacher was calling out for "Thomas DuVall." I didn't answer because my name was "Thomas Buchanan."

The Nun walked up to me and said, "Didn't you hear me call you?"

"My name is Thomas Buchanan," I replied.

Then the Nun said, "Your mother said your name is Thomas DuVall and you can read and write. So you don't belong in kindergarten! We are putting you in the first grade where you belong."

"My mother?" I asked.

"Yes," she said, "your mother! Now follow me, and I shall introduce you to your new teacher!" I followed, but I was thoroughly confused. "Mother" was gone by the time I looked around for her.

The Nun was sympathetic but said that reading and writing were more important than playing with blocks in a sandbox. To this day I regret not having been able to finish my Mighty Castle (groan). Kindergarten was now a room across the hall. No blocks here! No sandboxes, no toy trucks, no dolls! In less than an hour, I went from a master builder and architect to a common letter and number writer, making circles and boxes over and over and over again. *Wow,* what a drag! I was so upset that the teacher had to actually come over to me, physically take me by the arm, and move my arm around in a circular motion while I held the pencil. She did not notice that I was in shock and unable to move. She thought I just didn't know how to read and write.

My teacher's name was Sister Mary Nazareth of the Oblate Order of Nuns. She was as pretty as a picture. If she had not been a Nun, she could have easily been a movie star or could have at least appeared on the front of some religious cards as Mary, Mother of God (as far as I was concerned). My Cousin Cynthia Clark Johnson, a great kindergarten teacher who carried on her mother's teaching tradition, reminds me of Sister Mary Nazareth. I was coming out of my shock and falling in love. I was in love with the teacher, and she was a Nun! What a crush I had! Her voice was like music to my ears. She was as gentle as a lamb.

She had a slight southern accent that added to her charm. She stood before the class to give us our morning exercises—hands in front, now hands out to the side, now hands over your head. Well that hands-over-your-head thing she did caused her shawl-type garment to rise up and reveal a beautiful bust line, I thought. I was surprised, as I did not think that Nuns had breasts! That just made her more beautiful to me. She actually made me forget all about kindergarten. She now had my undivided attention. All I had to do was look like I was having difficulty, and she would just stroll over to my desk and help me. It was great!

Later that day, when Sister came home from work, I told her that my teacher said my name was DuVall and not Buchanan. Sister said, "Your grandmother enrolled you in school under her maiden name. But she is in heaven now, and I am your mother, so hurry and get used to it, OK?" She said this with a smile. I said OK and asked her why everybody called her Sister. She said her brother, Willie, always called her Sister, so everybody in the neighborhood and around the house called her Sister, too.

Sister (I mean Mama) said that Buchanan was Grandmother's maiden name. I then remembered that my grandmother had enrolled me in school, but why had she said my name was Buchanan if my name was DuVall? And where did the name DuVall come from?

So I said to myself, *Oh well, DuVall is easier to spell!* Buchanan has eight letters in it. Was DuVall my father's name? If so, where was he? Mama said I would be meeting him soon.

About a month later, Mama told me to get dressed because I was being taken uptown to see Santa Claus. She was taking me to see Santa Claus at Kann's Department Store, located at Seventh and D Streets NW, but Grandma and I did not like Kann's because its Christmas décor always seemed lackluster. Hecht's Department Store, located at Seventh and G Streets NW, went all out with its window displays and toys. I told Mama that Grandma always took me to Hecht's to see Santa, so I refused to go into Kann's and decided to throw a temper tantrum by stomping, screaming, and yelling. She grabbed me with one hand and started spanking me with the other hand! The louder I yelled, the harder she hit me. And while she was hitting me, she was saying, "I am your Mother, and you better get that straight in your head now, or I will be hitting you like this until you do!" Then she hit me again (POW-POW). "Do you understand?"

"Yes, Mama, I understand!" And from that day to this, I have never been hit that hard by anybody, so I still call her Mama!

A few weeks later, the initial shock had waned, and I was back in school. I had been looking around the classroom and was becoming aware of the local characters I would be spending time with for the next nine months.

One fellow in particular was a dark brown-skinned boy who was always being sent to lie down under the record player. He would crawl under there and watch us do our reading and writing until he eventually fell asleep. This routine went on day after day, week after week. I was driving myself crazy trying to make sense of this routine without asking someone to please help me understand it. I thought that it was very strange. Nobody else seemed to notice or show any concern about this, so I decided to ask around. The story I got from the students was that he had the "sleeping sickness." His name was James

Skinner, I was told. I was only four, but for some reason, I just could not convince myself that he had sleeping sickness, as he did not look sickly to me.

One day I was selected by the Nun to pass out the morning work to the class. I saw this as a great opportunity to speak directly to Skinner and see what he had to say. I got down on my hands and knees, crawled under the record player, and handed him his classwork.

He said, "I can't take it."

I asked him why not.

He replied, "I'm not allowed to learn!"

"Why aren't you allowed to learn?" I asked.

He said, "Because I don't know who my real father is. And if I don't find out soon, they are going to expel me from school."

Wow!! That was worse than the sleeping disease rumor, I thought. I was in shock and disbelief; this couldn't be happening! Jimmy Skinner was a nice boy. He was a very soft-spoken and mild-mannered individual, and I could see on his face that he wanted to join us in our reading and writing. I just *had* to ask the Nun why Skinner wasn't allowed to learn with us. The Nun stated that it would not be fair to him because he was an "illegitimate child" and would soon be sent home. *Wow,* I thought, *I don't know who my father is either! They could put me under there with him.* I suddenly became frightened that the teacher was going to ask me what my father's name was. I was a nervous wreck in the first grade!

Sure enough, a few weeks later, poor Jimmy Skinner was **gone**, another "short-term relation!" But, in my case, I was called out of the classroom and into the hall and told "not to worry" because my expenses were being taken care of by a "benefactor." I said to myself, *What is a benefactor?* I was confused by the Nun's secrecy because she did not tell me who my benefactor was. I did not tell Mama what the Nun told me outside the classroom. But I wondered, *Who or what is a benefactor, and who is paying for me to be here?* I was called out of the classroom every year until I graduated nine years later and told not to worry because my educational needs were being taken care of by my benefactor. Since it was whispered to me in private, I thought it should remain private. I didn't even say anything to Mama about it!

What a traumatic experience that first year in Catholic school had been! WOW!! First my army truck was stolen, then I was abruptly moved into kindergarten, then my grandmother died, then my name changed, and then Jimmy Skinner vanished from class. And who was my father? **What was I going to do?**

Another "character" in the first grade was Bernard Gross. Bernard Gross would eat anything! He didn't care where it came from or what it was—he would just eat it. No questions asked—no matter how old it was or who was eating on it before he got hold of it! One day we were going through a vacant lot, and one of us saw a cookie lying on the ground. It had fallen out of a nearby trash bag. One of the guys yelled, "Let's give it to Bernard Gross and see if he'll eat it! Let's rub a little more dirt on it to make it look even worse."

"OK!" we all agreed.

Lo and behold, Bernard Gross was coming toward us with that silly grin on his face, as if to say, "I know y'all got som'pin' good on you!" So right away, we offered him the "The Cookie." He grabbed it, looked at it, and swallowed it! Wow! We hadn't even gotten a chance to speak first! We were stunned. We stopped calling him Bernard from that moment on. We just called him *GROSS* after that. We also agreed to stop giving Gross anything to eat, because nobody wanted to be a party to contributing to his death.

St. Vincent de Paul had no playground like the White Catholic schools had, so the school had to block off the street to traffic on I Street between Second and Third Streets SW. The girls jumped double Dutch rope, and the boys played tag. On rainy days we stayed in the classrooms and had free time. The girls played games, and the boys drew nasty pictures of boys and girls trying to make babies. Back then the boys thought the girls had penises too, so they thought that rubbing the penises together was how babies were made. I did not take part in this Art form, mainly because I was in doubt of this procedure.

Boys and girls were never allowed to play together. Many of the boys carried a piece of string in their pockets; we would all play Indian string games. (This is a lost Art form in which you take a piece of string, tie the ends together to form a loop, wrap it, twist it, and intertwine it to form recognizable objects, and never let the string leave your fingers. Examples of such objects are "the cup and saucer," "the baby in the rocker," and so on.) Then there were other string games called capture-and-release tricks. These types of tricks required one of the boys to have someone stick his hand through an opening the boy had created with his string trap. The arm would get caught in a loop that seemed impossible to get out of, and with a clap of the hands, the whole thing fell free and became a loop of string again. It took some maneuvering and thought, and the boy had to be able to undo the structure by repeating the steps and clapping his hands together. Then the whole thing became undone, meaning it became a loop of string again, with no knots except the knot that held the two ends together.

There were free hot lunches for a little while, but then they abruptly stopped because of World War II, the school said. What had we kids done to cause the school to take away our lunches? I missed those nice warm meals, especially when it got cold outside. (Oh well, the poor had to pay more and get less!)

Thanksgiving was upon us, and the whole class was preparing to do some holiday artwork to take home. There were pictures of Pilgrims, cornstalks, pumpkins, horns of plenty, and turkeys with all those feathers and that red piece under their necks. I had trouble with the turkeys because it looked like their brains were on the outside! The teacher said all this artwork had to be colored.

She started passing out the drawings when she suddenly realized that she did not have enough to go around. That meant that whoever had mimeographed the work sheets had counted the seats in the class instead of the heads. Guess who did not get a picture? Right, a couple of my buddies and me did not receive the work sheets. I decided I could draw a picture by looking over the shoulder of someone else.

Lo and behold, there must have been ten or more students who did not have a picture to color and wanted me to draw them one too! Nobody wanted to be left out, it seemed. I was overwhelmed with requests. Fortunately two other boys volunteered to help with the drawings. Their names were Thomas Davis and Frank Pinkney, and they were good too. Everybody soon had a picture to color.

The class was now at fever pitch, and everybody was busy trying to win the right to have their work displayed on the board and to win a prize for the best work. "Time's up!" said the Sister, and we turned in our work. The Sister took a show of hands on whose work looked the best, and the class could not decide between the three remaining pieces. The teacher called it a draw between Thomas Davis (a lanky, bend-in-the-knees-when-he-walked kind of guy who sort of reminded me of Abe Lincoln; as a matter of fact, Thomas Davis was later chosen to play Abe in the Negro History Week performance when he was in the third grade), Frank Pinkney (a red-headed Black guy with big freckles), and me, Thomas DuVall (a skin-and-bones dude with a runny nose). The first prize was a box of candy that we three boys shared with the whole class.

I asked the teacher if the whole class could display their work on the board because they had all worked so hard. She agreed, and *everybody's* work went on display. That made the whole class a winner! Now the teacher was happy, the class was happy, and the parents were happy to see all the artwork done by their children. That was a real "BLAST" for the class!

The next day, Sister Mary Nazareth called Thomas Davis, Frank Pinkney, and me up to the front of the class. She asked the three of us if we would be willing to stay in class on our lunch hour to draw Thanksgiving designs on the blackboard with the colored chalks she had. Frank Pinkney immediately said no and returned to his seat. Thomas Davis and I stood fast. (They used to call us the "Two TDs.") The teacher seemed very pleased with us. She dismissed the class for lunch and left us alone with this huge empty blackboard staring at us. The classroom was deathly quiet, and we were still standing in the same spot where she had left us. We could hear the noises outside of children at play—boys yelling, girls screaming. Thomas Davis screamed, "What are we doing up here? We gotta be out of our heads! We are standing here staring at a blank blackboard the size of a football field on our lunch hour!"

I finally spoke, "We gotta do this thing now or we'll be ridiculed! Let's go *crazy* in here for a while! Look at all this chalk and all these different colors. Ma-a-an, o man! We can have a ball, so come on," I said. "Tell you what! You take the far right side of the board, I'll take the far left side, and we can meet in the middle."

He said OK, and we were off and running. For one solid hour, all you could hear were the heavy scratching and scraping sounds of the chalks that were steadily being moved across the board. We were so busy that we hardly spoke. At times things would get tedious, and we would sigh out loud and glance at the clock. It seemed like forever before we saw where we were finally going to hook up in the middle. We finally reached the point where our lines were meeting and the drawing was becoming complete. We were amazed at what we had done in record time, but Thomas Davis was visibly upset that it had cost him his lunch hour. For some reason I was too gratified to be concerned with missing lunch.

The bell rang, and the class filed back in. Sister Mary Nazareth's mind was blown! She said our drawing was "beautiful," and the students expressed their appreciation for the brightly colored decorations of Thanksgiving time. I turned around to look and realized that it *was* a pretty sight, especially on Thomas Davis's side. This guy had a gift for color. *It was a miracle,* I said to myself. The teacher rushed to the door to get the other Nuns to come see this mural that the "two Thomases" had drawn, and they all began to flip out!

The next day the teacher once again called Thomas Davis and me to the front of the classroom. This time she told us, "The other teachers came in and saw your wonderful work and wanted to know whether you would also be willing to decorate their blackboards." However, since the Mother Superior felt it would be unfitting for a four-year-old to go to the seventh- and eighth-grade class to decorate the board for twelve-year-old students, Sister Mary Nazareth said, "It will have to be done during your lunch break!"

Thomas Davis spoke first. He said he did not want to give up another lunch hour to draw.

"What about you, Thomas DuVall?" the teacher asked.

"I'll do it," I said.

The classroom became very quiet after that, and even the teacher seemed a little surprised. She asked me a second time. I answered, "Yes, I'll do it!" (I should have known then that something was **wrong** with me but guess I was too young to realize it.)

When I got back to my seat, Thomas Davis said to me, "Are you crazy? What about your position as shortstop? Don't you care about your team? The only time we get to play is on our lunch break! You are going to cause us to lose this game!"

"I won't let you down, I promise," I said. But I was wrong; my shortstopping began to *slip* as the artwork improved, so the team had to cut me loose. There were at least three other classrooms, and it had taken two of us an hour to do one room. That would be at least five or six lunch hours I would have to sacrifice.

"Thomas DuVall," Sister Mary Nazareth asked, "are you sure you don't mind giving up these lunch hours, especially on nice sunshiny days? You would have to eat your lunch while you work, you know."

"OK!" I said.

The next big project involved the coming of Christmas. The Nuns gave me pictures of the Scenes of the Nativity, especially mistletoe, holly, stables, camels, the three kings, and so on, to use as source material to decorate the boards. I had quite a library file to work from.

By then I was getting static from some of the other guys in class. "Have you lost your mind? How can you give up the one time in the day when you can go out to play or at least be outside!" they would say. They could not understand why I was smiling so. (Neither could I!)

When I didn't have to draw, I would go out to play, but it was difficult to get chosen to play ball. When I did get chosen, it was because they needed one more player to even up the sides. If there had been anyone else near, they wouldn't have chosen me at all. I can't blame those guys, though. I had made a choice, and I was responsible for it, so it was back to the chalk for me.

All I knew was that the finished product was always a "TURN ON," or maybe I was just a "chalk junky." Not only that, but I was on my own. I got to decide where to put things, and if I didn't like it, I could change it. What more could a four-year-old kid ask for? So maybe I never got to finish my castle, but I did get to draw a few murals on the blackboards. It was a very good year except for the bloomers and stovepipes I had to wear. What a drag!

Bloomers, Stovepipes, and Knickers

From about age two to about age five, my brother and I wore unisex-looking underwear called bloomers—we pronounced them "bluh-mas"—under our clothes, which made everybody smell like urine all day long. I hated them because they didn't have a cutaway hole for the penis. It was as if to say that boys under the age of five didn't have penises. It seemed like we had the habit of holding our pee as long as we could so that we could play just a little longer, and that would cause us to run for the bathroom at the last minute. We would have to stand there and unbuckle our belts, unbutton our flies (three or four buttons), take down our pants, take down our bluh-mas, reach for our "Timmy-Tommies" (this is how we referred to the penis in my family!), and then try to reach the urinal before we finished peeing and wetting all of our clothes. It never ceased to happen! On the other hand, I saw the girls just pull up their dresses, pull down their bloomers, and squat, and then they were off and running! We were still standing there trying to get it all together so that we could exit with some kind of dignity.

In the winter it was even worse. We boys had to wear snowsuits, which were heavy, woolen overall-type pants that had suspenders attached to them. Then we would put on snowsuit jackets and were good to go. Well, as luck would have it, by the time I'd get to school, I'd have to go so badly that I'd run straight for the boy's room. I'd be holding my breath! First I'd have to take off the jacket to get to the suspenders. Then I'd have to take the suspenders off and pull them down around my knees so that I could get to the fly and unbutton it. Then I'd remember I had *bloomers* on, so I'd have to take the pants down so that I could get to the damn bloomers and pull them down. Then I could get to the Timmy-Tommy, but by that point I was already urinating down my pants leg.

On one such occasion, I was soaking wet from the waist down. (You have no idea how awful wet wool feels.) I actually saw steam rising from the wet wool. I had to get out of those clothes. Even my socks felt wet. I leaned against the bathroom wall and started removing my snowsuit. I had to keep on the wet stovepipes. (Stovepipes were what they called the above-the-knee trousers that boys wore in those days.) *My stovepipes were a dark color, and unless people looked closely, they might not notice the wet area,* I said to myself. But I had to walk fast so that nobody would have a chance to look closely.

I got to the classroom, and the teacher was calling me to the front of the class to explain why I was just getting back to my seat! I blanked out after that and could not, for the life of me, speak of the events that had taken place earlier that morning. They say that when the brain can't take any more pain, it just shuts down until things get better.

I hated the clothes that these grown-ups had us parading around in. Now that I was five years old, I had to wear knickers! What are knickers? They are trousers that either button, snap, or have elastic just below the knee. Knee-high argyle stockings must be worn with them. (If you have ever seen a picture of George Washington or Benjamin Franklin, you must know they wore knickers and long stockings.) They were a nightmare to me! I had skinny legs, so the stockings were always down around my ankles. I walked around all day long pulling up my stockings. One day I got the brainy idea of using rubber bands to hold up my stockings. It felt great—no more bending over all day long pulling up the stockings. A few hours later, I was having pains in my legs. The pain got worse and worse. It got so bad that I had to sit down and conduct an investigation. Lo and behold, it was the rubber bands! They had cut off the circulation in my legs, which were swelling up! So it was back to pulling up the stockings every few minutes until spring-time, when we could wear our stovepipes (short pants) if we preferred.

There was one good thing that came with the knickers: the underwear. Now that I was five, I was allowed to wear these things called Jockey shorts. They had an opening in the front that allowed us to get to our Timmy-Tommies without having to pull our underwear down to our knees to take a leak. *These were a great idea,* I thought. They made me feel like we were moving on up! My brother was not yet five, so he was still wearing bloomers. I was seven years old before I was allowed to wear long pants. It was like waiting a lifetime to hide these skinny legs of mine. Oh, happy day! For real!!

I soon found out that I was not the *only* one who liked Sister Mary Nazareth. A young White Priest (who was always blushing), Father Cohen, also liked her. He was a nice guy and was handsome too. We all liked Father Cohen; I even felt a father-son, biological attraction to this man and noticed a resemblance between his mannerism and presence and mine. I would not have been surprised if he had come forward and admitted he was my real Father. Even to this day, as I write this story, I feel a tug at my heartstrings whenever I think of him.

We all knew he was crazy about Sister Mary Nazareth. He would beam and blush the whole time he was there. He seemed to favor the brown-skinned beauties, I guess. I know I wanted to call him "Daddy." He would always visit our class, even when he did not have time to visit the other classes. We children were pleased that Father Cohen and Sister Mary Nazareth were enjoying each other's company. We wanted them to marry and stay together forever. They would have made a beautiful couple. And we all agreed that their children would all be just as beautiful (this shows you how the beautiful and innocent minds of children work). However, I am certain Mother Pious got wind of it and went about having Sister Mary Nazareth shipped out!

Sure enough, one day the Mother Superior, Mother Pious, came to the classroom and asked Sister Mary Nazareth to step outside into the hall for a minute. When Sister Mary Nazareth came back, she did not look good. We felt so sorry for her. She announced to the class that she would be leaving soon but that the teacher replacing her, Sister Mary Marion, was very nice.

Father Cohen had eyes for Sister Mary Nazareth. They should have sent HIM away, if anything, because he was the "pursuer"—not Sister Mary Nazareth! She was always real cool and polite to Father Cohen! This was a sad day for all of us. We all loved Sister Mary Nazareth very much. She was sent away to Mississippi. Father Cohen was crushed too. He was never the same after that. He eventually handed in his resignation and was sent to an all-White Parish, as he'd requested. I did not know what Parish, but he went.

By the way, in those days we knew of only one Black Priest. We found out that he was always "living out of a suitcase" and was never assigned to a Parish. We were dismayed about this situation and could not figure out why a Black Priest would accept the fact that he would never be assigned to a Parish.

It was then that I realized any aspirations I had had to become a Priest "died" when Father Cohen left. What a way to end the first year in Catholic school.

The body count: army truck, kindergarten, James Skinner, and Sister Mary Nazareth—gone, but not forgotten!

CHAPTER 3

Summer Vacation

I was five years old and on summer vacation. My brother Roland would be three that month, and Mama was eight months pregnant. A few days later, Mama brought a man home and told us he was our father. His name was Hugh Sheffer DuVall, and he was the son of a Minister and Pastor of a Baptist Church in Clifton Forge, Virginia. I did not think I looked like this man. He had thicker limbs, and his hair was different from mine. He had thin lips, and my lips were puffier. He had a widower's peak and a low brow line. My hair was very curly, and I had a high brow line. He had short stubby toes, and my toes were long and narrow, but Roland's physique was similar to our father's (I thought), so I asked Mama again, "Is this my real father?"

Mama looked at me and said, *"Yes!"* But I was not convinced.

Nonetheless, I liked "Hughdy Duball" or "Speedy Duball," which his male friends would call him a lot. He had a great sense of humor and a manly, hardy laugh that made me laugh too. I asked one of his friends why they called my daddy "Speedy." He looked at me and said, "Your father used to drive around Washington, DC, with a white scarf around his neck waving in the wind, and he was always driving over the speed limit. So we nicknamed him 'SPEEDY' after 'Barney Oldfield,' the first winner of the Indianapolis 500-Mile Race." Daddy did love to drive. He would take us on long car rides through Virginia, and we loved it.

The boy who stole my truck no longer lived on the block. *Thank goodness*, I thought, as I definitely had no desire to set eyes on him ever again. To the left of me lived the Lucases—Roscoe (who was a good sketcher), Rudy, George, Melvin "Shave th' Razor," "Porky Pig," and two girls, Mary and Marian. Their mother, Ms. Lucas, made the best hot rolls in the area, and people would come from all around on Sunday morning to get hot rolls from her. Sometimes people would be waiting in line at her door. We could smell those rolls baking all over the neighborhood. It was something I looked forward to smelling. It made Sunday morning special to me.

I would even sneak out of bed at night, go to the bread box, grab one of those rolls, dash back upstairs, jump in bed, pull the covers over my head, and eat that roll "undercover." I would wake up in the morning with a head full of crumbs and a mother with a confused look on her face because she could not, for the life of her, figure out why I would have bread crumbs in my hair. I didn't have nerve enough to tell her of my newfound adventure. I kept up this practice until I was twelve years old.

I also had a new friend in the neighborhood who went by the name of "Fatso." I don't know why he was called Fatso, as he was neither fat nor skinny, but everybody called him Fatso. Kimble was his last name. Fatso and I did a lot of playing together.

Fatso and I used to meet on Saturday mornings on my porch. We would read comic books and then try to draw the ones we liked most—Captain Marvel, Batman, and Robin. For some strange reason, Captain Marvel was the biggest favorite. He had a real Italian look, and if he said his name, there would be a big SHAZAAAAAMMM and a big BOOOM-BAM! And he would turn into this Super Human Being and save everybody from harm!

Some of the older guys could really draw well. They could draw a lot of the heroes from memory. Roscoe Lucas and his brother, Rudy, were good drawers. I wanted to be as good as they were. They could draw anything and make it look real! I stood in awe of those guys. After a while, they stopped drawing. I heard Roscoe had a new girlfriend, so he was never around anymore, not like before anyway. But Fatso and I kept drawing until we moved away from the neighborhood.

I still draw, though not like before. Drawing makes me feel like I am in charge of what I'm doing, and there is a certain amount of responsibility that goes along with this charge. It involves trying to demonstrate that the object being drawn is something that has been looked at with a certain amount of observation and study. The finished product is the final analysis, in whatever medium, of what my eyes told my mind to do with my hand, and I had no choice in the matter but to let it happen. So be it.

One day my mother came to me and said that I was not to play with Fatso anymore because she believed he was a bad influence on me. Fatso would draw pictures of boys and girls coming together, and the boys and girls would have penises touching.

I did not see Fatso for several weeks. Then I ran into him walking down the street. I yelled at him, and he stopped. I asked him why I had not seen him around. He replied that his mother had told him not to play with me anymore because I was a bad influence on him! (Oh, no!) I guess his mother thought I had given him the penis idea. I told him my mother had said the same thing about him.

We stood there looking at each other for a few moments and decided to go play together.

Wow! We had a lot of fun that day and decided not to mention anything to our parents. One day my father saw us playing together and wanted to know my friend's name. I told him his name was Fatso. My father became very upset and wanted to know his real name. I told him it was the only name I knew. My father told me to ask him his real name. When I saw Fatso again, I asked him what his real name was, and he replied, "Fatso!" My father became very angry with me because he did not like nicknames. He said it was very improper to call a person out of his or her name. He insisted that I go to the boy's parents and find out his real name and address him as such. I did that, but Fatso would not answer to anything but Fatso. Even his father called him Fatso!

Fatso was a bit different from the other boys, maybe because he was always chewing on his tongue, even when he talked, which sometimes made it difficult to understand him. But I was used to his habit and had no trouble understanding him, which is probably why he liked me so much. I was willing to accept his quirk. I had a friend named George West who was always chewing on his shirt collar. He could even carry on a conversation with his collar in his mouth, and the harder we played, the harder he chewed! These guys were good playmates and made everything funny and fun.

We played with items like Popsicle sticks, marbles, bottle-top caps, yo-yos, penny whistles, baseball cards, and two flat sticks that we held between our fingers to snap out hand rhythms. We also had hair combs wrapped with wax paper; when we blew through the paper, the comb sounded like a wind instrument. These items could be found in every boy's pants pockets.

Bean shooters and slingshots were also the weapons of the day. The bean shooters were just soda pop straws that were cut in half and loaded with navy beans that were blown through the straw to pop you on the head. The distances those beans could be blown were phenomenal!

And they could really sting the person who was hit. The slingshot was a bit more sophisticated, so we did not use it on one another. It was made with a Y-shaped branch of a twig, a piece of inner tube tied to a shoestring, and the tongue of an old shoe. A stone would be placed on the tongue and pulled back as far as the inner tube rubber could be stretched; then it would fly. We used the slingshot to break bottles and knock tin cans off logs in a manner similar to a shooting gallery. We also made a lot of bows and arrows. *Every* boy had a bow and arrow!

Summer was coming to an end. Mr. Wal'er was still taking me to the barbershop, and there was talk of returning to school. My friends all went to different schools. Some went to Anthony Bowen Elementary; some went to Van Ness Elementary. I was the only kid on the block going to Catholic school. I discovered a stigma among my neighborhood friends about my going to Catholic school, which was that in Catholic school all kids got to learn about was religion all day long. I argued the point but was shot down as just a naïve kid! For those reasons, I didn't get into how I got to draw on the blackboards. *Why make it worse?* I thought.

Roland, Thomas (center), and Herbert in the backyard.

CHAPTER 4

Second Grade

It was the first day of school, and the house was abuzz. Mama told me she had made arrangements for the Davises to take me to school because she was now working for the Bureau of Engraving and had to be at work early. The Davis family lived at the corner of Half and M Streets SE. I would walk to their house, and Jack Davis, the oldest brother of my friend Thomas Davis (the Abe Lincoln-looking guy), and Bernard Gross would also walk with us. We would hook up with the Coates boys at South Capitol and M Streets. The Coates boys were Puffy Coates, Cookie Coates, and Steve Coates and their cousin, Baggy Leftridge.

Together we walked to school. It was fun. The older boys always cracked on the younger guys, and we liked it. We would walk up South Capitol Street to I Street, make a left on I Street past Randall Junior

High School, head across Delaware Avenue to Second Street, and then walk across Second Street to the middle of the block. St. Vincent de Paul—on I Street between Second and Third Streets—was an old red brick structure that was two stories high with a cross on top. Next door was the convent.

We arrived just as the Nuns were filing out of the convent to open the school doors. We filed in and walked into the assembly hall, where we would line up according to our grade. The boys were on one side to the right of the hall, and the girls were on the other side to the left. The Mother Superior, Mother Pious, a stern-looking, tight-lipped disciplinarian, would welcome us and inform us of what she expected throughout the coming year. I guess you could say she was reading the "riot act" to us.

We all saluted the flag and filed out. The boys went up the stairs marked "boys," which was carved in stone on the first step. The girls went up the steps marked "girls" (also carved in stone). So never the twain would meet. (Catholic school was the only place where I ever saw this kind of setup.) I was caught taking a shortcut up the girls' steps one day because the water fountain on the boys' side wasn't working. I got a good dressing down for it. *Boy!* I thought. *They certainly are touchy around here.*

We all filed into the classroom—the girls first and then the boys. It was the same situation as last year with the seating—not enough desks, and the ones that were broken were still broken. The big difference was that I was now on the other side of the room. I was on the second-grade side this year. The new teacher's name was Sister Mary Marian. She was not as pretty as Sister Mary Nazareth but seemed to be a very nice person.

She introduced herself and led us in the morning prayers, which consisted of the Our Father and a few Hail Marys. The Hail Mary was a strange prayer to me because I thought the boys and girls were saying, *Hail Mary, full of grace, the Lord is with thee. Blessed art though amongst women and blessed is the fruit of thy wound, Jesus.* Years later I learned the word was "womb," not "wound." It was still later that I found out what a womb was. I could not for the life of me picture Mary, Mother of God, with a womb. (My mother always said I was a little naïve. I guess this proved it.)

After the morning prayers, Sister Mary Marian announced that she was about to call the roll and that we should answer "here" to our names when called. The names were in alphabetical order, and when I heard Thomas Davis's name called, I knew I was next.

"Thomas DuVall!" she called out.

"Here!" I said.

She paused, called my name again, and asked me to stand up. *Oh no!* I wondered. *What did I do now?* I hesitated and then stood up. Sister Mary Marian broke out in the biggest smile and said, "Sister Mary Nazareth spoke so highly of you. She spent a lot of time telling me about how you *volunteered* to decorate the blackboards for her. I am so pleased to see you are back with us this year. Would you be willing to do the same for me this year? Now you don't have to if you don't want to."

I was flattered that Sister Mary Nazareth had done this. My heart skipped a beat as I thought of her. I looked at Sister Mary Marian, and she was still smiling. How could I resist such praise from one and a big smile from the other? So I said, "Yes, Sister, I would be glad to do it." Then she turned to the class and asked what they thought of it, and the class applauded. I was undone. I was also out of more lunch hours.

Sister Mary Marian went back to calling the roll, and when she got to the Gs, she called the name Jean Guy. It was a name I remembered from last year, but this time I took notice. She was very smart in class, as I recalled, and she always had pigtails and was soft-spoken. I guess I looked a little too long at her this time, because I immediately fell in love with Jean Guy—I mean head over heels in love! Was it love at first sight love? I figured the good Lord didn't want me to grieve the loss of Sister Mary Nazareth, so He sent me Jean Guy. I loved the way she walked; she had excellent posture. I loved the way she talked, so soft-spoken and sensitive. I loved the way she used her eyes and seemed to be so aware of her surroundings. I loved her brain and the fact that she was so alert, self-assured, and modest. I was in *love*! Just knowing I would see her in class was enough to keep my attendance record perfect.

Talk about incentive! Roll call was now complete, so we prepared for the first lesson. The first lesson of the day in Catholic school was Catechism. That's when we learned the difference between a mortal sin and a venial sin. Dumb me. I thought venial had something to do with veal.

The Nun drew three milk bottles on the board. She colored the first bottle black and said, "This is a *mortal* sin." She colored the second bottle gray and said, "This is a *venial* sin." She left the third bottle white and said, "This is a *clean soul* that is sure to go straight to heaven."

"*Asperges me, Domine, hyssopo, et mundabor: lavabis me, et super nivem dealbabor.*" ("Thou shalt sprinkle me, O Lord, with hyssop, and I shall be cleansed; thou shalt wash me, and I shall become whiter than snow.")[1]

The black bottle was the worst kind of sin. Those who committed black sins would burn in hell forever, and those who committed gray sins would burn for a little while in a place called Purgatory, where the fire wasn't so *hot*. Once they were "burned" clean, they would be reevaluated and allowed to go to heaven. That sounded horrible to me! I was definitely not going to be doing the **"black thing"** but was kind of *fuzzy* about how I was going to always tell the difference between the white and the gray. I figured there might be a moment when I couldn't be a white soul, but if I could be a little gray until I could get

---

[1] The Aspérges of the Traditional Latin Mass

to confession, maybe I could avoid the "black" fire! I guess that made me a "Purgatorian," right?

A few weeks later, Father Cohen made his first visit to the class, but this time he was not his blushing, handsome self. As a matter of fact, he looked rather pale. He was visibly disheartened. I felt kind of sorry for him, because I could see his heart was full of sadness and pain. He posed his routine question, "How many of you boys are going to be a *Priest* when you grow up?" We all raised our hands. His usual response was one of great satisfaction; however, this time he barely responded.

I also overheard him tell Sister Mary Marian that he had put in a request to be sent back to his original Parish (which was an all-White Parish). He also told her he had never wanted to come here in the first place. We were all hurt by this announcement. We all thought he liked being here with us "coloreds!" I guess we were wrong. *But Sister Mary Nazareth was a Black woman! What kind of denial was this?* I thought to myself.

Now back to the reading and writing. "I saw Scottie. Scottie saw me. I saw Spot. Spot saw me. Scottie saw Spot. Spot saw Scottie. Scottie ran Spot up the tree. 'Come back, Spot,' said Jane. 'Come back.'" The teacher had us reading aloud. Jean Guy and I were the best readers in the class, and the teacher was always calling on the two of us to read aloud to the class. I enjoyed seeing Jean Guy rise from her desk to read. Her voice was music to my ears.

The lunch bell rang, and we all filed out to eat and play. I told my friend Cookie, who was standing next to me, that I liked Jean Guy. That was a mistake, I found out!

He belted out, *"BLACK Jean Guy?"*

"What do you mean 'Black Jean Guy'?" I said.

He replied, "Can't you see how Black she is?" (Sure enough, she was Black.)

"So what!" I said. "She is the darkest, the prettiest, and the smart-est!" She had slanted eyes, pretty long eyelashes, and pretty lips (with a slight under bite). Her skin was silky and smooth, and she had a sleek, tapered figure. The more I looked at her, the more beautiful she became. I turned to my friend (who was the *same* complexion as Jean Guy) and said, "You mean to tell me you can't see how pretty she is?"

He replied, "She's just *too* Black for me!"

She was an intelligent, neat, and well-dressed girl, but the students were trying to tell me and others that something was **wrong** with her because she was dark-skinned.

The next thing I knew, everybody was teasing me. "Thomas likes *Black* Jean Guy! Dada, dada, da-da!" They saw *only* her complexion, but I saw her whole being. I had just learned another lesson in life—people see only what they want to see. It was a painful yet eye-opening experience. However, I was undaunted!

Thanksgiving was approaching, and I was looking forward to some blackboard artwork. I also asked about Halloween. Sister Mary Marian explained to me that Catholics did not celebrate Halloween the way non-Catholics did. She explained that Halloween had once been a religious holiday known as Hallowed Eve or Holy Eve. The Church celebrated this day by holding a Mass in honor of all the Saints and Souls that had passed on. Hence, we had to go to Church that night, and it was a "midnight mass," so most Catholics did not trick or treat. Nonetheless, my friends and I did squeeze it in when we could. Maybe this was one of those gray *venial* sin areas I was concerned with.

I figured that I could trick or treat and then go to confession, say a couple of Hail Marys and an Our Father to purge myself, and be back on the street in good standing. I guess this kind of thinking definitely made me, once again, a "Purgatorian!"

Wintertime was now upon us, and we were about to learn a new routine—how the hats and coats would be collected and taken to the cloakroom. A boy and a girl were to be selected from each aisle each day to do this, starting with the first seat of each aisle. The teacher selected the first names and said, "Boys, give your coats to Frank Pinkney, and girls, give your coats to Barbara Eazell." As soon as the teacher turned her back to walk away, the boys started whispering about who they hoped would be the girl they picked up coats with! The cloakroom was located directly across the hall from the classroom, and when the teacher stood at her desk, she could not see the cloakroom.

Now the boys were already conjuring up what they were going to do if they hooked up with this one or that one. I had eyes for only one, and when I sized up the selection method, I had as much chance as a snowball in hell for hooking up with Jean Guy. There was just too much skipping of seats. So each day, I had to sit and listen to each guy's wild story about what happened with this girl or that girl in the cloakroom. Most of the stories were made up to keep things interesting, I bet! In retrospect it's hard to believe everybody was hugging and kissing when they got into the cloakroom.

Many, many weeks later, the teacher called out two names, "Thomas DuVall and Jean Guy, collect the coats and take them to the cloakroom." I almost wet myself. She had to call me twice! I looked at the faces of the other boys in my class, and their expressions seemed to say, "This is it, Du'ball."

As I collected a coat from one guy, he said to me, "Jean likes you."

"Get out of here!" I said. And now I was headed for the cloakroom. Jean Guy, walking in front of me, knew I was following her.

The cloakroom was about six feet wide, six feet deep, and eight feet high. It was made of plywood that was painted brown and had a door that could be opened and closed from the inside. About a dozen hooks and a few wooden fold-up chairs were placed along the walls. The hooks were really too high for a second-grader to reach, and each hook was already overladen with the coats of the older students who would get there before us. We looked at the chairs. The chairs were also covered with coats, and coats were all over the floor! There was hardly *room* even for the two of us to stand. Plus there was no light installed in there, so the door had to be open for light to enter.

She looked at me, and I looked at her and started feeling weak in the knees. She said to me (in the sweetest lyrical tones), "Let's try and throw the coats over the ones on the hooks first, and the rest we'll try to place on top of the piles of coats on the chairs!"

My knees were shaking, and my throat was dry. I managed somehow to say, "OK," though my voice cracked. (I couldn't believe how much my legs were shaking! What was going on?) I turned to her and chokingly said, "Have we been in here a long time?"

She looked at me and softly said, "Close the door, and they won't notice."

Oh no! I said to myself. "But there won't be any light in here!"

She said, "We will be able to see!" (Oh no!) So I closed the door.

Everything went black, silent, and still for a moment. Once my eyes adjusted, I could see her standing there in front of me. She was just looking at me, and all of a sudden, I reached for her, and she came closer. The next thing I knew, we were embracing! Well if she was going to let me hug her, maybe she would let me kiss her. I kissed her! Unfortunately I overreached a little and lost my footing on a coat that was lying on the floor. With both of my feet caught in the coat, I was forced to put all my weight on her, and she had no place to go but backward over the chair with the biggest pile of coats. The chair slammed into the wall of the next classroom, and the pile of coats fell into the coats piled on the hooks and knocked all the coats off the wall hooks.

Now we were on top of the coats that had been piled on chairs and underneath all the coats that had been on the hooks. "Oh no," we both said. We started digging ourselves out. Once we were on our feet again, we immediately began picking up coats.

Jean said, "Now we have been in here a long time!"

I said to her, "Go back to the classroom, and I will finish putting up the coats!"

She said OK and left. I continued to reassemble the cloakroom. It took me a few minutes, and when I finished, I stuck my head out of the cloakroom door. Who did I see but Sister Mary Martha, the teacher from the classroom whose wall was banged by the chair.

It was then that I noticed Jean Guy leaning against the wall by our classroom door. "What's wrong?" I whispered to her in a fit of confusion. She told me that someone had locked the door to the classroom, so she couldn't get in. I asked her if she had knocked. She, a bit annoyed, answered, "Yes!" Then Sister Mary Martha came over and knocked good and hard, and the teacher came to the door. Sister Mary Martha told Sister Marian that she found the two of us standing out in the hall and asked where we had been. We told her we had been locked out.

Sister Martha told Sister Marian that she had heard a noise, had come to investigate, and had found the two of us in the hall. Sister Mary Marian wanted to know who could have locked the classroom door. The whole classroom was noticeably quiet.

Sister Mary Martha returned to her classroom. About an hour later, she returned and asked Sister Mary Marian to step outside in the hall for a minute. The classroom became very still. Usually, when the teacher left the room, the students would talk to each other or act up somehow, but now the students did not make a sound. It was as if a sentencing were about to take place.

Sister Mary Marian returned and stood before the class and said she had an announcement to make. She stated that from then on, two girls would pick up the girls' and boys' coats. All the boys looked at me for the answer. They wanted to know if I had spilled the beans! But why in the world would I have ratted on Jean Guy? They finally got the message. We later found out that Juanita Davis (a.k.a. Lena the Hyena) spilled the beans because she was the homeliest and the meanest. Nobody was kissing her, so why should there be any kissing? She might have been the one who had locked the classroom door. She had a crush on John Smith, the *"handsomest"* boy in class with the *curliest hair,* and neither he nor anyone else would give her the time of day, so she was always upset and vengeful (a Cruella DeVille type).

A few weeks went by, and one day there was a knock at the class-room door. Sister Mary Marian answered the door, and the woman identified herself as Mrs. Guy, Jean's mother. Sister Mary Marian turned and asked Jean to come forward. The three of them walked out into the hall and began to talk. The pencil sharpener was near the door, and all of a sudden, all the girls had to line up to get their pencils sharpened. I decided to get on line with them. When my turn finally came to sharpen my pencil, I could see Jean's silhouette and could tell she was in pain. Her head was low and slightly to the side. I felt pain in my heart. I was torn between feeling guilty for being clumsy and angry at the way things were being handled.

The door opened, and Jean came back and went to her seat. Sister Mary Marian resumed her lessons for the day. I looked at the Sister's face for some kind of compassionate glance. All I got was ice. I knew that I had to speak to Jean to find out what the verdict was, but how? They were all watching now, the students, the Nuns, especially the Nuns. Their job was to keep us apart, and they went about it devot-edly. However, I did get an opportunity weeks later.

One day we had to work at the blackboard together, and I was able to whisper to her. She said to me that they would let her stay here at St. Vincent de Paul until the Easter holidays, and then she would have to find another school to attend. She also said it would be an extra hard-ship for her mother, who lived near this school but would now have to travel all the way up to St. Augustine's in Northwest Washington. I felt depressed, powerless, guilty, angry, and heartbroken. Easter came and went. I returned to school and faced the fact that there was no Jean Guy to exchange smiles with. What a kick to the head that was!

It was back to the books and blackboard Art. I had to get out of second grade. There were too many memories now. One thing for sure was that I was *never* gonna have another crush or get emotionally involved with anyone for the rest of my life. No, sir! There would be no more jerking on the heart strings for me! I was not interested in the who or the what from then on. *"Forget it,"* I said to myself. Then I thought about being in the third grade without Jean Guy and fell apart all over again. God bless her soul, wherever she is.

I began sizing up the activities going on in the third- and fourth-grade classroom. They looked like a pretty wild bunch over there to me—especially the boys! I saw them giving the Nuns a hard time and a rough road to travel. One day we were all in line to go to our classrooms when the fourth-grade boys started shooting staples at the girls with their slingshots, and the girls were all screaming, ducking, and running. The Nuns went after them, and the boys ran into the boy's restroom, laughing and yelling to beat the band. The Nuns did NOT pursue them into the boy's restroom. They just stood at the door and called for them to come out. The boys pulled similar pranks for weeks, and no matter what the crime was, all they had to do was run into the boys' restroom, and they were SAFE. What a sweet deal that was. Even I took advantage of that.

Soon there was a big announcement: the third- and fourth-grade classroom was getting a new teacher. Her name was Sister Mary Carmel. Sister Mary Carmel didn't smile; that was the first thing I noticed. She swaggered like a man—the way she swung her arms and all. Nonetheless, the boys came in with their slingshots one day and decided to break her in. I was already in the boys' restroom legitimately. All of a sudden, I heard this loud crash at the door. About eight to ten boys came tumbling through the door, laughing and falling all over each other. They had *made it* to the boys' restroom.

There was a sharp rap on the door that sounded like a policeman's nightstick. I heard Sister Mary Carmel's voice say, *"Either you come out now or I'm coming in after you!"*

Then there was a scuffle among the boys to get their Timmy-Tommies out as if they were about to take a leak. *"I know she won't come in here now,"* I heard one of them say.

Sister Mary Carmel said, *"Ready or not, here I come!"* She came in swinging hard and talking loud. I could hear her say, "You better put 'IT' back in your pants if you got 'IT' out, because if 'IT' gets hit, I am not going to be responsible."

I had never before heard such hollering and screaming and jumping around! Her timing was perfect. They could not get their Timmy-Tommies in fast enough. One boy ran to the urinal with his ding-a-ling out; she whacked him across his "able-sugar-sugar," and he jumped *straight* into the urinal. It swas chaos in there! She didn't even look at me as I walked out and left them to their folly. She had turned a safe haven into a torture chamber. Those boys *never* tried that one again! Yes, sir, she broke that one up! That was my first brush with the new teacher. I would have her next year in the third- and fourth-grade classroom. What an introduction!!

The body count: army truck, kindergarten, James Skinner, Sister Mary Nazareth, Jean Guy, and Father Cohen—gone, but not forgotten.

CHAPTER 5

Summer Vacation (1939)

Mr. Wal'er (Grandma's friend) took me to the barbershop until I was seven years old. When I turned seven, Mr. Wal'er said to me, "Thomas, you have reached the age of reasoning. You are now old enough to go to the barbershop on your own!" It was only three or four blocks away from the house, so I walked on my own. That was a big deal to me and to Mr. Wal'er; he knew I had to negotiate that intersection at South Capitol and M Streets. The barbershop was located at Third and M Streets SW. I lived on Half and M Streets SE., because South Capitol Street divided east from west.

It was a lot of fun going to the barber's with Mr. Wal'er because he would get into all the topics that were being argued or discussed. A little beer was always on the scene, and Mr. Wal'er would always let me taste his beer and say, "Jus' don't tell your mother!" I didn't realize how much I was going to miss him.

The barbershop was called Ben Ross's Barbershop, and Mr. Ross, who was fifty or sixty years old and had a big potbelly, was the head barber. Mr. Wal'er's instructions to me were to wait for Mr. Ross's chair and not to go to any other barber because he knew how to cut my type of hair and anybody else was just going to mess it up. I said OK and followed his instructions. My turn finally came, and I climbed up onto the special seat that they used to cut little children's hair.

While I was sitting there waiting for him to start, a man rushed into the shop, handed Mr. Ross a big cigar, and said, "I'll give you this cigar if you promise me you won't eat it!"

Mr. Ross looked at the cigar and said, "Wow! This is an expensive cigar!"

The man said, "Yeah! That's why I don't want you *chewing it up!*"

Mr. Ross said, "OK, I promise." The man walked away. As soon as the man walked out of the shop, Mr. Ross took the cigar out of his pocket, took a *big* bite out of the cigar, and started chewing it up. With a mouth full of cigar pieces, he came over to me, put the barber's drop cloth around my neck, and started combing my hair.

Mr. Ross put his face in my face and said to me (with his breath stinking like tobacco and saliva), "You have nice hair!" There was a long pause, and after a little more combing, he asked, "Do you have any sisters?"

"No, no sisters," I said.

After another long pause and a little more combing, he asked, "Well…ah…how old is your mother?"

I was thinking, *Say what?* I thought that was a bit much, so I answered, "I don' know!"

After another long pause and a little more combing and some snipping, he said, "Well…ah…how old are *you?*" he asked.

"I'm seven!" I said.

"Well…she can't be that old then, if you're only seven. That would put her say…aroouuund…thirtyish anyway. That's a *nice* age! What's her name?"

"I don' know!" I said.

"Well…what do *you* call her?" he asked.

"I call her *Mama!*" (I could not believe I said that.) He got quiet after that.

After a few more attempts to get more info out of me over the summer months, Mr. Ross decided he did not want to be bothered with me rejecting him and began turning me over to another barber working in his shop. That was fine with me because I was getting tired of him too; besides, his breath made me sick to my stomach anyway.

The other barbers were not as good as Mr. Ross and had the same routine as he had. I got chewed out at home for allowing some other barber to just mess over my hair. When my parents confronted Mr. Ross, he told them he could no longer promise he would always be available for my hair. Now none of the barbers wanted to be bothered with me, nor did I want to be bothered with them.

I got to a point where I hated going to the barbershop because I hated being pumped for information. I used to call it the hair routine. The barbers no longer paid attention to instructions sent by my parents. Whenever Mama wanted to send me to the barbershop, I would think up an excuse to avoid going, so my hair just got longer and longer. The first day of school was fast approaching, and Mama said I definitely had to get a haircut before going back to school. I said, OK. *But that will be the last time,* I said to myself.

My brother Herbert was born that July. The man Mama said was my father looked like Herbert. I thought to myself, *I don't think I look like him, but I can see Herbert and maybe Roland in him.* I didn't suspect Father Cohen to be my father now, but I did feel Mama would have preferred a Catholic man of the cloth. Would Mama have messed around with a Catholic man of the cloth? Some did, and there *were* secrets in the Church; the first grade had certainly taught me that much! At least Hugh DuVall was the son of a Baptist man of the cloth.

I was told that mixed-religion families could have insurmountable family problems. Even though I did not think I looked like Hugh, Mama said I was to call him Daddy. I did as I was told, but from time to time, I would ask my mother if Hugh DuVall was really my father. She would always reply, "Yes, Thomas!" I would then ask her why I had hair on my arms and legs when nobody else did. She said it came from her side of the family. I saw nobody with hair on their arms and legs on *her* side of the family either. I also had a big toe that was unlike anyone else's in the family. I began to feel I was annoying Mama with these questions, so I left it alone (for the moment).

I thought Hughdy (as Mama called him) was a likeable guy with a wry sense of humor and a hardy laugh. He had a great flair for clothes and wore boutonnieres, cravats, cummerbunds, and embroidered initialed handkerchiefs. He spoke as if he were reading poetry; every word was spoken eloquently and precisely. His handwriting was highly stylized and full of serifs and curlicues. He was a dandy of a figure. He was also good at poker, we found out, and was very lucky. I heard him say one day that he was the best poker player in the Washington, DC, area.

He always took us for long drives on Sundays. The speed limit was fifty miles an hour on the open road back then.

CHAPTER 6

He Made Me Hate My Name
or
Thomas, the Cat Killer

Around the time I was seven years old, somebody was killing cats in the neighborhood. For some reason, people in the neighborhood decided that Thomas DuVall was the cat killer. Someone said that they had seen me swinging a cat around by the tail, so that was why I was the suspect. Mama questioned me about this, and I told her I would never kill anything, much less a cat. I loved cats and dogs. I did admit to dropping a cat to the floor because I had been told that cats always landed on their feet and wanted to see if that was true. It was true, so that was that for me. I was crazy about the little stray kitten I found one day, but Mama would not allow me to keep the kitten. It broke my heart, but it did not make me vindictive. The suspicion remained, and cats were being stabbed to death and buried in shallow graves. The women in the neighborhood were furious and greatly disturbed. I had no idea who would do such a thing but knew it was *not* me. People started calling me "Thomas, the cat killer." I was given a bad name, and everybody treated me with suspicion and scorn.

Months went by, and I was sick of the accusations. One day I was passing by the house of Reverend Davis (who I suspected was a self-ordained Baptist Minister), when his son, Ralph, who was about a year or so younger than I was, asked me if I could come into his yard to play with him. Reverend Davis was a very strict disciplinarian who never let Ralph play with the other children in the neighborhood. Ralph always had to play in his yard by himself. I felt kind of sorry for him, so I said, "OK, I'll play with you for a little while!"

We played for a while, and the whole time he was playing, he carried this dinner fork around in his hand. Every now and then, he would sit and stab into the dirt with this dinner fork. I eventually asked him what was he digging for and why he didn't he use a shovel. He said he would show me why. He put the fork in his pants pocket and said, "Wait here until I come back, and I will show you why I need this fork."

He went away and came back with this little kitten. The kitten seemed a little nervous to me, and it remained in a crouching, close-to-the-ground hunch. I kept watching the kitten as he looked at me as if to ask for help. But I figured maybe he was just nervous. All of a sudden, Ralph grabbed the kitten around the neck and stabbed the kitten in the neck with this dinner fork until the poor little thing was dead.

I could not believe my eyes! I was *mortified*! I could not speak and could not forget the way that poor little kitten had looked at me just before he was butchered. He had been trying to get me to help him escape his fate at the hands of this son of a preacher man! My God, what kind of family was this? I JUMPED UP so fast that it startled

Ralph. I told him that for months I had been accused of killing these cats while he had been walking around *above suspicion* because he was the son of a preacher man! Ralph just looked at me as if to say, *"SO?"* I told him I was going to expose him to the neighborhood and that I wanted my name cleared of this devilish thing! He gave me a challenging look, as if to say, *"So, who is going to believe you? My father is a Reverend!"* I felt like I was going to vomit! I ran all the way back to my house and sat by the window to wait for Mama to come home so that I could tell her what I had discovered. That boy had shown no sign of remorse. Maybe that's why his father was a preacher; he probably knew he had an evil son, so to hide the *real* truth, he pretended to be a man of God. What a lesson that was for a seven-year-old to experience! Even though the word got around that I was *probably* innocent, it did not clear my name altogether; people just called me "Tom Cat" right up until I moved away to a new neighborhood some five years down the road.

Ralph probably turned out to be a real serial killer. Who knows? I just hope I never see him again, in life. The funny thing was that I kind of liked the sound of the nickname Tom Cat! (This was before *Tom and Jerry* cartoons for me.) My first *Tom and Jerry* show had me saying to myself, *How do they know about that, especially the parts where the mouse takes advantage of the situation by destroying things around the house and the housekeeper accuses Tom of breaking something?* Poor Tom could not speak on his own behalf, so he would be thrown out of the house as punishment! I could relate to that. I knew just how he felt.

Roland, Mama, and Thomas.

CHAPTER 7

Third Grade

Summer was over, and we were all back in school. I was in the third-grade class, and Sister Mary Carmel was my new teacher that year. She was a stern, frightening, and awesome sight. She even had a slight mustache. We just *could not* believe she was not really a man. She walked like a man and talked like an Army Drill Sergeant.

We started the day with the usual morning prayers—an Our Father and a few Hail Marys. Then she called the roll in alphabetical order. I listened for Thomas Davis's name to be called and knew I was next.

"Thomas DuVall!" she called out.

"Here, Sister," I answered.

She called my name again. I answered, "Yes, Sister?"

"Stand up, Thomas DuVall!" she said. I stood up slowly and pensively. "Sister Mary Marian has spoken so highly of you, Thomas, and I have seen your artwork and would like to know if you would be willing to do the same for us this year. Now you know you don't have to, but we would certainly appreciate it if you did."

I was too scared to say no, so I volunteered to do it. She responded, "You still have to give up your lunch hours because we can't have you doing artwork during class periods." I said I understood. This time I told my mother that I would be doing artwork on my lunch hours again this year. She *flipped out* and asked me how long this had been going on. I told her I had done it in the first and second grades too.

My mother immediately picked up a pen and paper and started writing a letter to the Pope in Rome. She demanded that this thing be stopped immediately, if not sooner. Then she told me she was mailing the letter that day. That's when I spoke up. I told her I had *volunteered* to do it. She was shocked! She dropped the pen on the table, and the letter fell out of her hand.

"What did you say?" she asked.

I said, "I volunteered to do it."

She was visibly perplexed. "Well, what do you know!" she said. "I don't know what to say! Son, are you telling me you want to do this?"

"Yes, Ma'am, I want to do this," I answered.

She stared at me for a moment and then started tearing up the letter. *"What can I say?"* she said. "I am confused *and* impressed. I am also proud. However, you understand that you don't have to do this."

"Yes, I understand, Mama, but I enjoy it very much, and the school enjoys it too."

"OK!" she said.

Everything was going along pretty well in class, but my hair was getting longer and longer, and I was not combing it. One day Sister Mary Carmel said to me, "Thomas DuVall, your head looks like a *feather bed*! If you come in here tomorrow with it looking like that I am going to comb it *myself*!" I told Mama what she said, and Mama said it looked like a *sheep's BUTT* to her.

The teacher had to leave the room one day, and the rowdy classroom started to sing this song (to the tune of "I Ain't Gonna Study War No More"):

> Oh you can't get to heaven
> With curly hair,
> 'Cause God don't want
> No sissies there!

Then everyone in the class would chime in to sing the chorus:

> Oh you can't get to heaven with curly hair,
> 'Cause God don't want no sissies there!
> I ain't gon' lea-eave my Lord no more!

WOW! I hadn't known that if I had curly hair, I was a sissy and couldn't go to heaven. *Wow,* I thought, *I've never heard that before.* But John Smith, who was also in the class, had curly hair. I wondered why they never messed with him like they messed with me. His hair looked exactly like mine. What in the world was going on? I soon found out that John Smith's family was very active and visible in the Catholic community, so the children didn't want to mess with that family. They did not know *who* I was. They also knew John Smith was from Half and M Streets SW, but I was a "Southeast boy." I was from Half and M Streets SE, so maybe that's what it was. I never said anything or protested because my mama had told me that sticks and stones may break my bones, but names will never hurt me. I remained silent.

The boys soon decided to jump on me and beat me up. I guess they were following the bully because they were afraid to do otherwise or they were just *tired* of singing! They beat the snot out of me. I was thinking to myself, *What in the world is going on?* When I got home, I would get another beating for looking like I got beat up!

"Boy! What in the world happened to you?" my mother would yell. "Look at your new coat. The sleeve is gone. And where's the collar? Don't you realize that was a brand-new coat?"

"Mama, I don't know what happened to the collar, but I thought I put the sleeve in my pocket," was all I could say. That was when I felt the first wallop.

Poor Mama thought I was mismanaging her hard-earned money. This was during World War II, and times were hard, especially for Colored folks. She would beat my butt for looking like I had gotten my butt beat. I felt like I was getting beaten coming and going and didn't even know what it was all about. I kept thinking, *Is it really about HAIR?* Until I was about eight or nine years old, that's what my life was like. I was tired of this hair routine. I thought, *The class can sing the song all they want because I don't care.* I even liked the tune. I just made up my own verses and sang along with them in silence.

I was beginning to notice the hair of everybody in school. The boys were referring to their stocking cap press as "BOSS MOSS." It made the ringlets of hair lay close to the head and created little waves; I thought that was clever. I even tried it myself. The girls were another story. They were talking about GOOD hair and BAD hair and how to avoid showing their "kitchen" to the public! (The kitchen is that area at the back of the neck where the hairline stops. It is this area that is said to revert back to nappy "first" after having your hair STRAIGHTENED!)

On Saturday afternoons in my neighborhood, you could pick up the smell of hair being "fried" in almost every house. Every now and then, a scream could be heard as a *red-hot* comb burned some poor soul. My mother was a good hair presser; she even had a few regular customers. The most *frightening* thing to me was to watch my mom press her *own hair* with those blazing red-hot combs so close to the scalp. I could not bear to look, so I would find something to do outside. I wasn't going to hang around.

Juanita Davis was a lively topic in 1942, when I was in grade school. She had practically no hair! It was basically fuzz. They said her hair was so short and nappy that every time her mother would buy her a new bow ribbon, she would have to send her to the store to buy glue to glue it on with! I felt so sorry for her, and it was apparent that she was not taking it well.

Juanita Davis was a skinny, shapeless girl. She was very plain looking, loped when she walked, *never* smiled, and had the smell of poverty and not bathing daily. She was madly in love with John Smith (the handsome boy with the curly hair), and he wouldn't give her the time of day. She was so disturbed by his aloofness that she decided to pick a fight with him and made the mistake of taking her coat off first. That's when he hit her. Her arms were caught in her coat, and she was defenseless. She fell over backward, and her butt hit the ground.

She was crushed. I felt sorry for her; she was sitting on the ground soaked with tears. Nobody moved to help her. John Smith laughed out loud and walked away. I went over to her, helped her to her feet, brushed her off, and helped her put her coat back on right. She never looked at me and never said thanks. I turned to John Smith and said, "You didn't have to hit her! She was only trying to get your attention!" He looked at me like I was crazy.

Poor Juanita wanted somebody with GOOD hair. *For her children's sake,* I thought to myself. Most of the boys preferred girls with long, straight hair, it seemed. I had a flashback to the barbershop, where the barbers pumped me for info on whether I had sisters and who and how old my mother was because they had deduced from my curly hair that the females in my family must be fine. The people in my family had all kinds of hair, and I had never heard a mumbling word about hair one way or the other. But now I was hearing classifications of hair types that would astound a zoological taxonomist. Why there was bad hair, kinky hair, frizzy hair, curly hair, beady hair, wavy hair, blow hair, knotty hair, Indian hair, somewhat straight hair, ain't too bad hair, and GOOD hair! (Yeah, Man!!) A good grade of hair was *preferred* in those days before Black was beautiful. People were seeing the hair before they saw the person, and then they saw only what they "wanted" to see, not what they needed to see.

I have never looked at a girl's hair first. I always look at the eyes! There is something mystical about the eyes! I wouldn't care if she was bald. I do seem to have a natural pull to braids (with no extensions attached). Maybe I am old-fashioned, but there is something so clean and fresh looking about braids (or "plaits," as some people refer to them).

As I was about to enter my teens, I was also checking out the older brothers. They thought that if they could straighten their hair, they could get the SLICK CHICKS and maybe even get into SHOW BIZ! Cab Calloway, for example, really had the girls worked up, the way he would throw his hair around and all. The brothers wanted some of that same action. During his famous bow to the audience, Calloway would allow his hair to fall over his face and then throw his head back. All of his hair would fall back without his having to touch it with his hands. Adam Clayton Powell Jr. had a huge sister congregation. They were swooning at the way he would throw his hair around when he was charged up with the Scriptures. Then there was Nat "King" Cole, with such all-time hits as "Mona Lisa," "Unforgettable," and "They Tried to Tell Us We're Too Young." He made it OK for men to have their hair gassed. Plus, it got him on TV with his own show for a spell. Even Rochester had a konk (chemically straightened hair)! Poor Sammy Davis Jr. didn't help things. The brothers wanted to be slicked up for the SISTERS (not for each other). The sisters were looking FINE as WINE, and the brothers wanted to be noticed, so they started gassing their heads.

To get this straight-hair look, they ingeniously concocted a homemade substance of Red Devil Lye, potato mash, and some other convoluted-sounding stuff. They'd hook up a garden hose to a sink to water down their heads because as their heads dried, the lye would commence to burn their scalps (and I have seen some nasty burned scalps). Sometimes I could hear their blood-curdling screams all over the neighborhood, as they would yell, "Oh, Jesus! More water, more water! Hurry, hurry, yeah, yeah, more, more!"

Nonetheless, they were willing to do all this because it was going to make their hair STRAIGHT! (*Wow!*) The White man saw this slaughter, decided he could make a safer product for the boys, and put something on the market called "KING KONK." They jumped on it! The downside of this was that when their hair wasn't freshly KONKED UP, it really looked KONKED OUT!

I told my mama that they were still teasing me, and she replied, "If they lay a hand on you, you better fight back. I can't keep buying you jackets for some other mother's son to rip up! So if you don't want a whipping when you come home looking like that, you'd better start defending yourself!"

"Yes, Mama!" I said. I stopped singing along with them (in silence!). Maybe they thought I was a *sissy* because I willingly gave up my lunch hour to draw. While they were singing, laughing, and making jokes, I was saying to myself, *Sing all you want, just don't touch the clothes! Because if you put your hands on me, I'm fighting back!* And I had no problem telling them that. I was not smiling! They eventually settled down, and peace was restored. When Mama noticed how nice I looked one day when I arrived home, she commented, and I told her I was following her instructions.

Nonetheless, I was getting a bad reputation as a "hitter" and being punished for it at school. I didn't care, however, because I was getting *praise* at home for taking the necessary precautions to protect my mother's clothes. They eventually sent for my mother about me fighting in school. When she got back home, she asked me if I had started any of those fights.

I told her, "I have never started a fight; I just hit them after they hit me first."

She then looked at me and said, "Son, *never, ever* start a fight. But if someone strikes you *first*, you strike back. And if they are bigger than you, find yourself a two-by-four or an old tree trunk and *defend* yourself! But if *you* strike first, I shall *never* forgive you."

"Yes, Mama!" I said. I got the picture. I also told her that that's what I was doing. For some reason the Nuns would *never* see anyone hitting me but *always* saw me hitting someone! My punishment for getting caught hitting was to be called to the front of the class and made to face the wall and punch it continuously with my fists until the *teacher* got tired. I did not care because Jean Guy was not there to witness this, anyway. I really missed her.

Then it was back to the reading and writing. Sister Mary Carmel was a very demonstrative teacher. She pressed so hard on the chalk when she wrote on the blackboard that when she called on someone to erase what she had written, the student had to use a *lot* of elbow grease to erase her markings from the board. There was something intimidating about her demeanor. She intimidated all of us except Barbara Eazell, who was always raising her hand first when the teacher called on the class to answer a question.

For example, the teacher would ask, "Who was the first president of the United States?" Barbara Eazell's hand would shoot up in the air, and she'd wave frantically to be the first one to respond. The teacher would call on her to give the class the answer.

She would reply out loud with such vigor and confidence, "Abraham Lincoln!" The class would break out in laughter.

"Barbara, sit down," the teacher would say. Then she would call on another student to give the correct answer.

If the teacher called on the class a hundred times, Barbara would respond immediately a hundred times, though never with the *right* answer. The teacher was visibly perplexed. It got to a point where the teacher stopped calling on her first. She would try to skip around the room for new hands raised. Trying not to obviously look like she was ignoring Barbara, she occasionally would call on Barbara to respond. "OK, Barbara, how much is five times five?" Barbara would exuberantly and *immediately* reply, "Thirty-five!" It was a hopeless situation, it seemed. Nevertheless, Barbara Eazell was undaunted.

As time went by, Barbara came to realize that the first thought in her head was not always the correct thought. She was a hard worker who always attacked her work with zeal and zest. She would always finish her work *first*, only to have the teacher say, "Barbara, there is plenty of time for you to go back to your seat and give this assignment a little more thought before handing it in. You still have plenty of time left."

She never made the honor roll, but I am sure she got an A for class participation. She was a sweet person who was somewhat naïve and a bit rambunctious. Charles Schultz, the creator of the comic strip *Peanuts*, must have had a Barbara Eazell in his class in school and decided to call her "Peppermint Patty." Barbara Eazell was definitely a "Pure Spirit." I pray she found her niche in life. God bless your soul, wherever you are, Barbara.

Sister Carmel was pleased with my progress in class and decided I was smart enough to skip to the next grade. She started giving me fourth-grade work, which I seemed to be handling okay—especially in spelling. I became a good speller. History, geography, and religion were no problem either, but penmanship and math were a struggle. This confused the teacher because she could not understand how a person who could draw so well could not write legibly. (I could not figure it out either!) However, calligraphy, especially the old English script that the entire class had trouble deciphering, was a piece of cake for me. My biggest struggle was the times tables. I could not for the life of me remember all the multiplication tables, especially the eight and nine times tables. Whenever the teacher would call on me to give the answer to a flash card on those times tables, I would break out in a cold sweat.

One day Sister Mary Carmel was using flash cards with the class. She held up the card "9 x 9 =" and called, "Thomas DuVall!" I was unable to come up with the answer. She called me up to the front of the class. Then she told me to face the class, and I did. The next thing I knew, she bent over behind me, grabbed me by the cuffs of my pants, and tried to lift both of my legs off the floor simultaneously!

Knowing her reputation, I thought she was trying to do some bodily harm. What did I do? I thought to myself, *I'm not going to let her hurt me because I don't know the answer,* so I resisted. I would not let her manhandle me like that and became determined that my two feet would remain *planted* on the floor. As big and strong as she was, I managed to somehow keep at least *one* foot on the floor. She finally got the message and, panting for breath, said to me, "Return to your seat!"

With tears running down my face and my nose running like a faucet and no handkerchief, I was a sniveling, sniffling, snarling mess. I had no choice but to go for the sleeves of my shirt. So I wiped my tears on my right sleeve and wiped my nose on my left sleeve. (Luckily it was a long-sleeved shirt.) I wanted to disappear from sight. Now I knew what the word "embarrassing" meant. Wow! Now I had to walk down the aisle past all those girls whose mocking expressions seemed to say, "Look at the crybaby!" I thought, *I'm glad Jean Guy is not here to see me now, boy oh boy!*

I had been taken completely by surprise, and it had scared me to death. I had resisted because I saw my head hitting the floor! She called up another boy and did the same thing to him. He immediately placed both his hands on the floor so that she could lift his legs into the air. Now he was standing on his hands.

The teacher asked, "What is nine plus nine?"

The class responded, "Eighteen!"

She released the boy's legs, and he stood up. "Now how much is nine times nine?"

The class responded, "Eighty-one!"

She said to me, "Now, Thomas, that should make it easy for you to remember." She then sarcastically said, "I thought *all* boys knew how to stand on their hands, but I guess I was wrong."

The teacher could have at least *announced* what she was about to do, rather than just grabbing at my ankles like that. I can't remember that boy's name, but I remember seeing him walking on his hands during recess. He had everybody's attention. Why hadn't she called on him first?

To this day I have trouble with the answer to nine times nine, but I am now in my seventies and of (somewhat) sound mind. I can see what her point was. (My mama always said I was a little slow.) Yeah, Ma! I may have been a little slow, but I was determined not to let her harm me. Nevertheless, I still can't stand on my hands!

Sister Mary Carmel was somewhat of an entrepreneur. She had taken it upon herself to open a candy concession stand in front of the school and sell candy to the kids while they played. She even had a credit system going so that we could get our candy even if we didn't have ready cash. She kept a record book, so if we were delinquent in paying up, she had her way of dealing with us. She sold BB Bats, Mary Janes, Kit-Kats, candy kisses, nut bars, Peppermint Patties, and other kinds of candy. She was called the *Cavity Queen.*

She was also the school "security force." If there was a disturbance of any kind, especially fights of any nature, the Nuns would ring this bell, and Sister Carmel would actually roll up her sleeves, swagger to the rescue, and handle it. It was like watching Batman, cape and all (the headpiece the Nuns wore had a scarf-like tail that flapped in the wind as if they had wings on their backs), sans the Batmobile. The kids somehow found out what her name was before she took her vows as a Nun. It was *Gertrude Curtis.* All the students immediately started calling her Gertrude. From then on, it was "Gertrude this" and "Gertrude that." She was the hardest hitter of all the Nuns. When Gertrude hit us, we knew we were hit. She seemed to enjoy hitting too!

She would hit us and steadily talk at the same time. *"And don't bring your parents down here because I don't want to see 'em!"* That's what she would say; those were her *signature* words. She also would roll up her sleeves as she was coming after us. Gertrude was a sight to behold.

CHAPTER 8

The Spelling Bee

The Christmas holidays were over, and we were back in school. After we said our morning prayers, Sister Mary Carmel greeted the class and announced that she had wonderful news for us. The fourth-grade students of St. Vincent de Paul had been selected to represent the school in a citywide Catholic School Spelling Bee. The spelling bee was going to be broadcast live on station WOL up on Wisconsin Avenue. "You will be competing with St. Ann's for first place," she said. *WOW!* we thought. She then said that St. Ann's was an all-White school, and the students were sharp, which meant we were going to have to work hard to make our school look good. No matter what, we knew we had to work hard, and with Sister Carmel in charge, we knew we were in for some drilling!

Spirits were running high in the fourth grade, and we were *steadily working at it*. Sister Mary Carmel had narrowed the spellers down to about nine—seven girls and two boys. There was a lot of dictionary homework and lists upon lists of study words. Sister Mary Carmel gave us a good rule to remember: first *pronounce* the word, then *spell* the word, then *say the word again*. That was a good rule! We also had to practice and memorize a *victory song* that we would have to sing if we lost, praising the victors in their struggle to win. It was a long song with many lines and verses. The song was pretty, and those girls really sounded good singing it! I was singing too; we all had to sing, and sing we did.

Spring was in the air, and we were on our way to radio station WOL to compete in the citywide Catholic School Spelling Bee, which would be broadcast *live* in Washington, DC! We arrived early to be on time. We had to stand outside the studio door until we saw the red light over the door that displayed "ON THE AIR" go out, and then we could enter.

We entered a large room that had two very long tables, one on each side of the room, and chairs that were arranged so that the two schools would be facing each other. In the middle of the floor was a table with all the prizes that would be given out. I saw some really nice things on that table. We were all abuzz talking about the things we saw as prizes. We had never seen such nice things for classroom projects and learning aids and especially had our eyes on the little *radio* that we saw. We had always talked in class about how nice it would be to have a radio for our class projects. The radio stations used to broadcast specials over the air that would help with class assignments on governmental and historical events.

At the other end of the room was a smaller table where the Master of Ceremonies, or MC, sat. He greeted us and announced his name. I cannot remember his name, but his voice was one that could be heard at any time of day on WOL. We all recognized his voice and now knew what he looked like. He reminded me of Ted Mack of *Ted Mack's Amateur Hour*, but he looked and sounded exactly like Mac McGarry from the Saturday morning quiz show for DC-area high schools, *It's Academic*. Following the spelling bee, every time I saw McGarry on Saturday mornings, I had to stop what I was doing and stare at him until he made some kind of gesture that I could point and say, NO, he is not the guy.

The students from the opposing school eventually arrived and took their seats facing us on the opposite side of the room. The all-White students facing us sat there staring at us, some in disbelief and some with disdain, while others looked away with indifference. Some of them even looked flushed! The White Nuns never even acknowledged our presence. It was an *eerie* feeling. I figured one Nun would give some kind of hello sign or something to the other Nuns, but all I can remember now is the *silence* that permeated the room. It was as if we were behind a two-way mirror watching them and they didn't see us watching them. It was somewhat unnerving to me, but then again, what do you show your opponent—love and affection? Yes! Why not?

The MC told everyone to watch the sign on the wall; when it lit up, we were on the air, so there was no talking. The MC began to announce the schools' names and the rules of the game.

He said he would be giving St. Ann's School the first turn and when they *missed*, it would be St. Vincent's turn at the mike. He also said that the words would get harder as we proceeded and that a prize would be given for each word spelled correctly. The prizes got better as the difficulty of the words increased, so the harder the word, the bigger the prize.

The radio was set aside for the last and hardest word, and I had my eyes on that *radio* for the class. I don't even remember today what all the other prizes were. I did not care because my eyes were on that RADIO! (Boy o' boy!) The MC called out the first word to be spelled by the opponent, and they got it right. The second word they also got right.

We were thinking the words were pretty easy so far. The opponents took the first part of the bee and about a third of the prizes, but we were not concerned yet. Our eyes were on the prize—that RADIO! *For Phase II, the words will be more difficult,* we thought.

The MC started calling out words, and this time we noticed a weaker response from the other side. Was insecurity raising its ugly head? About two or three words into Phase II, the competition was faltering. They were down to their last team member, and he was not coming up with an answer. Out of desperation, he turned to the nearest Nun for help, and she *did* help him. She mou-u-u-u-thed the letters of the words by silently animating the sound of the letters. A big smile came over his face, and as she was lip reading and gesticulating, he was deciphering a vowel and got it right! WOW!! We were all *dumbfounded.* We waited for the MC to say foul! The MC just smiled and *congratulated* the boy. Then he presented the boy with his prize! We were all looking at each other. We thought, *Do you mean to say that the MC did not see that floor show they were putting on over there?* We *wanted* to believe that maybe he had not seen it, but we all *saw him watch* the pantomime-sign language performance of the cheating Nun!

The MC went back to his station. Without giving us a glance, he announced the beginning of Phase III. *Lord, have mercy!* I said to myself. *Am I dreaming?* Sure enough, the words got tougher, though no word he had called out would have been a problem for us. Oh oh! Once again, the first-choice speller was stumbling and stammering! She turned to the Nun, and the Nun immediately went into her routine. It was a sight to behold! The girl turned back to the MC and spelled the word as if she had known it all the time. She was a pretty White girl, too. You should have seen the beautiful smile on her face when the MC gave her the prize.

Now only a third of the prizes were left. I couldn't take it anymore and was looking for Sister Mary Carmel to say something to the MC! Sister Mary Carmel was busy telling me she saw it but couldn't say anything right then. *(What?)* *"But they were cheating; make them stop cheating, Sister!"* I said. She just looked at me and said nothing. I looked at her and said to myself, *I thought you were so BAAAaad. You're scared!* She wanted no part of tangling with the White folks. That was the look I saw in *her* eyes!

To our amazement and dismay, the White Nuns continued their lip-synching pantomime coaxing until every prize on the table was gone, except the radio. I just knew those Nuns, out of some sense of decency or morality or some kind of sign from GOD or *something*, would allow us a chance to take that radio with us. They had cheated us out of everything else.

Please, dear GOD, intervene here and help us help ourselves. That was my silent prayer; however, it was all in vain. The MC called out the last word, whose spelling we knew, and the students immediately turned to their Nun, did their favorite routine, and, presto, the radio was gone, just like magic! It was all over! The table was bare, and the champions were congratulating each other. Sister Mary Carmel *finally* spoke, "All right, children, let's all rise and sing the victory song to the new champions!" The words consisted of phrases like, *"Hail, you mighty Victors, this day is won, the day is yours, and we praise and pay honor to you, Oh mighty Victors!"*

I stood up, but for the life of me I could not open my mouth to sing. The other students sang and swayed. I was *shocked, dumbfounded,* and *frustrated.* I was also sick to my stomach. They tried to get me to sway with them by bumping into me, but I was stiff as a board. Sister Mary Carmel looked at me as if to say, "How dare you! *And* in front of these Whites." Not only that, but the White students had filed out of the room long before their song of praise was done, and they didn't look back to say good-bye! And to put the cap on the bottle, the MC walked out right behind them. The students from my school were still in the room singing and swaying, and I admit they *really* sang well and sounded great.

Lights began blinking in the studio, which was the signal to leave the area. We put our coats on and left as the last lights turned off. I took one more glance around the room and paused to see if I was going to awaken suddenly, only to realize I was *already awake*!

This was the year 1940, and television wasn't on the commercial market yet. Those Nuns took advantage of that fact, as they knew that people couldn't see them mouthing the answers over the radio. They knew the advantage being on the radio could bring. (I have looked at a similar quiz show recently and got the same feeling when I saw those children from the so-called ghetto schools or those schools in the middle of all-Black neighborhoods. Why not do away with this kind of show, which reveals the great inequities heaped on these schools on worldwide TV? If the producers can't show some kind of compatibility, why *"slaughter"* them with the world looking on? Remember that there is supposed to be "liberty and justice for all!") We had worked SO HARD for weeks only to be destroyed in thirty minutes.

When we got outside, we lined up in two rows, with the girls in front and the two boys bringing up the rear. Sister Mary Carmel walked to where I was standing and said, *"Thomas, you will never amount to anything in life unless you can change your attitude. You will always be living on the 'raggedy fringes of life'; you will be a drunkard and never amounting to anything!"* With that said, she turned and went back to the head of the group.

I was already broken, so I figured a little salt on the wounds was all I needed. What puzzled me at the moment was this: *what in the world is a drunkard?* On the way back to school, I was saying to myself, *I drink, you drink, we drink, they drink, I drank, you drank, we drank, they drank, I have drunk...drink, drank, drunk!* Those seemed to be the only parts of speech I could recall having ever learned. What was I missing? Was I out of school when they discussed how to use the word "drunkard" in a sentence? I was befuddled. When we got back to school, the first chance I got, I whipped out my English book and looked up the parts of speech for "drink." I did not see the parts of speech for "drunkard," so I looked in the back of the book for a reference for the word "drunkard." The word was not in the English school textbook! Now I was really confused! If the word wasn't in the schoolbook, where was it?

That night at the dinner table, my mom asked me about my day at the spelling bee. The first thing that popped out of my mouth was, "Mama, what is a drunkard?"

Mama said, "WHAT? You mean to say that that was one of the *spelling bee* words?"

"No, Mom," I said.

"Then where did you hear that word?"

"Sister Carmel told me I was going to be a drunkard in my life!"

She said, "WHAT?" Now Mama was on her feet. "Son, are you telling me the truth?"

"Yes, Ma'am!"

"Well, maybe you need to tell me why she called you that!"

"Yes, Ma'am." I proceeded to tell her all that had taken place that day. With each word I gave her, I could see the pain on her face as she felt for her child. She would shift from anger to disbelief, to sorrow, to horror, and back to just sheer anger.

Mama jumped up from the table and shouted, "She called you a *drunkard* just because you took a stand against *wrongdoing? You should have been rewarded, yet you were persecuted!* Get your hat and coat. We are on our way to have a talk with Sister Mary Carmel! Get up! You can finish your dinner when you get back!" she said.

We went to see Gertrude, and I was told to remain seated while she talked to my mother privately in the next room. Knowing Mama, I knew she was probably nose to nose with Gertrude. I can honestly say that I had never known Mama to step back from a good scrap, big or small.

On the way back home, Mama told me that she had to get that Nun straight on a few things. "The whole time I was talking to her, she was busy trying to make reference to the fact that I had on fingernail polish, as if *that* had something to do with my son's behavior. Where did they find her? What's her name again?"

"We call her Gertrude!" I said.

"What's the Nun's name?" Mama asked.

"Sister Mary Carmel," I said.

We returned to school the next day, and after we said our morning prayers, Sister Mary Carmel announced that the Catechism lesson today would be about heaven and how wonderful things will be there for those who make it. She said heaven was a place where all the souls went and that St. Peter, who would stand at the Gate and ask them to list all the good deeds they did while they were on Earth, would judge all the souls. Those who did any misdeeds would not be allowed to enter.

Somebody asked, "Can somebody go to heaven before they die?"

The teacher said, "No! You must die first!"

Somebody else asked, "Are the White people who cheated on the spelling bee going to be in heaven too?"

Sister Mary Carmel said, "*Everybody* will go to heaven—the Whites, the Blacks, and all others. And we will all get along up there. But *you've got to please God first!*"

I asked myself, *How come those Whites didn't seem to be bothered by how they treated others here on Earth? And why weren't they afraid of offending God? Why don't they have to please God too? I did not see any* fear *on their faces as they went about their diabolical schemes! They were as happy as can be! I was thoroughly confused! What do these Whites know that we don't know?*

Shortly after the spelling bee, I turned seven. The Nuns told me I was ready to receive my first Holy Communion because I had reached the age of "reasoning." I *must* have been *a drunkard* because I could not, for the life of me, come up with a reasonable (or sober) answer to this spelling bee *fiasco*!

WOW!! The experience had affected my whole being. I had just learned that there would be privileged Whites in heaven. I asked the teacher if they would be privileged up there too. She said, "We will all be *equal* in heaven, but you've got to die first." I said to myself, *Who in the world is going to be willing to die to find out if this is true? I don't know of anyone who has died and confirmed that to be true! I want to know why people can't treat each other right BEFORE they die, since life is supposed to be so "sacred."*

I made my first Holy Communion and shortly afterward became an altar boy. I liked getting up early in the morning and going to serve Mass because I didn't have to be on time when school started at 9:00 a.m. It made me feel somewhat privileged. The only thing that I had to get used to was the smell of that wine they served at the Mass. It was a pungent smell that lingered in my nostrils. In the beginning it would upset my stomach in the morning (so did coffee, for that matter). These grown-ups were weird! It's referred to as a "jump-start."

Sister Mary Carmel did not seem so awesome to me now. I was beginning to see her in a different light. She also seemed smaller in stature now, more like a female in Nun's clothing. Although she was still feared by many, I saw her as someone who had no problem beating up on her *own*, but like most Blacks, she saw some kind of aura around white-skinned people.

I still did the decorating and drawings for her class, but things were not the same. She no longer sent pretty girls up to the classroom to visit me and leave candy and stuff. The artwork was my one solace, as things all around me seemed superfluous and trivial. ART had been my saving grace, thanks be to God.

CHAPTER 9

The Booker T. Washington Banner

It was the year 1942, and we were into our second year of war with Germany. My brother Roland was now going to school with me and the other Catholic school boys from the neighborhood. I was eight years old and in the fourth grade. It was also my second year with Sister Mary Carmel—the one I called Batman! She called out my name and asked me to stand up. She wanted to know if I would be willing (in my spare time) to make a *banner* of Booker T. Washington (the noted Black educator). The banner was to be carried in a parade they were going to have along Constitution Avenue for "Educators' Day" or something like that. I think all the schools in the area were involved. She wanted Booker T. to be recognized as the role model for our school, so I said OK.

"Now, Thomas," she said, "you will have to figure out how to do it all by yourself, and I am sure you can get some of the boys to help you when you need it."

"OK!" I said.

When I got outside, I said to myself, *How in the world am I going to pull this off? I have never painted a portrait before, let alone a banner!* I thought about it all the way home and was oblivious to the traffic as I crossed South Capitol Street. A few blasts on the horn of a passing truck brought me to my senses as I ran for my life across that busy street.

I told Mama about my assignment. She said she would give me an old, white sheet that could be used as a banner, and I could paint on it. That got the ball rolling for me. I envisioned this banner being attached to two poles and figured the banner could be about eight feet long and four feet high. I went to the hardware store and bought a pint of brown paint for the skin tone and a pint of black paint for the outline of his face. With that done, I went about finding a picture of Booker T. at the library.

I began moving furniture around to make space in the living room to lay out my nice white bed sheet. I picked up the picture of Booker T. Washington and studied his face for a while.

I figured his face had to be at least two feet high to be seen in a parade. I took my pencil and a twelve-inch ruler and measured off two feet in the middle of the sheet. Next I began to draw a head in a vertical oval shape. (I also had a book from the library on how to draw faces.) Then I drew a line through the middle and drew in his eyes. Then I drew a line halfway between the eyes and the chin and drew his nose. Halfway between his nose and his chin, I drew a line and then drew his bottom lip on it. I went from there to his eyebrows. Then I drew his hairline in and drew a line through the eyebrows and another line under his nose. Between those two lines, I drew in his left and right ears.

I then began trying to model the mechanical layout into a likeness of some kind. That was getting to be a task that involved a lot of erasing. (Did you ever try to erase pencil marks from a bed sheet?) I finally got to a point where I needed a second opinion on whether or not this thing looked *anything* like him, so I called in members of my family, and they all had a look of amazement and disbelief! They said my drawing looked so much like him that it was spooky!

I spent the whole evening drawing and erasing, and then I had to do my homework and get some sleep. The following evening after school, I pulled out my project. Just as I had done before, I moved the furniture and spread out my sheet. I opened the can of black oil-based house paint and began to paint over the penciled lines of the face.

The next day after school, I was back at it. The black outline was dry. I moved the dining room table against the wall and spread the sheet out on the floor. I opened the can of brown house paint and began to lay on some brown paint. The brown was too brown, and I could hardly see the black lines of Booker T.'s features. It was then that I realized that I should have bought *real* artist colors for the job. But artist oil paints cost a lot of money, which I did not have, so I had no choice but to push on. I put as little paint as possible on the brush and sort of dry brushed the paint on. This technique made his eyes look like they were popping out of his head, but I dared not touch the white of his eyes. My family said it looked nice, so I pushed on.

When the paint dried, I went and got the two poles I had bought, took some carpet tacks, and nailed the sheet to the poles. I then rolled the two poles toward the middle and stacked the banner in the corner. The parade was the next day, so I would have to carry the banner from Half and M Streets SE to Third and I Streets SW. I opened up the banner to show the teacher. She said it looked fine. I asked for a volunteer to help me carry it in the parade. One of the boys in class came forward—I think it was Joseph Only (pronounced "Awnly"). We were off to the parade.

We assembled at Fifth and Jefferson Streets NW and waited for our turn to join the parade down Constitution Avenue. I looked around to see if another Black school was there, but I saw none. *Are we the only Black school?* I said to myself. I was also noticing the banners of the other schools. Their banners all had a nice professional look to them, though they had half-moon-shaped *holes* in them. Wow, our banner was going to look nice because we didn't have any tears in ours! (Poor me!) I didn't know that the whistle had been blown for us to join in the parade.

I unrolled our banner, and the students from St. Vincent de Paul fell in behind us. We got on Constitution Avenue and found there was a crosswind blowing about twenty-five miles an hour straight at us as we headed down the avenue toward the Monument Grounds.

The wind *grabbed* that banner and blew us both backward about four or five paces! The banner became a *SAIL*! We were blown into the marchers behind us. It was pandemonium there for a while, as we tried to get back in step with the band playing ahead of us. Joseph Only and I had to lean forward at a forty-five-degree angle to move forward. It was hard work! As we approached the corner of Sixth and Constitution, the sheet began to tear away from the poles! By the time we got to Seventh and Constitution Avenue, we were not only tired but also frustrated from trying to hold onto the poles while trying to keep the sheet from tearing away from the last two tacks holding it to the poles!

It was fruitless. The wind blew the sheet free of the last tack on my pole. The banner had now become a FLAG! I walked over to Joseph Only, grabbed hold of the flapping banner, and told him to tear the sheet from the remaining tack and just hold it up by hand. *That didn't work either,* so we each took an end of the sheet and wrapped it around ourselves. Then we tucked it under our armpits so that only the face was left showing and somehow walked from Seventh and Constitution to Fourteenth and Constitution Avenue. When we reached the Monument Grounds, we were dismissed from the parade. Joe had been a good sport about the whole thing. I had selected him to help me because he had a great sense of humor, and we had been cracking up the whole time we were marching. What a guy! Well, it was over now, and this probably would cost me my friendship. I dumped our wind-beaten banner in the Monument trash can. I then turned to Joseph and said, "Now I know why all the White schools' banners had those half moon-shaped tears in them! They were air vents to let the air blow *through* them! Boy, nobody knew to tell us that! (We were only eight years old!) I stood there waiting for Joe to crack on me for not having thought of that *before* the parade!

Joseph Only looked at me and said, "I'll race you to the top of the Monument!"

"You are on," I said, and off we went. We ran into a lot of the White boys who were also running for the Monument. It was the thing to do. We all had our bets going about who would be the first to climb all the way up without stopping. Wow! Now that was a lot of fun! Yeah, Jim!

Joseph Only and I timed ourselves. Hitting the first Monument step to the top and checking out the four directional windows in the observation tower before running back down the steps to the street below took us approximately one hour! We saw a lot of the same dudes we had passed while walking up, and they were still trying to go up. *They couldn't believe their eyes!* We waved at them as we headed down the stairs. Those gray boys (which is what we called White boys) were from out of town. The gray boys from this area would have been with us going down the stairs. A lot of them were good. Joseph and I had known what to expect, so we had paced ourselves. After all, we did this every other week or so, as we lived a short walking distance from the monument, which gave us the edge on things. I will just *never* forget the way those boys looked at us as we ran past them on the way down to the bottom! And that is how the day of the big banner parade came to an end. He who laughs last, laughs best!

Christmastime was upon us again, and I was preparing myself for the coming artwork to be done on Sister Mary Carmel's boards. Only this year something had been added. Every day when I was alone in the room, I got a visitor. The visitor was a pretty girl from another class who came in, placed money on the teacher's desk, and started a conversation with me. I answered all her questions, and then she walked out.

The next day it was the same thing. Another pretty girl came in and placed money on the teacher's desk, but this time she placed several candy bars near the money. She came over and struck up a conversation with me. I responded kindly but did not stop working. She eventually left.

The following day, a third pretty girl came in and placed money on the teacher's desk, plus a few candy bars. This time the candy bars were all different kinds. One candy bar was my *favorite* cavity maker, Mary Janes.

I was beginning to see some kind of pattern. My first thought was to eat the Mary Janes, but I didn't. The next day another girl came in the room and placed more money than before and more candy than before on the teacher's desk. As a matter of fact, it looked like a big amount of my favorite candy. This girl was even prettier than the other three were. She came over to me and struck up a conversation. Only this time I asked her who was sending the money and candy here every day, and she said Sister Mary Carmel was. I then asked if she helped out with Sister Carmel's candy operation. She said no and that Sister Carmel just picked girls at random and told them what to do.

I thought I was being tested for some reason. Old Gertrude was trying to get something on me. I thought she was suspicious of me. Why would a boy want to stay in the classroom alone unless he was up to no good of some kind? Maybe she was having trouble believing I had good intentions, but then why had she asked me to do it? I was confused. Nevertheless, the work had to be done, so I went back to work. Regardless of what her concern was, my concern was to finish this artwork. The girls continued to come with the money, the candy, the whole bit.

I finished the project, and the work looked great to me. The teacher and the class expressed their appreciation. The day before we started our Christmas vacation, Gertrude called my name and told me to remain after class was dismissed. She wanted to speak to me. (Oh, no!) What did I do now? The classroom was now empty, and she asked me to approach her desk.

"Yes, Sister?" I asked.

She said, "I sent those girls up to you with money and candy for weeks, and you did nothing. You didn't say anything out of the way to my girls and you did not touch the money or the candy. I am impressed with your honesty, so it seems I have you pegged wrong."

I asked, "Why me?"

She said, "We all know how mischievous people with artistic abilities can be, and I wanted to know if you were also mischievous." (Wow! I was being tested!) I thanked her and asked her for permission to leave.

CHAPTER 10

The Meatloaf Sandwich

Mama made meatloaf for Sunday dinner, so I knew I was going to get a meatloaf sandwich in my lunch by Wednesday of that week. I *loved* Mama's meatloaf, especially when she put mayonnaise on it—boy oh boy! Sure enough, on Tuesday night Mama was making me this sandwich. I watched her as she neatly cut it in half, wrapped the two halves in wax paper, and placed them in a bag in the refrigerator. She also made me a peanut butter and jelly sandwich, which was my "fun" sandwich. I said to myself, *I'm not going to touch my meatloaf sandwich until lunchtime. That way, I can smell it clean up until lunchtime.* Why did I say that? Because sometimes I ate my lunch on the way to school, especially if it was something I did not particularly like, but I always saved the meatloaf sandwich for last. I saw other boys doing the same thing. (I never saw a girl do that.)

On Wednesday morning I was on my way to St. Vincent de Paul Catholic School. I met up with the other guys, and we discovered that the older guys were not there. I asked where the older guys were. Somebody spoke up and said that all the older boys had gone to a retreat at the Church and we would have to get to school on our own by following the route they had given us. We followed the route until we got to Second and Delaware Avenue SW, where Anthony Bowen Elementary School was located. Then Philip "Cookie" Coates said, "Let's take the shortcut today because we are running a little late!"

Now the shortcut referred to here was an alleyway that was about midway between First and Second Streets, just off Delaware Avenue. Walking through the alley was a bad risk because some boys hid behind the fence there. When people walked by, the boys would jump over the fence and take their lunches. It had happened before. I myself had lost a few lunches cutting through there. The older boys used to walk us around the block to Second and I Streets to avoid "the alley," as it was called. The shortcut knocked off about two blocks, which would have taken us five minutes longer to walk. "OK, let's take the shortcut!" I said.

Because it was cold that morning, we figured they probably wouldn't be out there and took off through the alley. We were about halfway through the alley when we heard what at first sounded like a cavalry charge or a cattle stampede (minus the dust)! Over the fence came the raggediest, meanest, hungriest looking dudes we had ever seen. It was like a scene from a bad movie! There were at least six or seven of them, and each one looked worse than the other.

"*ALL RIGHT! Hand over the bags, and nobody gets hurt!*" the leader of the gang yelled out. We were only five guys and were scared stiff to the point of wetting ourselves! The oldest among us was not more than eight years old. The leader gestured to his boys to go collect the bags from us. They all gave up their bags willingly. When the gang member got to me, he reached for my bag but couldn't get the bag out of my hand. He stepped back and looked at me in *disbelief.* I was in disbelief too. He grabbed the bag again, and again he got nothing. He looked at me in a state of confusion. "Hey, Chief!" he said. "This one won't let go of his bag!"

The leader looked over at me as if to say, *"Wow! I don' wanna go over there!"* So he yelled back, "Just take it from his hand as I watch you!" The gang member tried one more time to take the bag from my hand but got nothing. I was in shock and knew they were going to crucify me for resisting. But I just could not give up my meatloaf sandwich, even if it cost me my head. I knew it was dumb and was angry with myself for being so stubborn!

Now this meatloaf sandwich was *sounding off*! My nostrils were full of its aroma, and a slight hunger pain ran across my stomach like a flash. It suddenly dawned on me that the gang member trying to take the sandwich didn't really want to push this thing any further. He had tried three times and gotten nothing. I could not BELIEVE my right hand was not letting go of this bag! I was more confused than the guy trying to *get* the bag.

The leader seemed a little reluctant to come down from his lofty position atop a large dirt mound to check me out. He also knew that he must come to me or lose face with his gang members, so he swaggered over to where I was standing and stared at me. Now I could see that he was smaller than I was. Standing out of striking distance, he said to me, "Hold up your left hand!" The lunch bag was in my right hand. I said to myself, *If I were the leader, I would have said, "Hold up your right hand,"* and then snatched the bag! But that was not what he had said. So I held up my left hand (which was *not* shaking). "Now let your hand go limp!" he said. I did that. He took a long look at my raised, limp left hand and saw that it was not shaking and said, *"Keep it up there!"* Then he walked away.

He went over to the four other guys who had given up their lunches already and said, "All right, all of you hold up your left hand!" They immediately complied, and I was amazed at what I saw. *Everybody's hands* were shaking like leaves on a tree. Cookie's hands were shaking the most. I was *flabbergasted*. The leader walked back to his lofty position, turned around, and said, "*All righ'*, I'm gonna let y'all go! So when I say GO, y'all take off outta here and don' look back! Now GO!" And off we went.

We were all quiet and stunned after that as we headed across that open field at Second and K Streets SW. We got about halfway across the field, and Cookie Coates said to me, "How come you didn't fight for my lunch?"

I looked at the other guys and saw that they were looking down and looked sad. I replied to Cookie, "You shouldn't have given up your lunch so easily." Then I realized that he was older and taller than I was and had been the first one to give up his lunch.

I felt sad because I was the only one left with a lunch. I thought that I would share my lunch between the five of us but wasn't sure how we could all eat one meatloaf sandwich. One boy yelled, "I hate meatloaf! What else you got?"

I gave half of my peanut butter and jelly sandwich to the boy who didn't like meatloaf. The second boy didn't want peanut butter and jelly, so I gave him the half of the meatloaf sandwich. The third boy took the other half of the peanut butter sandwich.

"Well I stood up for my meatloaf sandwich, so I feel I am entitled to at least half a meatloaf sandwich!" I said.

Cookie Coates immediately said, "I'll take the other half of that meatloaf sandwich!" That left me with graham crackers and an orange.

While they were all eating my lunch, I was busy telling them that the shortcut through the alley was a godsend because it cut out about two whole blocks. But in order to take advantage of it, we would have to operate as a unit.

"What do you mean, Duball?" a boy asked.

"I mean the next time we have to use that shortcut to save time, we *all* need to just hold onto our sandwiches and let *them* make the next move!"

"What makes you think that will work?" they all asked.

I said, "Trust me. OK?"

"OK!" they all said.

Several months later we were running late again and voted to take the shortcut to school. We hit the alley with brisk steps, and when we were about halfway through the alley, over the fence came the Anthony Bowen Bad boys. There were six or seven of them and five of us. They cut off our path, and the leader once again yelled out, "All righ'! Han' 'em ovah!"

"Freeze and don't say *anything*. Keep your lips *tight*, and above all, *don't* let go of your lunch bags," I said to my friends.

The gang members moved about us trying to get the bags out of our hands with no success. (I felt so proud of those guys for standing up to those raggedy lunch snatchers from the public schools.) The leader and his band were visibly *dumbfounded* (just as I had suspected). When they saw us standing there tight-mouthed and tightfisted, they decided it was best not to challenge us further. They all turned to the leader for further instructions. The leader shouted out to his cronies, "Let 'em go!" They all took three steps back, and we proceeded to walk on out of the alley with our lunch bags in our hands.

After we reached a safe distance from ground zero, I looked back to see whether they were following us, but they had disappeared. "Relax," I told everybody.

Everybody immediately asked, "How did you know that idea would work?"

I said, "I noticed how cautious those dudes and their leader were with handling me and how the leader wanted me to raise my left hand instead of the sandwich hand. That made me realize they didn't want to risk the possibility of getting hurt just for a sandwich! So all we had to do was show them that we were willing to take the risk of defending our lunches. They were not so willing to risk getting hurt over someone else's sandwich."

"'Duduball' (they called me), that was a GREAT idea!" So we swaggered off to school feeling triumphant. We soon received word that the Anthony Bowen gang was telling everybody that those Catholic school boys were fighting back! We never had any more trouble out of the Anthony Bowen gang after that.

CHAPTER 11

My Setback

Several weeks later Sister Mary Carmel called Henry up to the blackboard to solve a math problem she'd put on the board. Henry got up to the board, picked up a piece of chalk, and started to shit on himself! Now this ain't funny, because Henry had on short pants, and the turds were falling out of his pants, sliding down his leg, and into his shoes and socks! Henry was standing there facing the blackboard, so I couldn't see his face. Sister Carmel was on her feet. Henry turned his head in the direction of the Nun and looked at her. He had always been scared of her, but now he was *mortified*!

Sister Carmel yelled out, "THOMAS DUVALL!" (She scared me to death. What had I done?) *"Thomas DuVall, get up here!"*

"Yes, Sister?"

She pointed her finger at me and said, "I want you to walk this boy home!" (This boy was bigger than I was.)

I said to the Sister, "But he knows where he lives! Why can't he take himself home?"

"Because he has to pass by that alley where that gang hangs out and I heard you were able to handle *them*, so you can see Henry safely home!" The whole class broke out in laughter. "Now go!" *Who told Sister Carmel about that alley?* I wondered.

I looked over at Henry and saw that there was a big pile of warm feces on the classroom floor that he was standing in. It was also in both of his socks, and it was *sounding off* throughout the classroom (pee-ew!).

Henry lived on South Capitol and L Streets SE. He never said a mumbling word; he just sort of stood around and looked. I took Henry by the hand and led him out of the school. As soon as we hit the street, people began to notice this little boy leading the bigger boy by the hand. People also noticed that the bigger boy was covered with doo-doo from the waist down and that *flies* were following us. I was so embarrassed. I found myself pulling him along, trying to get him to walk faster. He was silently uncooperative.

We finally got to his house, but he would not enter the yard. I went up to the door and knocked. A lady who looked liked his grand-mother answered. I identified myself and pointed to Henry standing down near the gate, and she called him inside. Now I had to pass by that alley again to get back to school, which made four times that day. This time I was by *myself*! Everything was noticeably peaceful around the area, and I was beginning to feel a little more secure walking the streets of Southwest Washington.

A few weeks later, however, when I was walking past South Capitol and L Streets SE, two boys came out of the house next door to Henry's and ran straight at me. They started hitting and kicking me, so I started hitting them back in self-defense. I thought I was doing a pretty good job of defending myself, when all of a sudden the door swung open and another boy ran toward me and started hitting and kicking. I saw the boys' mother in the doorway and was about to attempt to seek her help when she suddenly said to the boys, *"Kick that yellow son of a bitch's ass!"*

That threw me into some kind of trauma. My arms dropped down by my side, and I lost the feeling in my body. I just stood there and was not able to lift my hands to fend off the blows. The three of them pounced on me until they were out of breath. I could not believe that a *mother* would allow this kind of foul play! What kind of world was this? Now I was a yellow son of a—what? What was a "bitch"?

Jean Guy was dark-skinned, and we had liked each other. This mother had three dark-skinned boys, and they hated me! I had done nothing to deserve that beating, yet I was beaten good! I looked back at the mother again and saw the face of the mother of the boy who had stolen my army truck. I kept this whipping to myself; I just didn't want to discuss it with anyone, not even Mama. Meanwhile, I decided to look up the word "bitch." I found out that a bitch was a female dog.

That meant that the woman was putting my mother down while her sons kicked my ass! Wow! I never walked past South Capitol and L on the east side of that street again, and nobody ever knew why—until now. How old was I when this happened? I was only eight years old.

Back at school we were preparing for final exams, which meant I would be finished with Gertrude for good. The average student had to spend two years with this Nun, but because she had skipped me from the third grade to the fourth grade, I had to spend only one year in her class. I don't think I could have handled two years with her.

Final exam time had finally arrived, and summer vacation was just around the corner. We were all scrambling and cramming for those final exams. Our incentive was that we would be finished with *Gertrude* and that next year it would be the fifth grade and a different teacher.

Once we took our final exams, we were all on pins and needles. A week later Sister Carmel announced that she would begin to read aloud the final grades of those who had passed and those who had not. She read off all the names of the students who got As, then Bs, and then Cs. Good gracious, I had not heard MY name yet! Maybe she had forgotten me? She said, "Now I shall read off the names of the students who got a D on their report cards: Thomas DuVall, Puffy Coates, and Donald Johnson!" (In Catholic school a D in any *one* subject meant the student had to repeat all of the subjects for one more year.) I knew why Donald Johnson and Puffy Coates were kept back; they were the dumbest guys in class. They stayed back *every* year! I thought I had been getting good grades. What in the world had happened?

I just had to raise my hand to ask the Sister why I had failed. She said that I had flunked long division and that that would mean repeating *everything* over next year. I asked, "Couldn't I just take long division over since I got an A in all the other subjects?"

"No," she said, "you will repeat Religion, English, Geography, History, Mathematics, and all other assignments for the coming year. Those are the rules. Class dismissed. Have a safe summer."

I was traumatized. I couldn't believe I had to spend *another year* in this Nun's class! And what was I going to tell Mama? It usually took me about a half hour to walk home, but that day it took me an hour and a half. I could barely move my legs. It was a big effort just to put one foot in front of the other. When I finally reached the front door, I felt exhausted. I had to throw myself against the door in order to get it open. I went straight to my room and dropped. I lay there for several hours. I heard Mama come in from work and knew it wouldn't be more than thirty minutes before she would be calling me to dinner.

About thirty minutes later, she said, "Thomas, your dinner is ready. Wash your hands, and come to the table!"

"Yes, Ma'am," I said and started moving to the sink to wash my hands. I washed and washed them, and they were now super clean.

"Thomas, what are you doing?"

"Nothing, Ma. I'm coming!" I left the report card on the bed and proceeded to the table.

While we ate there was no mention of report cards, so maybe she wouldn't remember that it was report card day. As soon as she swallowed the last mouthful, she said, "Thomas, isn't today report card day?"

"Yes, Ma'am."

"Well where is your report card?"

"I, ah, left it upstairs!"

"Well go get it!"

"OK," I said. I took off up the stairs, picked up the card, and gave it to her.

Mama looked at the card for several minutes and said in an unbelievably low voice, "You *didn't* pass? What happened? I thought you were doing so well in her class?"

"I thought so too, Mama!"

"Why didn't you tell me you were having trouble with math?"

"Mama, I see you working so hard and just didn't want to burden you."

"Well, you see where that got you, *don't* you? So now you have got to look at that woman for another whole year! I bet you will be asking for my help from now on, won't you?"

"Yes, Mama!"

"Well now you are at the grade you should have been in," Mama said. "So you will put in two years with her like everybody else had to do." The way Mama talked to me made me feel a little better about things, and I promised her I would pass next time.

From that moment on, I began seeking Mama out for help with my homework. Sometimes she would nod off while I struggled with a math problem. I got to a point where I would not disturb her until I really needed her. Those were painful moments for me. I was being a burden, I felt, so I studied hard in order not to have to lean on Mama so much.

CHAPTER 12

Five Pennies

I was playing in the front yard with my two brothers, Roland and Herbert, when a neighbor came by to see my mother about some matter. While waiting for her to answer the door, he reached into his pocket and gave us five pennies apiece. He then turned and went inside. We looked at the pennies and asked each other, "What in the world can we buy for just five pennies?" That wasn't even worth the trip to the store; though it was only a block away, it was a long walk for us youngsters not yet allowed to leave the front yard.

I decided to put my five pennies into a white envelope and seal it up. Roland and Herbert decided to do the same thing. Roland was listening to the pennies knock together inside the envelope when I said to him, "You ought not to do that because those pennies will eventually tear through and fly out everywhere! That has happened to me already." He ignored me and continued to shake the envelope. Sure as shooting, the pennies ripped through the envelope and went flying. Now the pennies were on the ground, and it was beginning to rain.

We stood on the front porch, gazing at the pennies getting wet in the rain. I asked Roland, "Aren't you going to pick 'em up?"

Roland looked at me and said, "I ain't picking up no pennies!"

Herbert and I stood there for several minutes, waiting for Roland to change his mind. But Roland was adamant and did not move, so I said, "Well I'm not going to pick 'em up for you! I tried to warn you about shaking them up like that. So if *you* are not going to pick them up, they will just lay there in the rain!"

Herbert broke ranks, walked out into the rain, and picked up each and every penny. Roland and I stood there with a look of surprise. Herbert walked back up on the porch with raindrops running down his face, picked up his envelope, placed the pennies in the envelope, and sealed it. He said not a mumbling word, and neither did Roland.

I just had to ask Herbert if he planned to keep the pennies. Herbert turned to me and said, "You heard him say he didn't want 'em!"

Well umpteen years later, I have a small house, Roland has a somewhat small house, and Herbert has eight houses and counting. There may be a moral to this story!

CHAPTER 13

Keep That Hat On

We were learning how to keep our hats on. Every day and any day we were home, we had to spend our waking hours outdoors, rain or shine!

One day it was raining outside, so we took it for granted that we would be playing inside. Mama eventually came downstairs, saw us in the living room on the floor, and with a puzzled look on her face, said, "Why aren't you all outside playing?"

We said, "It's raining outside!"

"You all have raincoats and rain hats! Go get them, put them on, and go outside!" We were in disbelief. "Move!" she said.

We jumped into our raincoats, rain boots, and rain hats and headed for the door. We stood in the rain, looked up and down the street, and saw *no one*. Roland said, "What are we gonna do?"

I said, "I don't *know*!"

Herbert broke for the door and began to bang on it, trying to get Mama to let him in, but Mama did not respond. He banged harder and cried louder, but Mama did not respond. Poor Herbert was dumbfounded.

We stood in the rain for a while, waiting for Mama to come to her senses. We eventually realized that Mama wasn't going to let us back in until lunchtime, and it was only about nine thirty or ten o'clock. I suggested that we walk up to the other end of the street and stomp in the puddles on the way. We took Herbert, who was still bawling with his head thrown back, by the hands and led him away from the door. We got to the corner and saw, lo and behold, there were a couple of other boys standing near the corner with their raincoats, rain hats, and rain boots on too! They had been collecting bottle caps to use as sailboats and were using a matchstick as a "sailor" to float them in a race in the rainwater that was running down the gutter to the sewer at the end of the street. We asked if we could participate, and they said, "Yeah! Just get yourself some bottle caps and remove the cork from them so that they will float better. Try to get a variety so that we won't have trouble distinguishing whose are whose." Then they explained the rules:

RULE No. 1: If your sailor got blocked or snagged by something falling into the water, you could not help it. It had to be left to the force of the moving water to dislodge it.

RULE No. 2: If your sailor got out of commission, you had to abandon ship. You could replace it with a new sailor by setting it in the water near the place of abandonment.

It sounded simple enough, I thought. It was still raining pretty heavily, and we had been playing for a long while. It was also quite adventuresome because there were always new and unpredictable things that would occur in each cruise downstream. A few more boys joined in, and we now had a full-fledged tournament going. We even had a few spectators follow us up and down the block as we went from Start to

Finish. We could hear the cheers go up when someone crossed the finish line. Just think, this couldn't have been done if it hadn't been raining! It was still raining when our mothers called us in for lunch. We took off down the street (not to get out of the rain), but to get to those sandwiches! (Thanks, Mom, for sending us out to play in the rain.)

Of course, this idea of Mama's applied to all weather conditions—it did not matter. We had snow clothes, rain clothes, and whatever else it took to survive outside, because we were going *outside*! In the winter we would have to put on our snowsuits, galoshes, hats, and gloves. Mama was *emphatic* about that and insisted we keep our *hats on*. She said, "If you keep your hat on, you will not get sick, regardless of the conditions!" She was right; we seldom got sick.

Master Ashiko Drummer Baba Moses Miannes (1904-1967). He was one of the personalities who inspired me to become a professional Drummer.

(Photo by Ronnie Brathwaite)

CHAPTER 14

The Cardboard Boxes

Big cardboard boxes have amazing possibilities. We discovered that we could use them to slide down a grassy hillside, like a bobsled on snow. We would open a big cardboard box up at both ends, get inside, get on our hands and knees, and pretend we were inside a tank. The cardboard box ends became the treads of the tank. We would have three or four of these big boxes used to ship cornflakes into supermarkets. We would face off at each other, haul off at each other, and try to roll over the guy facing us. Wow, that was a *lot* of fun. After a while the boxes would split open and the tank would be treadless and declared out of commission. It would then become a bobsled. We would take off for the highest hill or mound (which was the hill across the street from St. Vincent de Paul's Church at South Capitol and M Streets) to have bobsled races and then aim the cardboard bobsleds at each other so that we could have crashes.

Yeah, we really knew how to improvise and convert or metamorph things that had been thrown away or discarded on the street. That's what we did when we couldn't get the real thing. And that was how we spent our summer days (especially on Saturdays).

One particular Saturday we were all together and were heading for the big grocery stores. In those days they were known as "Sanitary Stores," but today they are known as "Safeway Stores." (Time marches on.) We were at the store and found that no big cereal boxes—like the BIG cornflake boxes—had been thrown out yet. Four or five of us could get in one of those boxes at one time. Can you imagine that?

We hung around for a while but were growing impatient, so we decided to take the smaller boxes and walk with them over our heads. One boy had a stick he had been hitting things with all morning; now he was hitting on the box that was on his head. Suddenly he said, "Hey, man, listen to this!" He rapped on the boxes on our heads, and it sounded like a drum head. We had stumbled upon a sound we could get that had us looking for a nice stick or twig to use as a drumstick. After we all found sticks, we started to notice the variety of sounds each box made. The thickest boxes, like the tomato boxes, the canned goods boxes, and the orange crates, had a nice solid tone when we wore them on our heads. We began stepping in time with each other.

That went on for a couple of hours, and then someone yelled out, "LET'S HAVE A PARADE!" So we headed back to our neighborhood on Half Street SE and started drumming up some support for this parade—all while *singing* and *drumming*!

Some girls came over and joined in. They all decided that they were Drum Majorettes and started strutting around in front of us and twisting their waists around with one hand on their hips. It was about noon, and we were making such noise that parents were throwing open their doors and trying to figure out how all this had gotten started. But we all noticed they were smiling, so we really put on a show then. We beat those boxes to a frazzle. And those girls were twisting themselves like nobody would BELIEVE! Finally the cardboard boxes began to fall apart, and the sound had depleted to a flapping sound. We stopped the parade with the agreement that we would meet the next Saturday and start all over again.

It rained the following Saturday, so we played rain games, but the sounds of those boxes are still ringing in my head. I am sure that experience was the motivating force behind my eventually becoming a professional Drummer and traveling around with various personalities and dance troupes for twenty-some-odd years (1953 to 1974). The noted personalities included Roland Cave, Michael Olatunji, Chief Bey, Mike Quashie, Harry Belafonte, Pearl Primus, Percival Borde, Solomon Ilori, Akwasiba (Joan) and Afida (Meryl) Derby, Maya Angelou, Esther Rolle and her sisters, Helen Haynes, Helena Walker, Julito Collazo, Jothan Callins, Randy Weston, John Coltrane, Moses Miannes, Yusef Lateef, Candido, Mongo Santamaria, Max Roach, Abbey Lincoln, Ray Mantillo, Ray Barretto, Babafemi, Baba David Coleman, Neil Clarke, Sam Turner, Paul Hawkins, James Alexander, Julio Miranda, Montague Pollard, Sule Greg Wilson, The Cardboard Box Drummers, and others.

The older boys on the block were all making "pony-horses" (as we called them) and riding through the neighborhood like motorcycle gangs, but this was more Western style. How did we make a pony-horse? Well, we went to the lumberyard and bought a strip of wood that was about six feet long and one inch wide by a half inch thick. Then we bought a piece of fine sandpaper and sanded it down nice and smooth so that when we straddled it, we wouldn't get splinters in our inner thighs. (That could be mighty painful!)

After the wood was all sanded and smooth, we put notches where we decided the horse's neck was and tied a ribbon there. The ribbon represented the mane. Then we made another set of notches to tie on the straps with which we held up the pony-horse's head. The straps were also used to tie the horse to a tree or fence in the riding position when we were not riding. There was a special way we had to ride this horse, according to the older boys. The trick was to raise the back of our stick, tap the ground, and immediately do a quick two-step pattern with our feet to make a sound like that of a horse trotting. I loved that sound and the posture the older boys had perfected from seeing so many cowboy movies.

This pony-horse fever went on all summer. The older boys would travel from neighborhood to neighborhood, but we younger guys had to stay within earshot of our parents. The older boys from the First and M Streets SE area once decided they were all going to ride through Half Street unannounced. They came through at a walk, not at a gallop, and every pony-horse was fully dressed. They were a sight to behold! They all had wooden swords that were well made with handguards and all. They really looked smart.

The older boys rode in front, and the younger boys brought up the rear. We all stood there dumbfounded. The First Street boys looked tough. After they disappeared around the corner of Half and N Streets SE, we knew what we Half Street boys had to do!

The older boys on the block immediately started choosing the frontline riders (ages twelve to sixteen), and the second line of defense was made up of boys from ages nine to eleven. I was in the eight-to-eleven lineup until it was discovered that I was good at making swords. They then put me in charge of the armor, and I was allowed to ride with the front-liners. In about a week, we were prepared to make a march through First Street. Everybody had a pony-horse and a sword. There must have been twenty or thirty of us, it seemed.

All of these preparations were made in secrecy, and on an unsuspected and unannounced day, we arose early one Saturday morning. We gathered our forces and ascended on First Street in full regalia and with maximum representation. We had everybody on the block running to look out their windows and doors at the Half Street boys as we paraded through their neighborhood in fine spirits on that bright early morning surprise. The expressions on their faces were priceless. It took us a good hour to do our demonstration, and then we disappeared as the sun rose higher, brighter, and hotter, leaving only a whisper of what had just occurred. A couple of days later, we heard from the enemy. They were daring us to appear on the next Saturday at the vacant lot that was between Half and First Streets. We sent a message back that we would be there on time.

Saturday morning arrived, and we were at the battlefield on time with swords drawn. We heard some yelling coming from the area of Greenwood's trucking garage at First and N Streets. Then we saw them coming out from behind the trucks. We met them head on. There was a lot of screaming and yelling and running around. The first line of defense stood its ground. I was somewhere in the middle and became the first casualty of the day when somebody whacked me with a wooden sword. I wanted to continue the fight, but the rules were that if we got hit by a sword, we were out of the fight. (I never even got to use my sword. I had worked on that sword for weeks! Oh well, so much for war games, I guess.)

Summer was drawing to a close, and my thoughts revolved around returning to Gertrude's classroom. I couldn't believe I'd be there for another whole year! Ugh!

CHAPTER 15

Fourth Grade

My brother Roland was starting his first year in Catholic school and was going into Sister Marian's class. I told him she was very nice and that he should have a good year with her.

I started my school year with a haircut, as usual. Sister Carmel started her class with the usual opening prayers and announcements. She also asked me if I would continue to draw on the blackboards this term. I said yes, even though I was no longer too enthused about it. There were a few new additions. My brother Roland was going to school with me now, and there was a new girl in the class whose name was Rosita Phifer. For some reason, I did not seem to like her. There was something tomboyish about her, it seemed. I did not know why, but she held my attention. There was also a new boy in my class. Sister Carmel announced the new students. The boy's name was Jeremiah T.

Gottsindamin. We all came to attention. *Oh boy, we are going to have fun with this guy's name!* That was the expression we all had on our faces.

Sure enough, when recess came and we were outside playing, somebody yelled out, "Hey, Gotsdamit! Get the ball, Gotsdamit, can you? Hey, Gotsdamit, we need you to—"

The Nuns were furious. "Stop calling him that!" they said. "His name is Gottsindamin."

"Yeah, that's what we said, Gotsdamit!" Then the Nuns heard the boys calling me "Duduball." What made it so bad was that Jeremiah and I were answering to these names. It didn't bother us one bit! (Heheheeeeeee!)

We had just returned to school after a record snowfall in the Washington, DC, area. We were all sitting in class when suddenly a snowball crashed through the second-floor window, and glass and snow went flying everywhere. The girls screamed, and the boys ducked!

When things settled down a little and we assessed what had just happened, Sister Carmel yelled out, *"Thomas DuVall, c*ome up here!" (What had I done?)

I got up from my seat and approached her desk. "Yes, Sister?" I said.

"I want you to tell me who threw that snowball through that window."

"Sister, I do not know."

She asked me the same question again. I tried to explain to her that since we were on the second floor, I could not see the street from my desk. She said to me, "You know very well who threw that snowball through that window, and since you refuse to tell me the truth, you will stay after school and scrub all the classroom floors and then oil down all the classroom floors." There were five classrooms. I was given two big heavy mops and a wash pail with a wringer on it. One mop was for the hot water, and the other mop was soaked in oil. I scrubbed all five classrooms and then went back to the first classroom, which was dry by then, took the mop soaked in oil, and coated the floors. This way the floors would not look water soaked.

I got home at around seven o'clock that night. Mama was visibly shaken. "Where were you?" she asked. "You weren't here for dinner! You have never missed dinner before. We have been searching the whole neighborhood! Answer me," she said. I started telling her about the snowball thrown through the window at school and how I had been punished for it. I told her my punishment had been to scrub all the classrooms and then oil all the floors and that I could not leave until it was all done.

Mama said that I was a poor liar and that my explanation was the worst lie she had ever heard, so she was going to punish me for lying to her. She gave me a good whipping and then sent me to bed without dinner.

The next day (Tuesday), I returned to school. That afternoon, I was given my mops and pail. This time the mops seemed heavier than before. I somehow pulled it off. I was dead tired, and it was dark outside already. I went to get Sister Carmel so that she could inspect my work. She said I had done a good job and allowed me to leave. I arrived home at around seven o'clock, and Mama was furious. She could not believe I was late again and had missed dinner again. She asked for an explanation. I gave her the exact same story I had given before.

She was flabbergasted. "You mean to say you are going to try the same lie again?"

"Mama, it's the truth!"

"Well I see I didn't whip you long enough the first time, so I will have to give you a good whipping this time."

Mama went to get the razor strap (a wide, thick, belt-like strap used to sharpen knives). She said, "Take your pants *and* underwear off! I am not going to waste my energy trying to hit you with clothes on." Poor Mama laid it on me this time. I had big welts on my legs, thighs, buttocks, arms, and penis! I cried until I could cry no more.

I was without breath, and so was Mama. She turned and walked out of the room without looking back. I fell asleep only to wake up the next day to see the scars of the previous night. Then I had to face Sister Mary Carmel.

Fortunately it was winter, so I was able to hide most of my welts with my long socks and knickers. I also kept my sweater on. On the way to school on Wednesday morning, all I could think about was *three more days of scrubbing and butt beatings, and all for something I didn't do! GOD, are you watching this? Can't you do something to help me?*

I walked into Gertrude's classroom, and she looked at me. The expression on her face was one of pleasure and exhilaration, as if the LORD was pleased with her for her handling of the evil seeds that were placed in her charge, in her classroom. I cannot remember anything that happened that day in school. I only remember Sister Carmel ringing her big brass bell at three o'clock sharp, meaning the day was over. "Thomas DuVall, your chores await you," she said. "When you are done, call me, and I will look over your work." I proceeded to get my equipment. Everything seemed to be heavier than the day before. I called on GOD one more time but got no response. Gertrude saw me pause. She said to me, "You'd better get started; I don't have all night."

I got started. Again I watched the sun set. It got so dark so early in the wintertime. It depressed me to hear kids running around outside having fun, waiting to be called to dinner, while I had to mop five classrooms twice; that was the same as doing ten classrooms once. When I was done, I would go home to get my whipping and probably no dinner. *Good Lord,* I prayed, *if you are for real, please help me help myself, because if you don't exist, then I am really all alone in this stinking world!* (That is an original prayer from an eight-year-old kid, Thomas Joseph DuVall.)

I finished my chores and went to get Sister Mary Carmel. She looked the classrooms over and then dismissed me. I got outside, and the night air seemed colder than ever. I buttoned all my buttons, hugged myself, and began the long walk home from Third and I Streets SW to Half and M Streets SE.

I arrived at home at around seven o'clock Wednesday night, and Mama was really out of it. She was completely perplexed and asked me to explain. I told her the whole story again, from the snowball through the window to the oil on the floors. Mama looked at me and said, "That's the same story you have been telling me for three days now."

I replied, "I know, it's a true story, and I have two days to go yet—Thursday and Friday!"

"Son, I whipped you Monday and Tuesday. Nobody in his or her right mind would tell the same lie three times and risk another beating. I am forced to say that I believe you! But for the life of me, that punishment sounds a bit harsh to put on an eight-year-old child! Why didn't Sister Carmel have the decency to inform me? And did I hear you say you have two more days of scrubbing and mopping to go for something you are innocent of?"

"Yes, Ma'am!" I said.

"Put your coat back on, we are going to see Sister Carmel."

"Mom, that's a long walk," I complained.

"Walk? We are going in a cab!" Then I heard my mother say, "That black rag she wears around her ass won't keep me off her if she won't leave my child alone!"

This time Mama was REALLY angry, and she let Gertrude know it! When we left the school, Mama said to me, "Do not stay after school tomorrow or Friday. If she says anything to you, ignore her and come home on time. I told her you were not to be punished any further." (Thank God for sending me Mama; now there were three of us—God, Mama, and me!)

I returned to school the next day to a peaceful school session. Sister Mary Carmel was her usual self. It was as if the previous day had never happened. When she rang the bell to go home, I was on my feet and out the door, and she never said a mumbling word.

I had all but lost interest in school. My grades were beginning to slip, and Mama was begging me again about bringing my grades up. I got three Ds on my last report card. The teacher sent a note home with my report card. It said, "Thomas has the ability to be a good student but is always *daydreaming*." She was right; I spent a lot of time looking out the window the snowball had come through. I became fascinated with the bricks and mortar of an abandoned building across the alleyway. I found myself making drawings of the old bricks and broken windows. I was escaping the classroom by making sketches of things outside the classroom. The sun seemed so sunny, and it gave new life to the ruins I could see from the window. Sister Carmel's voice was merely a sound I heard in the background.

One day a few weeks later, after we had said our morning prayers and were about to start our first lesson, the door was abruptly thrown open. In walked a blond-haired, freckle-faced White boy of about eight or nine years old. He took a seat in the front row. We all looked at Sister Carmel to see what her reaction would be. She pretended she didn't see him for a couple of hours or so and then said, "What grade are you in?" (I had never heard Gertrude speak softly to anyone before. Why, she did not even look like Gertrude; she actually sounded Angelic.)

He self-assuredly said, "The fourth grade!"

She then asked (in a singsong tone of voice), "Do you know what grade this is?"

He replied, "Yeah, it's the fourth grade!" (The boy seemed to know what to say, all right.)

Sister Carmel tried not to look perplexed. We students were even more perplexed, as we had known Sister Carmel for two years now and had *never* heard her say anything sweetly to any of us, yet now she was talking in a sugar-and-spice tone of voice. It was like watching an Angus bull sing and chirp in a high falsetto tone (on its tippy toes).

Sister Carmel tried to return to her lesson plan. She then decided to ask the boy his name. He replied, "Charles Smith." Right away we said to ourselves, *We have a "Charlie" (slang for a White boy) among us!*

Lunchtime came, and we were outside at play. Charlie was right at our side. We moved left, and Charlie moved left. We moved to the right, and Charlie moved to the right. We finally popped the question to him. "Aren't you White?"

Charlie abruptly said, "NO!"

We all said to him, "Well as White as you look, you could easily go to the White school only two blocks away. They've got a playground there! We don't even have a playground here. And the White school is not overcrowded. They have new books, and you can sit where you want to. Don't you want those things?"

"NO!" he said. "I don't want to go to school there! I want to stay here!"

We decided not to bug him any further because he was getting very annoyed. If he said he was not White, then he was not White; that was that. We returned to the classroom, and Sister Carmel was quite surprised to find that Charles had returned to class too. We all left at the sound of the big brass bell.

Several weeks went by, and Charlie was still hanging tough. What was really strange was that we knew Charlie was not registered to go to school here. Who were his parents? Was he a runaway? Nobody seemed to be concerned. We eventually accepted that he was determined to stay. My suspicion was that he was a sensitive kid who was not able to accept the vast inequities he had witnessed in his most tender years and wanted to make a statement about them. He seemed to be doing a splendid job at it. That was my opinion. Either way, I admired his tenacity and strong will, and he was fun to play with. He played like a real boy, took his licks, and had no problem dishing it out either. Yeah, Charlie was OK!

After Charlie had been with us for a month or so, an elderly woman appeared and told Sister Carmel that she was Charles's grandmother. She told the Sister that Charlie was White and that she wanted him to go to a White school. She came to take Charlie away. Charles was now screaming at the top of his voice, "I am not White, and she is not my grandmother!" The grandmother grabbed Charlie by the ear and they left. We already missed Charlie and wanted him to stay!

About a week later, Charlie walked back into the classroom. We were surprised and tickled. (Even Sister Carmel was smiling!) He looked neither left nor right. He walked to the seat he had first sat in. He didn't even speak to the teacher. He just wanted to do his work, take his recesses, make his grades, and go home. We never even knew where he lived because he had never told us. He was always well dressed and had his own money. Charlie stayed and finished the fourth grade with the rest of us. God bless you, Charlie, wherever you are! We will meet again in the happy beyond, I am sure.

It was now November, and The Feast of Christ the King, called the Sacred Heart Parade, was upon us. There was to be a parade down Constitution Avenue to the Monument Grounds. Sister Carmel told all the boys in class that we had to wear a dark suit, a white shirt, a dark necktie, and dark shoes and that we had to spend fifty cents to buy a flag that we all had to carry in this parade. While she was talking, I was preoccupied with some sketching I was involved in. When I got home that night, I told Mom that I had to have a white suit, a white shirt, a white necktie, and white shoes to be in this Sacred Heart Parade. Mama said to me, "Thomas, this is November, are you sure she said a white suit, a white necktie, and white shoes?"

"That's what I seem to remember, Mama!" Not many people had telephones in those days, and we were among those with no phone, so she couldn't call the school to check this out. Poor Mama went out and bought me the things I said I needed. She also said she drove herself crazy looking for a white suit in the stores. They all had the winter stock out, so a white suit was hard to find. (I didn't particularly want to be in the parade anyway.)

The day of the parade came, and I was all dressed up and ready to meet the rest of the school at St. Vincent de Paul's Church at South Capitol and M Streets at around 8:00 a.m. When I walked out of the house and got to South Capitol Street, I saw about two hundred boys standing in front of the Church, and they all had on dark suits, dark shoes, dark socks, white shirts, dark neckties, and a big American flag over their right shoulder. I could not believe my eyes! Sister Carmel was the first to spot me. She came over and said, "Why in the world would your mother send you here in a white suit? You're in a parade, and you show up dressed for Holy Communion? Didn't you give her my message?"

I told her that I had told my mother the wrong thing and that it was not her fault. Gertrude had a field day with me. I had given her the opportunity to avenge herself for the way my mother told her about herself. I suggested that she send me back home, but she would not hear of it. She then asked me for the fifty cents that she had requested us to bring for the American flag. I had forgotten completely about that too. I told her I only had a quarter my mother had given me to buy a hot dog (twelve cents) and a soda (seven cents).

Now she was really gritting her teeth. The flags cost *fifty cents apiece*! They were about eighteen inches by twenty-four inches and were attached to a long pole. "Give me that quarter and let me see what I can get for this," said Gertrude. She walked over to the flag man, gave him my quarter, and pointed me out to him. He reached into his bag and came up with the tiniest flag I had ever seen. It was three inches by six inches and could fit in the palm of my hand.

I asked Sister, "How am I going to wear this over my right shoulder?"

She said, "You should have thought of that before you left home. Now we have to try to blend you in among the others." It was an impossible situation. No matter where they put me in the crowd, I was noticeable! That white suit could not be hidden. In the meantime, I stuck my miniature flag in the handkerchief pocket of my jacket.

My arm was already beginning to cramp up on me. I noticed the other guys were not having the problem I was having because their big flag with the long pole allowed them to relax their arm by changing positions on the pole. I had no pole, so my arm was trying to hold a stick the size of a lollipop stick up on my shoulder. Sister Carmel, who was walking through the ranks like a Drill Sergeant, stopped in front of me and said, "Take that flag out of your pocket, and carry it on your shoulder like everyone else is doing!" I took my little flag out and held it up to my shoulder. I looked like a real idiot!

About an hour later, it was announced that we were about to leave for the parade assembly area. My arm was killing me at the elbow. All of a sudden, Sister Carmel ran up to me and said, "Thomas DuVall (I just knew she was going to send me home), we are going to place you behind the bass Drummer in the marching band, that way you won't be marching with the others."

The bass Drummer was the last person in the back with this big bass drum, and I was behind him. My face was on the same level as the seat of his pants. As a matter of fact, I couldn't see the bass drum because of the amount of space the seat of his pants covered!

After about another two or three hours, the parade started. The band proceeded first, and I was right behind them. All I could see of the parade were the hind parts of this bowlegged man's shiny, well-worn band uniform trousers as he hit this big bass drum. If this guy decided to pass gas, *I was dead*! In the meantime, I looked for Gertrude and couldn't find her anywhere, so the flag went back into my pocket. Then I could swing both of my arms in time with the bass drum! I looked behind me and saw my school about half a block away. How had they gotten so far behind? It didn't matter, as I was sticking with the Drummers. I was having such a good time walking with the band. The crowd thought I was some sort of mascot in white, and I could even hear some applause (or at least I thought so)! The music was swinging and steady, and we were all marching in step down Independence Avenue as we headed for the Monument and the finish line!

I was glad they hadn't sent me home. Then it dawned on me that Sister Mary Carmel had taken my twenty-five cents to pay for the doggone midget flag! Wow, that meant no hot dog, no soda, and no refreshments! I tried to sell the flag but found no buyers, so I headed for the Monument. I got to the entrance and ran into some of the guys from my class. We all had the same intention in mind: to *run* up the steps to the top of the Monument to see how long it would take. It was the *thrill* of the day! We ran all the way up, looked out the windows, and ran all the way down! To this day, I cannot believe we ran both ways! Then we walked home. We were all about eight or nine years old. We did that every year after that for the next five years. We even met other guys there from other neighborhoods doing the same thing, which made it more fun. Those were happy days.

There were no public playgrounds in the Black neighborhoods. The nearest public playground to me was at Fifth and New Jersey Avenue SE, just opposite Metropolitan Police Fifth Precinct, and it was for White children only. Those who dared would hide behind the hedges from time to time and watch the White kids swing and play on their sliding boards. They had two sliding boards—a small one for the little guys and a BIG one for the older kids. I was dying to get on that big one. I can even remember sitting in the rain in those hedges, waiting for a lucky break when there were no Whites about. I would make a mad dash for that big sliding board and do a quick swing, as high as I could propel myself, before being chased away by the local police or stoned and chased by irate Whites.

CHAPTER 16

Officer Cowan's Boxing Team

About a month later, one of the guys in class asked me to accompany him to South Capitol and M Streets, and I asked why. He said there was a guy who was going to be waiting there to beat him up. "I'm not afraid of him," he said. "I just don't know who he will have with him, and I don't want to be caught alone. I just want you to make sure it's a fair fight. Would you do that for me?"

I hesitated for a moment and then said, "Why did you pick me?" (I figured he could have asked one of the older boys.)

He said, "They told me you were a fair person, plus you live over that way."

So I said, "OK, let's go!"

We got to South Capitol and M, and sure enough, there was a guy waiting on the corner. The other guy said to my friend, "You said you would be alone!"

My friend said, "He is here to see to it that we fight fair. That's all!"

They took their jackets off and started their thing. Everything was going pretty well, but all of a sudden, the other guy slipped and fell. My friend saw this as an opportunity to get a few kicks in. He kicked the guy as he was trying to get up, and the guy fell over backward. My friend was about to kick him again when I stepped in and grabbed him to prevent him from kicking the guy a second time. My friend got annoyed at me for grabbing him and started taking pokes at me. I had no choice but to defend myself. I gave him a couple of pokes upside his head just to get him to come to his senses. While all this was going on, the guy on the ground got up and took off down the street.

All of a sudden, a cop appeared from out of nowhere and said, "All right, break it up!" My friend took off like a bat out of hell, leaving just the policeman and me. The officer had his hand on my shoulder. (I said to myself, *I'm going to jail for sure now; why hadn't I just run away like the others had?*)

"My name is Officer Cowan, and I am starting a Police Boys' Club here on this corner. How would you like to be on my boxing team?"

I was in shock. I thought I was on my way to reform school, and he was talking sports? "But I don't know anything about boxing!" I said.

He said, "I was watching you from the window. I like the way you handle yourself. You are a natural for a boxing candidate. I can coach you in what you need to know, and you can help me help others in the neighborhood. So what do you say? Is it a deal?"

I hesitated for a moment. Nobody had ever said these things to me before, and I knew I could use those boxing skills he was talking about. "OK!" I said to this Black cop. I joined the boys' club and the boxing club. We met every Wednesday at seven o'clock. I was tickled pink. However, I dared not tell this story to Mama—not yet, anyway!

One day Officer Cowan said to me, "Thomas, I am satisfied with your progress here and want to promote you to Lieutenant and give you an assignment."

"Yes, sir," I said.

"I want you to go out in the neighborhood and help me bring more boys into the club."

I said, "Okay," and off I went. I recruited my brother Roland, who was six years old, my brother Herbert, who was five years old, and two other guys, George West and his brother Donald. We all went out for the boxing team. Officer Cowan called the *Afro-American* newspaper and had them cover this story of his boxing team and the newfound Police Boys' Club for Colored boys at South Capitol and M Streets SW.

As I mentioned earlier, my man George West was a different kind of guy. Some guys would suck their thumb, some guys would chew their nails, some guys would always talk or cry, and some guys would always eat or pop bubble gum, blow their noses, or just get on your nerves, but George West was COOL! He only chewed on his collar.

Yeah, he would always have one side or the other side in his mouth. When he was fighting or thinking really hard, he would have both sides in his mouth. He could wear a collar out, especially when test time in school came around. Wow, he would be concentrating, and the shirt collar would be soaking wet when he was done. Nobody said anything to him about this because he always came up with the right answers or solutions. George even had me and a few others chewing on our collars when the chips were down—and it seemed to work, too! Not only that, but the collar didn't taste bad either.

George West always wore fisherman's rubber boots that came up to his knees, and they sounded like they were too big for his feet. They made a different sound when HE walked around the room in them. He was not tall, but if you closed your eyes and listened to his steps, you would think he was a big heavy dude. But not so. He would even wear them when the sun was shining.

George West was a thinker and a good friend, and we did a lot of fun things together with him wearing his rubber boots and wet collar. I had recruited him for the boxing team before I recruited my two younger brothers. George West and I stayed on the boxing team for the whole duration. I figured he was so good as a boxer because he was in the habit of keeping his chin tucked in, thanks to his collar-chewing habit. He was never knocked down from a blow to the chin, and I was dumb enough to perfect the same habit as my friend. We became so good that Officer Cowan made us his Boxing Lieutenants and Recruiters in the neighborhood, around South Capitol and M Streets SW.

One day Officer Cowan made a very sad announcement. He could no longer keep the Colored Police Boys' Club open because the man he was renting from wanted to open a business at the location and had served Officer Cowan with a notice of termination. Officer Cowan said he could not talk this Jewish guy into letting him keep the space for the Colored boys to have some place to go when school was out.

Officer Cowan then told us about Officer Barry's Colored Police Boys' Club up on Banneker Place NW and asked us to please continue to be members by joining the club and the boxing team there.

The *Afro-American* newspaper covered the story, and the DuVall Brothers (Roland and Herbert) were on in the center of the front page, boxing gloves and all, slugging it out! Mama came home with her copy in her hand and said, "THOMAS, GET IN HERE!"

"Yes, Mama!"

"WHAT is the meaning of this? I will not have you doing any boxing around here! My sons will not be walking around here with cauliflower ears!" she said. She was really upset. She called Officer Cowan and told him off. "I don't want my children on anybody's box-ing team!" she yelled. Then she hung up. Wow, I had really made a mess of that. She then turned to me and said, "If you don't care what happens to you, do not be dragging your brothers down with you!"

That Wednesday I went by the club. Officer Cowan was waiting for me. "I told you to get your mother's approval! Why didn't you do as I asked?"

"Because she would never have approved," I said, "so I figured I would wait awhile before I told her. I am back here to say that I want to continue boxing, but I must leave my brothers home."

He smiled and said, "OK, suit up!" So George West and I stayed on.

A few months later, Officer Barry called a meeting of all the members and announced that the boys' club was closing. As Officer Cowan had requested, we went to Officer Barry's Colored Police Boys' Club on Banneker Place. The Banneker swimming pool was still there. Now I had to take the bus and a streetcar ride to Wednesday boxing.

We met the Northwest guys, and they looked tough to me. But that Wednesday we did not box. We were having a marching band practice for the parade around the newfound Police Boys' Club, and guess who Officer Barry gave the BASS drum to? That's right, *me*. All of a sudden, I was back in the parade down Constitution Avenue, but this time I was *playing* the bass. I even found myself walking like that man I had walked behind. I stayed with the club for about three or four years. Then my family moved farther out in Southeast, and I fell away. I learned later that Officer Barry had passed on and the street had been renamed Barry Place. Now there is a McDonald's in that location.

God bless you, George West, wherever you are!

Summertime was around the corner, and we were all boning up for final exams—our only exit out from under Sister Mary Carmel, a.k.a. Gertrude. I was determined not to stay in her class for another year.

I was ready for the exams. I gave it my all. I held out handing in my papers until the bell rang for each exam's end. All the papers were in, and we went home. The next day she read off the grades of those who had all As, then Bs, then Cs, and then Ds. I grew concerned when she still hadn't called my name. *What's going on here, I haven't heard my name yet,* I thought. All of a sudden, she said, "THOMAS DUVALL!"

"Yes, Sister?"

"You passed, but I believe you cheated, so you will remain after everyone leaves and take this exam over in front of me so that I can see if you cheated." Wow! I was not yet free of her! I had one more obstacle to overcome.

Everybody filed out of the classroom. Sister Carmel said, "All right, Thomas, you may step up to the blackboard, and we shall retest you on your math exam." She had me write the problem on the board, and then I showed her step-by-step how I arrived at my answer. She was amazed at how I arrived at the answers to the problems, because I did not follow the steps and procedures shown in the book.

I used my own methodology and reached the same conclusions as the author. I solved the problem in eight steps, and the book solved it in seven steps, so she used this example to tell me how I must follow the book procedures because the author did not include any unnecessary moves or steps. Nonetheless, she saw firsthand that I had not been cheating and that I was being creative in my methods of deduction. We parted on an even keel, and I left her smiling. God bless Sister Mary Carmel, who did the best she could to keep me in check! I think that deep down inside, she came to like me.

WOW! I passed! I passed! I was out of there! Hello, fifth grade! Good-bye, Gertrude. *"Hail Mary, full of Grace! The Lord is with thee! Blessed art thou amongst women. And Blessed is the fruit of thy womb, Jesus."*

I was late getting home, and Mama was waiting for me. I told her how Sister Mary Carmel had kept me after school because she felt I had cheated on the final exam. Mama just shook her head and said, "That woman is incorrigible!"

CHAPTER 17

Purple and Yellow and Cowboys and Indians

When I was eight years old, my mother bought me a coloring book and a box of crayons. I was thrilled. I went immediately to work coloring page after page. I came across a clown that took up the whole page. He had on these big baggy pants with oversized polka dots. *Wow,* I said to myself. *I'm gonna color his pants purple and fill in the polka dots with yellow!* With the yellow in one hand and the purple in the right, I went to work. After I had finished filling in the pants with the purple, I immediately switched hands and approached the picture with the yellow. As I began to touch the picture with the yellow, I felt a twist in my stomach. I tried to ignore it because I was excited over my next application, yellow. I began to color the biggest polka dot on the clown's pants leg. My stomach was now churning, and I was beginning to feel a bit nauseous, so I paused for a moment.

I noticed that my skin, especially on my forehead, was feeling clammy. *Wow,* I said to myself. *What an inconvenient time to get sick—just as I'm about to put the finishing touches on my pet project! Maybe I can finish this off. I don't care what happens after that.* I paused for a while longer and began to feel a little better. I began hitting those polka dots with more vigor because I wanted to finish the picture before I started feeling any worse. I hit that polka dot with big, broad, bold yellow strokes, and the more I stroked, the worse I felt.

I was now vomiting into my left hand while trying to color with my right hand. I decided to make a beeline to the bathroom to vomit in the crapper. When I got to the toilet, I was fine—no sick feeling at all. I sat there for a moment just to be sure before I went running back downstairs. After about five or ten minutes of sitting in the bathroom, I decided to go back to my clown project. I was feeling fine, so I knelt down on the floor in front of the coloring book and picked up the yellow crayon. I looked at the large, unfinished polka dot. A sickening dizziness hit me square in the solar plexus! I paused again. *Was this going to be a routine?* I asked myself.

I decided to push on. I picked up the yellow crayon and approached the big unfinished polka dot. Immediately upon contact, I began vomiting! This time I was unable to hold it in my left hand, so it was running through my fingers and falling on my coloring book. By the time I got to the toilet, I was feeling just fine. Now I was in disbelief. What in the world was going on? Everybody in the house was still in bed because it was early on a Sunday morning. I had no witness to what was going on and dared not wake somebody up to tell them. They would have thought I had lost my mind, and I couldn't blame them, because that's the way I felt too.

Standing there bewildered in the bathroom, I said to myself, *Maybe it was just something that happened twice! Surely it wouldn't happen three times in a row.* I talked myself into trying to finish that clown's pants one more time. I went downstairs, picked up the yellow crayon, and began coloring. The more I colored, the more I vomited. I was sick as a dog. I was so sick that I could not get up the stairs to the bathroom, so I just lay down on the floor and crawled away from the coloring book. I was too weak to leave the room. I was a living mess; my eyes were watering, my ears were ringing, my nose was running, my stomach was cramping, and my head was spinning. Nobody could have told me I was not dying! I had resigned myself to the fact that my life was over. The house was still as quiet as a mouse. I thought, *They won't even know what happened to me, and I won't be alive to tell them what a mess I've made.*

Some time passed, and I was still stretched out on the floor waiting to get into hell (I figured nobody went to heaven feeling the way I did). Suddenly I began to feel better, so I jumped up and started cleaning myself up and wiping up the mess I had made while I was dying. I decided not to go back to the coloring book for a couple of days. I quickly closed the book and put it away.

I was dying to tell somebody what had happened to me. Mama eventually came downstairs, and I immediately started telling her about what had just taken place. She said that it sounded like something I ate and went about asking me what I had been putting into my stomach, so I dropped the subject. I told my friends about it, but they all laughed and started calling me "Weird Duball." Regardless, I did not try that purple and yellow combination again for many years. To this day I make it a point to avoid the two as a combination. Just the *thought* of it makes my stomach churn.

I wanted to continue pursuing my love of drawing and to share it with other children. The kids from my fourth-grade class were coming by the house to learn how to draw. I had a houseful of kids, but nobody was disorderly. Mama was really impressed with everybody's behavior. She was skeptical at first. She didn't see how I was going to maintain order. However, those who came really wanted to learn how to draw, and their attention was not diverted by anything. All I had to do was give them an assignment, and they went straight to work! (I was more impressed than Mama!)

Summer Vacation

Summer vacation was upon us. I was about eight or nine years old and living on Half Street SE. It was Saturday morning in the summertime, and the boys on the block were coming out to play. We boys seemed to be on the streets between 8:00 and 10:00 a.m. The girls all seemed to hit the street at around 11:00 a.m. or noon.

The boys would usually meet on the block about midway and map out what we were going to do for the day. We'd play until we could hear our mothers yelling for us to come in to do housework or run errands.

Someone would always yell out, "Let's play cowboys 'n Indians! Yeah, and Thomas can play the Indian!" They would all agree. This went on for weeks. In the beginning I didn't mind because I did have a bow and arrows, some of which I had made myself. But as time went on, I was able to get a Colt-44 long-barrel Peacemaker cap pistol like everyone else had, so now I wanted to shoot some "Indians" myself! But they all said that I was the one who looked more Indian than anybody else on the block, so I was to be the Indian. It was not their fault that I looked like an Indian, so why wouldn't I want to play the part?

"Why can't we take turns being Indian?" I asked.

They would all chime in, "But we don't look Indian, and you've got light skin, so you have to play the Indian!" With that said and done, they all drew their guns and shot me.

And that's the way it was. I soon decided that I would be the hardest Indian to kill, catch, or find. I was determined to be the fastest runner, the fastest drawer, the best camouflager, the greatest disguiser, and the best everything. I made my own rifle, my own knife and sheath, and my own stick horse. I was a fast rider and a straight shooter. I was the best Indian they had ever met. I even had a buckskin jacket that I wore everywhere I went, rain or shine, even to bed. I read about all the Indian heroes and warriors, their tribal names, and all the great battles and skirmishes. I was always one jump ahead of the "Black cowboys." I guess they figured that since they were always portrayed as "winners" in the movies, they did not have to work at being a cowboy. All they had to do was wear their guns, shoot at Indians, and win the day.

The situation eventually changed, and they decided the bow and arrow was the way to go. We joined up and made bows and arrows for each other. Then we had tournaments to see whose bow was strong enough to shoot at a distant target. We also had to climb trees to pick out nice supple branches that would have a good spring-back action to them. We spent many hours and days doing these things. Some of us had bows as tall as we were. We wore our bows across our chests as if they were medals of high achievement.

CHAPTER 18

Horse Racing and the Haunted House

I was now two months into being nine years old and I felt "born again!" That summer the other thing to do was horse racing. First we would decide who the "horses" were going to be (usually the younger guys). Then we'd take a piece of clothesline and run it around the back of the dude's neck and under both armpits and then even up the ends. In our left hands we'd hold the end that ran under the dude's left armpit, and in our right hands we'd hold the end that ran under the dude's right armpit. When we pulled on the left rein, the horse had to turn left, and when we pulled on the right rein, the horse had to turn right.

Now the rule for the horse was that he was not to turn right or left unless he was given a command by the jockey (the guy holding the rope) to do so. We'd go once around the block, and the first to get back to the starting line was the fastest horse. (Fortunately, the younger guys took pride in being the fastest horse in the neighborhood.)

I was a little unhappy with my brother Herbert. He was my horse one day, and we had run two or three races and had lost all three. He just didn't have any ZIP! Suddenly I remembered that Herbert was afraid of bugs, so while the horses were taking a break, I scouted the area for some kind of insect I could show Herbert just as the race started. Lo and behold, I found a dead June bug (a large Japanese beetle). I palmed the dead bug until the race started. We were falling behind the pack already. We were almost half a block behind when I decided it was now or never. I pulled up on my reins a little and yelled out to Herbert, "Herbert, look what I found!" He turned his head to see what it was I was trying to show him. When he saw the size of the bug I had in my hand, his eyes popped out of his head, and he took off like a bat out of hell!

I was struggling to hold onto the reins because of his sudden burst of speed. He was running so fast that I was regretting having done that. "Herbert! Herbert! Slow down!" I said. But Herbert did not, for a split second, slow down. As a matter of fact, the more I called his name, the faster he ran! I was trying to get him to slow down, but he thought I was chasing him. I was really feeling bad about what I had done. We were passing all the other horses, and for the first time all day, we were ahead of the pack. I could not believe what was happening. Could fear make someone a superhuman? Herbert was now half a block ahead of everybody, and everybody was in shock. They could not catch up with Herbert. Herbert won the race by at least fifty yards!

My brother Roland walked up to me and asked, "What in the world got into Herbert? I have never seen him move that fast in my life!" I showed Roland the bug I still had in my hand. He suggested I hold onto the bug for the next day's race. I tried to apologize to Herbert, but he was so happy he'd won that I was ignored. Herbert ran faster from then on. I no longer had to prompt him. He just needed to know he was capable.

Shortly after that Roland and Herbert started having bad dreams and would wake up screaming and yelling. Mama would give me a spanking because she believed I was telling them things to scare them and cause them to have these dreams. That went on for almost a week. I got the two of them together and had them tell Mama that I was not doing that. They did that (bless their souls), Mama took their word for it, and I was spared any future pain.

Horse racing was soon phased out, and playing homemade musical instruments was in. We made guitars out of cigar boxes and rubber bands and wind instruments out of combs and a piece of wax paper. We used rhythm sticks for hand jive percussion and penny whistles (flexible electric conduit tubes filled with water) to make an underwater flute sound. We'd all have harmonica and body percussion contests (the hambone) by slapping our chests and thighs while stomping our feet and humming a tune.

ALL: Hambone, Hambone, where you been?
ANSWER: Round the world and back again!
CALL: Hambone, Hambone, wha' chu see?
ALL: Big black monkey lookin' at me!

We even organized a parade and marched up and down the sidewalks while the grown-ups watched in amusement. Then it started raining.

The Haunted House

When I was about nine years old and living on Half Street SE, I would often walk across the Eleventh Street Bridge to Anacostia. It was like visiting another township; everything had a different look about it. The shops had a small-town look to them, and a lot of the houses were made of wood, rather than brick. But there was one exception: the house on Fifth and W Streets. This house sat on a hill and had big trees in its front yard. I found myself staring at it. For some reason I was intrigued by the place. It was deserted and run-down. I found myself wanting to go inside. I looked right and left; nobody was in sight. I entered the front gate and slowly walked up the hill toward the house. I kept looking around for someone to say something, but no one was about.

I walked up to the front door and found it open. I yelled inside, "Hello!" There was no response. If someone had answered, I would have asked for a drink of water. (In those days, all a kid had to do was knock on any door and ask for a glass of water, and someone would give it to him.) I stood there for a little while and then stepped inside. The place was in ill repair. I walked from room to room. The place was in a shamble. I stumbled across a small room off the kitchen that had a rolltop desk and a high chair like accountants used to use. I climbed up in the chair and sat at the desk, reflecting on how someone could have abandoned such a nice big house. I could see that someone successful, like a writer or a bookkeeper, must have lived there.

I sat there a long time. The whole time I sat there, I heard the sound of water running. I looked around and found a water pipe not far from the desk. At one time the pipe must have been attached to a sink. The sink was gone, but they had never turned the water off?

The floorboards had rotted away from the years of dampness and water damage. Seeing that water, I became even thirstier. I climbed down from the high chair and headed for the water pipe. I cupped my hands and drank. The water was amazingly cool and refreshing. I drank and drank. I returned once again to the high chair. I sat for a while longer, and something told me to go check out the bedroom.

I headed for the bedroom. There was a bed there with an old hand-carved headboard. The bed itself was the *strangest-looking* bed I had ever seen. Between the headboard and the footboard was only about three feet of bed. Had the house's owner been a midget? This aroused my curiosity immensely. I looked for other signs of the owner having been a dwarf but could not find a single thing. Everything else appeared to be for normal adult-size people, particularly the way the mirrors were hung. I left the house but could not get the size of the bed out of my head. I was intrigued!

That afternoon when I got back to the neighborhood, I started telling the dudes about where I had just come back from. They started telling me that house was HAUNTED! Nobody in their right mind would go in there, everybody seemed to agree.

"Why is it haunted?" I asked.

They said, "An old man died in there, and the family suddenly moved out and left everything in the house."

"They didn't take anything with them?" I asked.

"Nothing, they just *up and left!*" they said.

Wow! I said to myself. I didn't mention the short bed that I had seen. I figured I had said enough already. "Tom Cat" had now taken on a *new* meaning. Not only did I *kill cats*, but I hung out in *haunted houses*!

Well I guess that meant that I would be going back by myself. I wanted to get a closer look at that bed, visit my spot at the desk, and drink some of that cool running water from that broken pipe.

The following Saturday I got up at the break of dawn and got dressed. I dared not tell my brothers because they might have dreams about it. (Whenever my two brothers would have nightmares, Mama would give me a spanking because it must have been caused by something I said to them—something I said to them that made them have a bad dream.) So this was my secret mission. I did all my chores around the house and was out the door. It was about ten thirty or eleven o'clock when I headed for the Eleventh Street Bridge. I walked slowly across the bridge with my eyes glued to the water. Everything seemed so quiet and peaceful. I could hear the river water splashing up against the bridge's support. It seemed like it was taking me longer to cross the bridge this time. I finally crossed the bridge and headed up Nichols Avenue (now known as Martin Luther King Avenue) to

W Street. I turned left on Fifth (I think) and walked slowly up the hill to the spot where I had entered the grounds before. A sense of calm came over me. I thought about how everybody felt about this place and wondered why I didn't feel spooked. Was this what they called *reckless abandon*? I felt at ease in there and welcome, in a way.

I wondered if I should go back in there. What if something did happen? How would I explain *this one* to Mama? Then a little voice said, *You mean to say that you walked all the way over here for nothing?* This couldn't be for nothing, so I said to myself, *Here goes.* I walked slowly but deliberately up to the entrance. I called out, "Hello," but got no answer. I went in and headed straight for the master bedroom. The bed was still there. I carefully examined it to see if something had been altered to make the bed look like *half* a bed.

To my amazement I could find nothing to show an alteration. This meant the bed had been *specially* made for whoever had slept in it! I thought that this might haunt me for the rest of my life, but then again, why was the sight of a short bed bothering me so much? I proceeded to my favorite spot in the house, the rolltop desk and high chair. I climbed up into my chair, and there I sat, no paper, no pencil, just staring out the broken glass window at the overgrowth of weeds and shrubbery. I had the feeling some heavy writing had gone down at this desk. I could *feel it*! I sat there until the sound of the water again had my undivided attention. I felt myself getting thirstier and thirstier. I could not resist any longer, so I jumped down, went over to the broken water pipe, and started to drink. The water was unbelievably cool and sweet. I drank for as long as I could and as much as I could. I then went outside on the lawn. The trees in the yard were the tallest and the grandest trees I had ever seen. Everything was sparkling! I left there on a high. I said that if I ever got my hands on some money when I grew up, I was going to buy the place and fix it up.

Twenty-seven years later, on a return trip to DC to work with the Summer in the Parks program, I was teaching arts and crafts in the inner city. One of the stops along the route was the Frederick Douglass House and Museum in Anacostia, so I decided to take some of the kids over there to see the museum. Lo and behold, it was the haunted house I used to play in as a little boy! I could not believe it!

I immediately went to the master bedroom to see if that *short bed* was there, and there it was! I ran and got the guide to ask what the story was about the bed. He said Mr. Douglass had terrible back pains that prevented him from lying prone, so he had had a bed made that allowed him to sleep *sitting up*! I next asked the guide where the desk was that Mr. Douglass had used to write. The guide showed me the same desk and chair. I had come full circle!

My brother Herbert.

CHAPTER 19

Fifth Grade

The year I entered fifth grade was the year that Herbert was to start school and that Hughdy DuVall showed his "Baptist heritage" by deciding where Herbert would be going to school. We found out that Daddy did not like Catholic school, so no son of his was going to any Catholic school. He did not say anything about me and Roland, so Herbert must have been Hughdy's only son. He put his foot down, and Herbert was off to Van Ness Public School at Third and M Streets SE. Herbert was sick at heart. He just knew he was going to go to school with his two brothers.

But Hughdy had other ideas. Herbert became sicker and sicker to the point that he developed terminal whooping cough. Herbert was sick in bed more than he was in school. The doctors had given up on finding a cure for his condition. Then they lowered the boom and told Mama they did not expect Herbert to live another six months.

That night I visited Herbert at his bed and just stared at my poor brother. He was only five and was dying. Herbert was glad to see me, and I could see he was enjoying my company. Every time I said I was going, he would tense up. Suddenly I saw a light that seemed to brighten the room.

"Mama," I called, running to find her. I was so excited that I couldn't speak. I eventually said to Mama, "Mama, Herbert wants to go to school with us! I betcha if he knew he was going to be with us, he would get well, for sure!"

Mama looked at me real hard and said, "Maybe you are right, son. It's worth a try. I will talk to Hughdy when he comes home."

That night I told Herbert that I had spoken to Mama and that Mama was going to talk to Daddy. I said, "I am sure you will be going to school with us real soon."

Herbert started looking better already. He pulled his fragile self up and said, "I'll be ready!" Herbert is now in his early seventies and has hardly had one day of sickness from that day to this.

Hughdy saw then that he could not object any longer. He *was* the son of a Minister, and I am certain he saw the same light I saw around Herbert's head. I am sure this was the reason why the Church frowned on mixed (religious) marriages. He saw that his son wanted only to be with his two brothers. Religion/smiligion—Herbert wanted to spend the day with us!

In about a week's time, the DuVall Brothers were walking to school together. I walked into school, passed by Sister Carmel's class, and headed into the fifth-grade classroom, which was gloomy and dark. Then I realized that the fourth-grade classroom was on the sunrise side of the building. We were on the sunset side of the building. That meant this room would be without sunlight until after lunch—no more morning sunrise!

Our teacher was going to be Sister Mary Martha, and that Nun never smiled! She wore a frown *all* the time. She had been frowning so long that the muscles in her face were set, and she couldn't smile even if she wanted to. She was the Nun who had caught Jean Guy and me when we'd been locked out of the classroom. I am certain she was instrumental in getting rid of Jean Guy.

She called the roll and arrived at my name. "THOMAS DUVALL!" she said.

"Here!" I answered.

"Thomas DuVall, I know you have been doing a lot of artwork in the lower grades, but this is the fifth and sixth grade, and *you* will NOT be doing any artwork. This is the year you will be doing what everybody else will be doing. I don't need these boards decorated with anything but completed schoolwork."

"Yes, Sister," I said and thought to myself, *I need a rest anyway!*

Sister Martha quite frequently used the word "niggerism." She talked about niggerism behavior, niggerism on the street, niggerism on the playground, niggerism in the classroom, niggerism this, and niggerism that. I knew the word "nigger" but didn't know what the "ism" meant, so the first chance I got, I looked it up in the dictionary and found it: "-ism a. *the manner of action or behavior characteristic of a (specified) person or thing (animalism)* b. *abnormal state or condition resulting from excess of a (specified) person or thing.*"[2] Wow! Now I understood why she didn't smile! How could she smile with a vocabulary like that?

I sat across from Joseph Only. He loved to tell jokes, and so did I, so we were always laughing about something. He had a sister named Constance. She had a wild sense of humor! For instance Sister Martha called on Constance and asked her to give the parts of speech for the word "GOOD." Constance stood up and blurted out, "GOOD, GOODER, AND GOODEST." Then she and the whole class cracked up over what she had said. Sister Martha did not laugh. I could see

---

[2] *Merriam-Webster.com*

her lips saying "more niggerism" as she banged on the desk trying to restore some kind of order.

Joseph Only and I were beginning to get a reputation for being comical. The school was holding a talent show, so Joseph Only and I signed up as a comedy duo. He was the straight guy, and I was the goof. We had this routine in which he would ask me an intelligent-sounding question, and I would reply with a stupid answer. He would respond by hitting me over the head with a small stick. We were given enough time to tell three jokes, which meant I'd be hit across the head three times, so I got the dumb idea to get a man's hat. I found a paint can lid that I put inside the hat, thinking it would protect my head when he hit me over the head with the stick. We both agreed the paint can lid under the hat might do it.

We were queued to go on stage. Joseph Only walked out on the stage, and I was right behind him. We reached center stage, and Joseph Only turned to me and delivered his straight line (I wish I could remember the lines). I responded with the punch line, and he hit me over the head. WHAM! I actually saw stars and wanted to yell out loud, but that would have ruined the whole thing. I tried to pretend I was not in excruciating pain. The experience made me immediately realize I should have put padding between my head and the paint can lid. That metal lid was against my skull, and letting the stick hit that paint can lid had not been the way to go. He delivered the line for the next joke. I was hedging with my line because I was still reeling from the first blow to the head. I tried to tell him with my eyes not to hit me so hard. I gave the punch line, and he hit me across the head again. WHAM! This time I almost went down on my knees.

WOW! I could feel two knots on my head, and my eyes were beginning to water. I didn't think I could make it through the next punch line. (Boy o' boy!) What a fine mess I had gotten myself into! Joseph Only was doing an excellent job as a straight guy. I could hear the kids laughing in the audience. I was trying *desperately* to get ready for the last blow to the head. Joseph Only delivered his line. I hesitantly and somewhat halfheartedly responded with my line, and WHAM! He delivered the coup de grâce!

The children were on their feet in the audience. They had really enjoyed it, and we won the talent show. I was so dazed by the three blows to the head that I still cannot remember any of the jokes, nor do I remember what prize we won. My head was hurting for days, but I felt triumphant. Joseph Only said I should have said something, but I told him I didn't want to stop the show. (I had done it all for the love of Art!)

I was still an altar boy at that time, which allowed me to come to school late on the weekdays when I had to serve Mass. Father Smoot (pronounced "Smut") was the Pastor at St. Vincent de Paul and had sent for his brother, who was also a priest, to assist him in running the Parish. His brother, Joseph Smoot, had been assigned to overhaul and whip the altar boys into shape. He was a disciplinarian and very militaristic and wanted us to click our heels as we cut the corners around the altar and tabernacle.

We were marching around the altar as if we were guarding the Tomb of the Unknown Soldier, and we liked it. It gave us the opportunity to break the solemn Mass with a noise made by clicking our heels together. We also discovered that leather heels made a louder sound than rubber heels, so we all got leather heels on our shoes. We were always rehearsing our routines and memorizing our responses to all the Latin prayers. We would be tested and had to deal with morning inspections. Our shoes had to be shined, faces scrubbed, fingernails trimmed and cleaned, and so on, plus we had to get up at 5:00 a.m. to serve the six o'clock Mass and the eight o'clock Mass.

One Sunday, after I had served the twelve o'clock Mass and was headed back to the house, I saw some out-of-town buses in front of the Baptist Church at First and M Streets SE and was curious about what was going on there. I decided to walk past the Church to see what all the commotion was about. I discovered that there were out-of-town Gospel singers who were about to perform for the congregation. The singers included the Dixie Hummingbirds, the four Blind Boys, The Gospelaires, The Progressive Four, and others. I had heard these guys on the radio, and here they were in person. The next thing I knew, I was sitting in the pew, patting my feet and clapping my hands with everybody else. There was plenty of fried chicken, potato salad, punch, and watermelon, and the place was rocking.

The whole floor of the Church was moving up and down. The floor of that Church was even bending in the middle, and I think I was the only one who noticed. Everybody, and everything, was in motion, and I was being taken "on a ride"! I was there for several hours, and then the preacher told everyone to come back at four o'clock for the evening services. I decided I would leave and come back later. What a difference that was from the services I was used to! The Catholic service was a joke compared to what the Baptists were doing. Catholic music seemed spooky compared to the songs sung by those brothers and sisters, who were "putting down!" I could not get the music out of my head! I was singing and clapping all the way home! *I'm going back tonight,* I decided.

I now had a new routine. As soon as I finished my duties at St. Vincent, I would make a beeline for the First Street Baptist Church. I did this for several Sundays. One Sunday I was spotted going into the Baptist Church by someone from school. When I got to school the next day, Sister Martha called the roll, and when she got to my name, she said, "THOMAS DUVALL, STAND UP! You were seen going into that Baptist Church! Those people are worshipping the Devil in there, and you are going straight to hell if you don't discontinue going in there." She then called me up to the front of the class, picked up a bucket of holy water, dipped a pestle-like object into the water, and doused me with it in the sign of the cross. My face was dripping with water. I wanted to go for my handkerchief but dared not. I wasn't sure if I was allowed to wipe holy water off.

I was thoroughly confused! I saw the same huge picture of Jesus Christ there that I saw at my Church! How could He be the Devil on one side of the street and God Almighty on the other side of the street? As the water evaporated slowly, I pondered the complexity of this condemnation. I could not, for the life of me, *feel* condemned!

As I sat there, the answer came to me. The Baptist Church had two services for some reason. I decided I would go to the four o'clock service so that nobody from school would see me. The next Sunday I went to the late service. The singing began, and the floor started pulsating to the beat of the music. I did not have to pat my feet because they were bouncing off the floor anyway. All I had to do was just hold on!

When the preaching started, I would use this opportunity to move around the Church to check out the watermelon table for a slice of watermelon. Afterward I would grab a chicken leg or two and then go back to the watermelon table. When the next singing group came on, I would run and find a seat. They did not have safety belts in those days, so little guys like me just had to hold on when things started rocking again!

This went on for a while. Mama was unsuspecting because I was always home in time for dinner. I wanted to ask her why the Baptists spent the whole day in Church. They came in the morning, stayed all day, went home, changed clothes, and came back and stayed until bedtime. That was all day and half the night! They also kept passing the basket. The food was out of sight! And every so often somebody would get possessed, and the nurses would have to walk him or her around the Church to calm the person down. I still loved the singing groups, but the long-winded preaching and lengthy services were wearing me down. At least the Catholics did their thing in an hour and then the congregants were out of there!

This went on for several weeks until I was late for dinner one Sunday, and Mama asked her twenty questions. I could not lie, so I told her I had lost my appetite because I had eaten at the First Street Baptist Church. She was discombobulated. "What in the world were you doing in a Baptist Church? And you were EATING? THOMAS, what's going on? *WHO* took you there?" she asked.

"I went by myself," I said.

"Why?" she asked.

"Well," I said, "everybody seemed to be celebrating Jesus Christ's birthday and all, so I thought I would join in the celebrations. At the Catholic Church, everybody seemed to be in mourning, so after each mourning there should be some celebrating, right?

Mama looked at me and said, "Son, you cannot serve two Gods. You were born a Catholic, so please stay a Catholic, at least long enough to finish your education. Then you can join any Church you want to. But once a Catholic, always a Catholic." I could not understand this reasoning. Hadn't Mama married a Baptist? If she was so religious, why did she overlook certain things? Was she in love with someone as a Catholic? Had she been rejected by a Catholic Ministry and then married into a Baptist Ministry? What was wrong with these grown-ups? Why couldn't they see clearly?

I stopped going to the Baptist Church—going inside, that is. But nobody had said I couldn't stand around outside! Therefore, it was not unusual to find me leaning against the fence that surrounded the wooden-frame Church at First and M Streets SE on any given Sunday afternoon. Was I trying to enjoy the best of both worlds?

I was able to learn the titles of the songs by listening to what the chorus was singing. One of my favorites was "Them Dry Bones."

> The foot bone is connected to the ankle bone.
> The ankle bone is connected to the chin bone.
> The chin bone is connected to the knee bone.
> The knee bone is connected to the hip bone.
> The hip bone is connected to the back bone.
> The back bone is connected to the neck bone.
> The neck bone is connected to the head bone.
> Now listen to the word of the Lord.

That was sheer genius to me! There was so much harmony! It was amazing to me how *nice* things could get *squashed* in the push to be accepted.

"Spring is sprung and the grass is riz; now where the hell the flowers is!"

Easter was upon us, and the entire Parish was preparing to have Easter baskets on display. Mama bought Easter baskets for my two brothers and me. The women boiled and dyed the eggs all day Saturday. The baskets were fixed up with six hard-boiled multicolored eggs on cellophane grass and jellybeans spread around a chocolate bunny sitting in the middle. The women were well prepared.

Come Easter Sunday after Mass, we were all expected to go home to pick up our baskets and meet back at Church for an Easter egg roll. I heard the big boys say, "I'm not walking around with no basket swinging on my arm!" *Yeah!* I said to myself; I could not see myself doing that either. One boy said, "I'm putting mine in a shoe box!" *Hey, that's an idea!* I thought. So I went home and told Mama that the boys in school were going to carry shoe boxes. She said, "That is ridiculous!" I told Mama I was not going out with a basket hanging off my arm.

"If the boys prefer shoe boxes, I am with the boys, Mama," I insisted. Mama conceded, and I was glad. I went to the picnic, and to my surprise, all the boys swaggered up with shoe boxes under their arms. Only the girls swung their baskets on their arms. (A man's gotta do what a man's gotta do!)

Boneyard and Baseball

I was back on the baseball team and on the playing field, as I didn't have to worry about doing any lunch-hour murals! I was trying to regain some of my athletic prowess. We all picked up the baseball equipment—a ball with no cover on it, a bat without a neck on it, a catcher's mitt with no pocket padding, and a worn-out first-base bag. We headed for the vacant lot at Second and I Streets SW to get some raps in before Gertrude rang the fire bell.

I was standing at bat, ready for the ball to be pitched to me, and someone hollered out, "Hey, Boneyard, put your shirt back on!"

Then a girl who was from another class walked up to me and said, "Here, this is for you!" This girl caused an uproar from the boys because she was preventing the pitcher from throwing the ball. She was persistent, so I took the bag from her. She left, and I threw the bag under the tree, saving it until I finished striking out. Once I struck out, I returned to the bag and opened it. It was full of candy! Everybody wanted to know who was sending me candy and interrupting the game to do so. I gave everybody some candy, and we ate it on the way back to school.

The next day the same thing took place! The girl walked up to me and gave me a bag of candy, turned, and walked away. I said to myself, *I wonder if Sister Carmel is trying to make up to me for the way she's treated me for two years.*

I needed to know for sure, so I yelled to the girl, "WHO gave you the candy?"

She yelled back, "Rosita Phifer!"

"Rosita Phifer?" everybody said. (That was a shockaroo!)

"The tomboy?" someone shouted.

I was thoroughly confused. Why would a tomboy send me bags of candy? The next day it was the same thing. It was getting to be embarrassing, and all the guys were making jokes about it. "You better eat your candy, or Rosita is going to kick your ass! Hahaha!" they yelled.

This went on all week. I decided to follow Rosita out of school, and when we turned the corner away from school, I called out to her, "Rosita! Wait up a minute." I caught up to her and asked her if she was the one sending me candy on the playing field. She said yes without batting an eyelash. I told her that it had to stop because the boys were all laughing at me. It was embarrassing to me. "Why are you doing this to me? I want you to take this candy back!" I said. She looked at me and refused to take the candy back. I could see in her eyes that she was hurt. I was yelling at her, and she was about to cry. Her eyes were welling up with tears, and I was really confused. I stared at her for a moment and tried not to look puzzled. She was still swelling up. I felt like I had to do something to make her feel better, so I asked, "Can I walk you home?"

I found out she lived way past my house in Southwest, down past the old War College and in an area we used to call "Buzzard Point." They had built a project area down there during World War II, and we called it "Simple City." Even the cops were afraid to go down there!

I walked her home, and on the way we talked. I discovered that she was not at all tomboyish with me. She was now smiling, and it was a nice smile. I realized I had never seen her smile so much before. Was I beginning to like her? I said good-bye at the door and started home.

The next day I received more candy. Knowing Rosita would refuse to accept it, I gave it away to the guys on the field. The following day she and two other girls appeared on the sidelines. I got distracted and struck out at bat. (She always showed up when I was at bat!) They stood around until Sister Carmel rang her alarm bell. I recognized one of the girls from my class and decided I would speak to her about Rosita. Her name was Doris Barnes. I explained to Doris what was going on and told her that I needed some input on what to do about Rosita. She said, "I am having a problem with her too; if one of those Nuns sees us walking away from the girls' area to visit the boys' area, we are all going to be expelled! I'm not going to do it anymore!" I told her I was glad to hear that and filled her in on what had happened to Jean Guy. That cooled things down, for a while anyway.

Now that I was a little older (nine to ten years old), I seemed to be becoming more aware of my family's lifestyle. My dad used to take us to see a farmer friend of his down in Virginia, which was a short ride from DC. Whenever the farmer and his family would see the car coming up the road to their place, they would all run away from us and try to hide. I could see on their faces that they were fearful! When we got close enough to identify ourselves, they would look so relieved. I finally had to ask my father, "Why do your friends run and hide whenever they see us coming, Daddy?" I had to ask him why twice!

Daddy looked at me for a moment and said, "They are afraid for their lives! Some of the local Whites have been harassing them because my friends don't want to sell them their land. My farmer friend and his family love their little homestead, and the Whites want them to sell and move off that land."

WOW! What kind of world is this? These poor Colored folks can't even relax in their own home without somebody threatening them, I thought to myself. "Is he going to sell, Daddy?"

"He says he'd rather die first!" answered my father. I started saying a prayer to myself asking God to please not let anything bad happen to those kind and gentle people. I loved visiting them. They made me feel good.

On the way back home, I pumped Daddy for information about White people and why they were so troublesome. He started telling a story about how he had been on the road one day and witnessed an accident. "I got out to see if I could help the injured. There was someone lying in the road, so I went to that person first and saw that it was a young White girl. She had a very bad cut on her leg. It was an artery, and she needed a tourniquet. I started taking my shirt off to make a tourniquet when this White man walked up to me and said, 'If you touch her, you are a dead nigger!'"

My father said to the White man, "But she has a cut artery on her leg, and if I don't help her, she will die!"

The White man said, "Just don't put your Black hands on her!"

"Then what did you do, Daddy?" I asked.

"I just stood there helplessly and decided to wait there until the police arrived. When the police got there, the girl was already dead!" My father stepped up to the White officer and said, "I could have saved her life, but this man told me he wasn't going to let no nigger touch no young White girl! I could not believe he was going to let her die, but he did."

The White officer turned to the White man and asked for his driver's license and other identification. The cop was pissed off. My father said he turned, got into his car, and drove off. My father then said to me, "I want you to know just how far they can carry their stupidity!"

"Yes, sir!" I said.

My father was soon drafted into the Army. He cried when he got his notice. He was definitely no soldier, but he went. He said they had given him a choice to join the Army or go to jail, so he packed his bag. We were so proud of Daddy. He sent us a picture of himself in Army clothes, along with a recording of his voice. He sounded so unhappy. We all cried and played it over and over again until we could hardly hear a thing. Mama took it away from us and said, "We have worn the poor thing out!"

A few months later, Daddy came home on a pass. He was in uniform and said he had three days' leave. About two weeks later, Mama put her foot down and said Daddy had to go back to the war. I overheard Mama tell Aunt Thelma that Daddy was AWOL.

I asked Mama, "What's an AWOL?"

She looked at me and said, "How long have you been standing there?"

"I just walked in, Mama! What's an AWOL?"

She knew how proud I had been when I saw Daddy in his uniform, and Daddy was trying his best not to be in uniform. As a matter of fact, I had his soldier cap on then and wore it every day. The khaki cap was now at least three shades darker than the rest of the uniform because of my use of it. Mama had been caught trying to shield me from the truth.

"Your father is absent without leave—AWOL. I'm sorry, son. I didn't want you to know. That's why he has been inside so much here lately. You may have to help me talk to him before things get worse."

"OK, Ma! What do you want me to do?"

"Go get your brothers, and the three of you and I will confront him together."

"OK, Ma."

We all got to Daddy, and Mama said, "Hughdy! We have decided that the best thing to do is to turn yourself in and tell them we held you up and now we are letting you go. That way we will all feel better." Daddy said OK and sent me with his uniform to the cleaners to get it cleaned and pressed. Roland polished his shoes, Herbert polished the brass, and Mama fixed a good meal. Boy, could she cook!

Daddy sent me to the cleaners to pick up his uniform, and it looked great. When I got home, Daddy was ready to put on his uniform and discovered the hat was missing. He could not believe it! We were all about to panic. I ran out of the house and retraced my steps to the cleaners. The people at the cleaners told me the hat had been pinned to the uniform when they gave it to me. I went back to the street to search but found nothing! Boy oh boy, I was really feeling bad now. I couldn't believe I had ruined a good family plan!

When I returned home, everyone was on my case. They knew I had worn that cap every day and slept with it on. The cap had *never* left my head for two weeks! I couldn't blame everybody for looking at me out of the corner of their eyes but swore to God I did not covet my father's cap. Daddy was beginning to show some signs of weakening and had removed his shirt. It was too late that night to shop at the Army/Navy store, so we all sat down to a great going-away meal. We agreed to start anew in the morning. We scouted the area for an Army cap. We eventually found a cap that fit, but Daddy said it had the wrong color band. He said he was in the infantry and that they wore a blue band, but this one was orange. Mama found a way to change the band, which required a lot of hand stitching. She finally finished the job, and Daddy was off to the war. We heard from him a few weeks later, and he said everything was going OK and they were shipping him out to Seattle, Washington.

"Mama, that is a port of embarkation!" I said. "They are sending him to jungle warfare! I can't picture Daddy in anybody's jungle."

A long time went by, and we didn't hear from Daddy. In the meantime, it was back to standing in long lines for things like sugar, meat, shoes, and other goods. Everything was rationed, and we had to stand in line for ration coupons before we could get in line for the goods. It was rough, especially in the winter months, and I felt so sorry for the sick and the elderly standing in those long, slow-moving lines. But what could we do? It was the war!

Back at school Sister Martha still had not smiled. School seemed slow to me now, and I had developed other interests. I spent a lot of time in the libraries reading books on adventure, discovery, and travel. I still didn't like math, so math was a drag. Religion class was a bore, reading was uninteresting, and Latin was dull. Geography was a snap—I could deal with that one. It was the only subject holding my attention. Other than the final exam, it was an uneventful year, except for the sound of boys getting their hands hit with rulers by Nuns for doing one thing or the other. THAT went on constantly, and if we pulled back and made her miss our hands, the blows were doubled. No boy would dare flinch or snivel. I know I didn't, even when I was dying inside!

During our free period, the boys would draw pictures of airplanes shooting down the "Nips" or the "Krauts," as the enemies were frequently called. We also passed notes to one another. We'd get caught every so often and take the blows to our hands like men. I barely passed. Mama made her comments, and I promised her I'd do better.

Summer was upon us again (thank God), and I was planning to have some fun somehow. I had been working on my soldier collection all winter. I now had shoe boxes full of comic book soldiers, from Cavalry to Commandos. I also had homemade tanks, airplanes, and ships—the whole works. I was just waiting for a good rainy day to pull them out. My whole bedroom became a "theater of operations"—sometimes two bedrooms. One bedroom would be the Pacific theater, and the other bedroom would be the Atlantic theater. Beds became mountains, blankets became terrain, and the open floor became an ocean. Everything was ready, and the invasion was planned—destination: Berlin! The mission was to put Hitler under arrest for genocide. (I'm sure I was blowing everybody's mind in the family.) I was in my own world. It was also interesting how well the family tolerated this whole effort. I guess nobody was interested in stopping anything that was about stopping Hitler! This went on for the duration of the war—until 1945.

CHAPTER 20

The Monument Grounds' Big Art Show and Contest

When I was about eleven years old, I saw in the *Times Herald* newspaper that they were having a grand Art exhibit and contest to be held on the Monument Grounds and were inviting local Artists from the DC metro area to participate in the event. The theme was World War II. This was in 1946; the war had ended in 1945. I showed it to Mama, and she thought it was a good idea. She even suggested I draw something about the Negro soldier. I agreed. I entered the contest, not knowing what to expect. I went out and bought a small set of watercolors and a watercolor pad from Woolworth's five-and-dime store on New Jersey Avenue and N Streets SE. I needed some reference material and decided to go to Jerry's Surplus Store at Ninth and F Streets NW to look at the uniforms and fighting gear and form a good mental picture of the equipment I wanted to portray in my artwork. I saw a book, picked it up, and, lo and behold, saw that it had everything I needed to know about soldiers. The soldiers were dressed in full field gear and carrying weapons. The book was called *FM 22-5, The Army Basic Training Field Manual.* I bought it immediately and headed back to the house.

As soon as I got back to the house, I started laying out an idea I'd been thinking about all the way home. With a pencil in the right hand and the book in my left hand, I started sketching a soldier with a steel helmet, fatigues, a backpack, an entrenching tool, a pistol belt, a canteen, a first aid kit, and an M1 rifle on his shoulder.

I stepped back to look at what I had done. He looked kind of lonely standing there. The sketch needed some kind of a background or something. *I got it!* I thought. *I'll put a big American flag waving in the air behind him!* I sketched in the flag. It looked great to me! I showed it to Mama, and she said it looked great to her. That was all I needed to hear. Now I had to paint it carefully.

I broke out my fifty-cent watercolors. A brush was included. (I thought that was a big deal!) I mixed up a little brown and started filling in the face with a thin transparent shade of brown. It looked great. Then I mixed some green with a touch of brown and painted the fatigues and field equipment. Next I started mixing up some blue. I painted the blue around the outside edge of each star; this way I wouldn't have to fill in the stars—all forty-eight of them, to be exact—because the paper was already white.

I cleaned the blue paint from my brush, loaded up on the red paint, and filled in all the red stripes, starting from the top. I stepped back again and looked at it. *Does it need something else?* I wondered. I stared at that picture for what seemed like hours. Then I saw what it needed: a nice, bright, golden cord swinging in the breeze from the top of the flagpole. I drew it in and painted it yellow with orange accents. I stepped back again. It was beautiful! I had spent about two to three hours per day on the painting, which took me about a week to complete. When it was finished, I signed and dated it. I went back to Woolworth's and bought a frame for my painting (eighteen inches by twenty-four inches). I titled it **The Negro Soldier**.

I filled out the entry application, gave them my age, and mailed it in. A few weeks later, I received a reply stating that I had been accepted! They gave me directions for where to deliver my artwork and the date when I should show up with it. **"Wow!"** I said. "I'm in an *Art Exhibit* on the Monument Grounds! Hey, everybody, look at this! Where *is* everybody?"

The day to deliver the artwork arrived. I delivered the painting, and they gave me a map showing me where to find my piece in the exhibition.

On the opening day of the exhibit, it rained like crazy! The next day I was up early and made my way to the Monument Grounds. I took out my map and saw that the piece was located midway between Fourteenth and Fifteenth on Constitution Avenue. When I found the location, I could not believe my eyes!

The painting had been destroyed! Had the picture been left out in the rain? It looked so bad I did not stop; I just kept walking. When I got to the corner of Fifteenth and Constitution, I did an about-face and walked back to the picture. This time I stopped at the work *next* to mine (I could not get myself to stand in front of my disaster). I stood there for several minutes, stealing side glances of my painting every now and then while giving the appearance that I didn't notice my picture at all. Since every Artist there was standing next to his or her own work, I had to act like I was just a *spectator,* rather than a *participator.*

Oh well, I thought. *I'm here now, so I might as well check out the rest of the show.* The show was full of great artwork, and veterans themselves had created a lot of it. I was out there *all* day! I saw other watercolor artwork there, and something then caught my eye.

I noticed that all of the watercolor pieces were covered with glass. Nobody had told me that I needed glass on my watercolor because my artwork might get caught in the rain! Watercolors were not waterproof! Regardless, I was there in the midst of some beautifully executed artwork and was the only child participant there, Black or White, from what I could see.

Surprisingly, I did get an "Honorable Mention" for my contribution. I thought that was noteworthy. They must have judged the work before the rains came, or perhaps they thought I was being *avant-garde*! The person who won first prize, I remember, was a veteran who had lost his leg fighting in the South Pacific.

The sun was beginning to set, so I collected my piece and headed back to Half Street SE. I vowed to do more research and to use the knowledge I had just gleaned from those who knew what to do for the next time!

CHAPTER 21

The Hustling Blues

One day my cousin Sammy came by the house and said to me, "Let's take *your* allowance and buy some *Afro-American* newspapers for a nickel apiece; then we can sell them for seven cents. We get to keep all we sell. So I figured that with a dollar, we could buy twenty papers and sell them for seven cents apiece, which came to one dollar and forty cents. "OK, let's go!" I said. I figured it would get me out of the house and around the neighborhood without Mama wondering where I was all the time. "Come on," I said. "Let's go over to the Southeast House."

The Southeast House was located at Fifth Street and Virginia Avenue SE. We walked, and it was an adventuresome event. We got to talk to other boys from other streets and exchanged information with them. This was a great idea! We could sell papers to our neighbors and to weekly customers. Once we served our immediate area, we then could fan out and hit other streets. We got to learn all the streets in nearby Southeast and Southwest Washington and always had a little scratch in our pockets.

One week Sammy could not make it, and I was left with a decision to make: should I try to work these streets by myself or stay home and risk not getting my quota sold? I decided to hit the streets; after all, I was pretty much a familiar figure in the area. I said good-bye to Mama and was headed for the door when Mama said, "I wouldn't stay out late, Thomas, if I were you!"

"OK, Mama," I said and I was off.

All evening long things were going great. I was popping papers like I never had before. I even went back for more papers! My second round of paper sales was tapering off, and my time was running short. I made a (tough) decision to go over to the Randall Junior High School area to try to make a few more sales before the sun went completely down. This decision was a gamble because it was a rough neighborhood. I did OK until I got to the big empty athletic field that I had to cross to get back home. The sun had just gone down behind the horizon. That empty lot looked like it was the size of the Atlantic Ocean.

I pointed my feet toward the open field and started out. My concern was that somebody might have noticed that I was traveling alone. I had never realized that the field was not lit at night. About midway through the field, I saw about five or six figures coming toward me. I was not too concerned because I figured if anybody was coming after me, they would be coming from behind me. These figures seemed to be coming toward me, so I continued on.

All of a sudden, the figures that were coming toward me started fanning out around me. I knew then that I was in trouble. My heart started racing and pounding in my throat. I tried to swallow, but my throat was too dry. I looked over my shoulder and saw that I was past the point of no return. There was nobody at all back there. I changed my direction by about thirty degrees to the right. They also made an adjustment. I began whimpering and breathing harder. I kept walking, though my legs said run. I was afraid that if I started to run, either my hard-earned coins would jump out of my pockets or the papers would get wrinkled and would not be sellable. *Just run,* my mind said, but I kept my course. That was a mistake.

Just as I knew they would, they encircled me. "All right, empty out your pockets!" the leader said. I didn't budge. The next command was "TAKE 'IM!" They all started punching me in the head, and I fell to my knees, still grasping the pocket that had the most money in it. That made 'em madder, so they tried to tear my pocket off while hitting me in the head and kicking me in the behind. I tried to get a look at those guys. I recognized one or two of them from the Anthony Bowen School gang. I also remembered that voice.

I couldn't take any more of this mistreatment, so I loosened my grip on the papers, and they grabbed them all. I was on the ground in the dirt and decided to loosen my grip on the money. They were scrambling for the money when all of a sudden I heard a girl say, "Take your hands off that paper boy, NOW!" Then I heard all this commotion going on right above me as I lay on the ground. All I could make out were some girls putting their feet in those boys' *asses*!

I heard one girl say, "And he's cute too!" I was now up on one knee and looking around at these Black angels from heaven kicking the natural snot out of these guys. The guys were on the run! Two of these sisters lifted me to my feet and brushed me off. While this was going on, two other girls recovered my papers and money from the boys they'd run down.

WOW! These girls were only four in number and were about the same age as the boys (ten to twelve years old). *At least five or six boys looked a bit older,* I thought. After they got me all squared away and back on my feet, they decided that it was not safe to allow me to go home alone. I told them I deeply appreciated what they had done but didn't mind seeing myself home. One of the girls looked at the papers and said, "This is *The Afro American* newspaper he was selling! Those niggers ought to be ashamed attacking a Colored newspaper boy! We are gonna kick their asses again for this! Come on, girls. We gonna walk you home first, though!"

That was the proudest moment of my life so far! Four "Black Guardian Angels" escorted me safely to my door and threw me a kiss good-night! I knew then that I would be putting my life on the line any day for the rest of my life for the sisters. God bless them, one and all!

Now that I was eleven, I decided to get a paper route so I could deliver papers door to door in the daytime. I discovered a *Daily News* station around the corner from school. I went around there after school and applied for a job. The *Daily News* was the only newspaper hiring Blacks as paper boys. *The Times Herald, The Washington Post, The Star,* and *the Evening Star* were for "Whites only."

I spoke to the Manager, who said I was in luck because a boy had just quit, so I could take his place. I was tickled pink. He took me out on the route so I could become familiar with it. The route covered Third and I Streets to K and Fourth Streets and down Fourth Street to M Street SW. It was a poor neighborhood, but I was ready to go to work. I had about seventy-five to eighty customers. I was given a well-used, never-been-washed canvas newspaper bag to carry my papers in. I had no idea how heavy eighty newspapers could be on one's shoulder. I was struggling down the street saying to myself, *It will get lighter as I go because I am throwing out papers as I walk.* But I discovered that the shoulder was giving way before I could offload the papers.

I returned to the station after I had delivered my papers and asked the Manager how I could go about getting a wagon like the others had. He said I would need twelve dollars to get a wagon. *Gracious sakes!* I said to myself. *I have never had that much money in my life!*

"Maybe your parents can help you; in the meantime, there is an old wagon tied up outside that nobody uses anymore. If you return it before you go home, you may use it."

I soon found out why nobody was using it—it was completely worn out. The wheels leaned out from the wagon, were extremely noisy, and made for a rickety ride. Big nails had been used in a futile effort to hold the boards of the weather-beaten old wagon together. But at least it gave my poor shoulder a break.

The paper was three cents a day and about seventeen cents a week per customer. On collection day (Thursday night), I collected as much money as I could, and that money went back to the Manager to pay for my paper bill. If I didn't collect enough money on Thursday night, I went back out Friday night to pay my paper bill. I went to every house and could not collect enough money to pay my paper bill.

I returned to the station and explained to the Manager that I still was not able to collect enough money to pay for my papers. The Manager said that I should turn over all that I had collected and go back out Saturday to collect the rest. "And remember, you are not to keep a single cent for yourself until after you have completely paid off your paper bill!"

I went back out Saturday and knocked on all the doors of the customers. I could hear some of them in the house, but they would not answer the door. Those who did answer the door asked me to come back the next Saturday! I was out all that night and was not able to collect enough money to pay my paper bill.

Monday came, and the Manager told me how delinquent I was in paying my paper bill! He told me that he expected me to have this bill paid for on Fridays and that I could collect for myself on Saturday. I said to myself, *I am into my second week and don't have a dime to spend on myself.* The second collection week, it was the same routine: the same people didn't pay, and I had the same paper bill problems and heard the same speech from the Manager. The third and fourth collection weeks were the same. I said to the Manager, "Is there some way you can maybe speak to the people who won't pay me?"

He said, "Tell them you will cut them off if they don't pay!"

"OK," I said.

When I told them they would be cut off if they did not pay up, their reply was, "Cut it off then!" Then they slammed the door in my face. I asked myself, *What kind of Black adult people am I servicing here?* I needed to know what it was I had gotten myself into. I'd spent four weeks working and had nothing to show for it. The only thing I'd learned was how it felt to get hollered at and have a door slammed in my face. I wondered, *Why do my people have such a bad taste for each other?*

I told Mama about my paper route experiences, and she said, "Sometimes it's best just to walk away, son."

I went back to the station and told the Manager I was quitting. One of the boys standing there asked, "What route do you have?"

When I told him the route, he said, *"Good gracious!* That is the worst route in the District! Them people *never* pay their bills down there; you can forget it!"

"I just did!" I said to him. "So for the rest of the summer, I will just chill out."

My friend Fatso came by the house and said that Mr. Johnny was retiring from his job and was going to buy a horse and wagon he could use to sell fruit in area neighborhoods. He suggested we go over to see Mr. Johnny and tell him we wanted to apply for the job of door hopping for him. Then he wouldn't always have to jump off the wagon so much, and it would be fun for us to ride behind a horse-pulled wagon. I said, "Yeah, man!"

Mr. Johnny agreed to take us on board. He told us to meet him at the stable at 6:00 a.m. to help him harness up the horse and hook him up to the wagon. The horse's name was Johnny. That's what Mr. Johnny called him, and he had a knot on his head just like Mr. Johnny had on his head! *Maybe that is why he named him Johnny!* I said to myself.

We got everything hooked up and were off to the farmers' market to pick up the bushels of fruit and veggies to be sold that day. Mr. Johnny filled the little baskets called pecks and called out loud, "Vegetable man, get your fresh fruit and veggies here!"

The women would come to the doors and say, "Over here!" That would be our cue to jump off the wagon, grab a peck of fruit, and run over to the customer. The lady would dump out the peck and examine the fruit. If she liked how it looked, she would give me money for the peck. Mr. Johnny would pay us fifty cents a day and give us free fruit. It was a GAS (slang for fun)!

That evening when I got home, dinner was ready, so I went straight to the sink to wash my hands for dinner. When I passed by Mama to sit down at the table, Mama turned to me and said in an alarmed voice, "Goodness gracious, boy, you smell like horse manure! Get away from that table. You need to take a bath, change clothes, and then come to dinner! Go! Go!" So I went. I didn't realize that sitting behind that horse, which kept raising his tail and farting all day long, was ruining my family's dinnertime.

I enjoyed working on the huckster wagon. It took us well out of our neighborhood. We did a lot of sightseeing and enjoyed the ride, but the horse farts had to go! This horse seemed to be enjoying it. Every time he would raise his tail, we wanted to jump off the wagon! That was the roughest part of the job. I had to bathe every day before dinner or quit my job. Fatso and I started learning the huckster's cry:

Red o' de' vine
I gotta plug 'em all de' time
sweet as honey
and just off de' vine
see that lady standing in th' do'
wishin' she had a watermelon

'n eat it on the flo'
Red o' de' vine, I gotta plug 'em all th' time!
Sweet as honey 'n jus' off de' vine.

I loved to hear the hucksters sing chants of their wares. Even now, I sing the chants when I smell melons.

I was having a ball! And then one day, I was delivering a peck of fruit to an elderly lady, and she asked me to step inside. I stepped inside, and she took the peck of fruit and turned it over on the table. She counted seven pieces of fruit, and three of them were rotten. I was embarrassed. She turned to me and said, "What's going on, Thomas? The last three pecks have been like this, and I can't afford it! I have very little money, and I become very upset when I throw away almost half of what I've bought. Do you fill these pecks yourself?"

"No, Ma'am. Mr. Johnny won't let me anymore! He says he'll pack 'em, while we just run the route."

"Thomas, you take these bad ones back and tell Mr. Johnny I said if he wants me to pay for a peck, he will have to replace the bad ones."

"Yes, Ma'am!" I said.

I ran back to the wagon and told Mr. Johnny what Miss Kay had said. Mr. Johnny looked at me and said, "Why did you let her turn the peck over?"

"She took it out of my hand and emptied it out!" I said.

Then Mr. Johnny said, "I don't want you to allow the customers to examine the fruit before they pay for it. If they squeeze the fruit and then don't buy it, then nobody else will buy it either."

"But, Mr. Johnny, this fruit isn't pinched, this fruit is rotten!"

He shouted at me, "DON'T LET THEM EXAMINE THE FRUIT!"

It was becoming a vicious cycle, as more and more people were beginning to complain on my route. I tried my best to pack a few pecks and stash them in the corner of the wagon for the customers that I knew were going to examine them, like Miss Kay. I also noticed that my friend Fatso didn't seem to be having any problems on his route. I made it a point to talk to Fatso when Mr. Johnny was out of earshot.

"Fatso," I asked, "how come you don't seem to be having any problems?" He said, "I just don't let them touch it until it's paid for."

"Yeah, well I tried that, and they are saying if they can't examine the contents, then they aren't buying Mr. Johnny's rotten fruit! So I've been trying to get decent fruit up to those elderly people." Fatso looked at me in a puzzled way. Maybe there weren't any senior citizens on his route.

One day Mr. Johnny caught me fixing a peck of fruit. He immediately accused me of stealing and fired me! When Fatso got back to the wagon, I explained to him that I had just been fired and told him why! Fatso was visibly upset. He ran to Mr. Johnny and begged him not to send me back home. Mr. Johnny said, "All right, but he has to start selling the fruit I give him, or I can't use him."

I told Fatso that I was ready to quit anyway because I was not good at what I was being asked to do. I could not take advantage of those poor people. They deserved better treatment than what Mr. Johnny was willing to give.

With the war effort still going on, there was more money to be made in scrap iron. Mr. Johnny decided he would stop selling fruit and do what he said he would never do, which was haul scrap iron for a living. He said the horse would suffer from trying to pull such a heavy load. I guess he had to do something though. The horse eventually died from being overtaxed, and Mr. Johnny had to retire to his front porch, where he whittled himself to death.

I joined the scrap paper brigade and collected old newspapers for the war effort. I made about three cents a pound and always had a little money in my pockets. They rewarded us paper collectors with stripes to wear on our sleeves, just like the soldiers wore. Every time we would reach a hundred pounds or so of collected newspapers, we would earn a stripe. I had a couple of stripes and was proud of myself. I was able to buy things for Mama on holidays like Mother's Day, her birthday, Christmas, and so on. I was so pleased with being able to buy things for Mama because it made me feel grown up!

The war was finally over, and Daddy would be coming home soon. Uncle Ricky had come home months earlier. He was a driver in a transportation company called the Red Ball Express. I asked Uncle Ricky why they called his outfit the Red Ball. He explained, "The Army took blood from the soldiers for a blood bank in case someone was wounded and needed blood. When they took blood from the Black soldiers, they would put a red dot on the bottle so that it would not mistakenly be given to a White soldier. It was thought that if a White soldier got Black blood put in his system, his system would become tainted and he would lose his precious claim as a 'White.' He would also have to suffer all the disadvantages of being Black. Black blood was considered dirty and unfit for White people."

"WOW!" I said. "I've been living for eleven years only to find out I've got dirty blood!" I could not *believe* it! I didn't *feel* dirty! Boy oh boy, now I felt sorry for the White soldiers because if they believed that, they would most likely die if our blood was all that was left. And I felt just *fine* with Black blood!

The war had been over for months, and Daddy still hadn't returned. Mama said, "They have everybody on standby alert for the next six months, just in case the Japs try something."

Sure enough, about six months later, Daddy came home. But Daddy was different. He was never home much, and when he did come home, it would be past our bedtime. He came home late for dinner one night and had other people's clothes draped over his arms and three hats on his head. He said things like, "I am the best poker player in town! I beat the clothes off everybody in the game! They had to go home in their underwear!" He went on and on, and his breath was foul!

Mama was so upset and embarrassed. Daddy called me upstairs to count his money for him; he said I was a good counter. He pulled out all this balled up money from all of his pockets and threw it on the bed. "Count it for me, Thomas," he said, "and then give it back to me."

"OK," I said. I counted the money and gave it to him, and he put it under the rug near the bed. I went downstairs and told Mama how much money Daddy had.

Mama said, "It would help if he would just give me some of it." I was crushed by that statement! How could Daddy not give Mama any money for his family? How could he be my father? Didn't all this mean there was a possibility that he was not my father? I felt pain when I thought he could do such a thing to Mama and not feel guilty about it! Mama deserved better than that. Roland and Herbert may have looked like him, I thought, but my hair and lips were not like his, so maybe he wasn't really my father.

The next day Daddy got up and could not find his money. He called me and asked me if I had seen his money. I showed him where it was, and he took it and walked out of the house. I asked Mama if he had given her any of the money. She looked at me and said, "No, he did not, son."

The following night, Daddy came in and called me upstairs to count his money. I came up and started counting, but this time for every four dollars I counted, I dropped a dollar on the floor. He was passed out across the bed and couldn't see the floor. I finished counting the money, but before I woke him, I picked up all the money off the floor and put it into my pocket.

"Wake up, Daddy, here's your money!"

"How much is it, Thomas?"

"One hundred dollars, Dad!"

"OK, give it here, and thank you."

I stood there until he hid it under the rug. Then I said good-night and left. I ran straight to Mama and said, "Mama, I got something for you. Look!" I gave her a fistful of money.

"Goodness gracious, son! Where did all this money come from?"

"Daddy likes me to count his money, so I counted some out for you."

"Why did you do that, son?"

"Because you need it and Daddy didn't give you any before, so I took yours off the top!"

"But won't your father find out?"

"He falls asleep, and I tell him what I need to tell him."

This went on for weeks and weeks. Mama accepted the money because Daddy was not sharing it with her. I told her not to worry because he was unsuspecting.

One day he called my brother Roland upstairs to count his money. I told Roland what I was doing for Mama, and he did the same thing. Mama was tickled that we were looking out for her. Poor Mama.

Daddy got worse instead of better. Weeks later Daddy came home earlier than usual. He had no coats or hats with him this time, and he had been drinking. He ran into the bedroom and went straight for the drawer where Mama kept her little stash. He could not get it open, so he took a screwdriver, jammed it into the drawer, and forced it open. He then grabbed the money and hurried off up the street. I was in shock. Daddy had robbed Mama of her little nest egg? *WOW!!* I couldn't believe he could do that. *This man can't be my real father,* I thought to myself. *I cannot believe this man can do this to his wife and say he loves us. I would never do that to Mama! Is this what whiskey does to your brain?*

When Mama came home, I painfully told her what I had witnessed. She broke down and cried. She had been saving that money for a down payment on a house. She saw the busted drawer and fell to her knees and wailed. I was stunned. I went and put my arms around her, and we both sat there on the floor crying. Then she suddenly spoke. "That is the last straw! Thomas, we are going to move away from here," she said. "I was saving that money to buy a house in a nicer neighborhood, where you can meet nicer people and go to nicer schools." She cried some more and said, "This time we are going to put the money in the bank under my name, where it will be safe," she said.

A few years later, she had us packing. Mama was serious. Daddy was going to come home to find an empty house. We later heard he was shocked when he came home. Mama had left the house to Aunt Thelma, who was already on the premises, and she was sworn to secrecy about our whereabouts.

I was able to understand exactly how Mama felt. I still had doubts about whether Mr. DuVall was my real flesh-and-blood father, but I could not ask my mother again because that would lead her to think I did not believe her. But his toes were definitely not like mine, nor were my hands as thick as his. In retrospect I do have a few good memories of Hughdy DuVall when he was home. He had a great sense of humor that kept us in stitches, especially when he tried to dance. He had to be the worst dancer in the world; talk 'bout two left feet!

CHAPTER 22

Sixth Grade

Summer was over, and we were back in school again. I was in the sixth grade, and it was my last year with Sister Mary Martha. Sister Martha was still her scowling and never-smiling self. I sat in that class all year without remembering anything we learned.

I do remember her telling me that I passed but that I must have cheated. She stood me up in front of the class and searched me for hidden answer sheets. She made me roll up my sleeves and examined my arms, the palms of my hands, and my socks. She even opened my shirt to see if I had marked it with the answers. She finally gave up and said to me, "Because I didn't find anything doesn't mean you didn't cheat!" I told her I did not cheat on any exam, and I was out of there. I wanted to say to her that the only thing I had learned from her was the word "niggerism," which she used daily, but I was cool!

Rosita (the girl who sent me bags of candy at the baseball games) had invited me to visit her during the summer months. She especially wanted me to visit on Wednesdays when they would show current movies at the community center down in the Simple City or Buzzard Point area of the southernmost part of Southwest.

Of course, I had to get permission from Mama to go. When I told her where I wanted to go, she was flabbergasted. "Son, I don't think that's a good idea!" she said. "That's a pretty rough area down there to be going by yourself, don't you think? And it will be good and dark when it's time for you to come home. I just don't feel good about it."

"I'll be all right, Mom, I promise you!" She hesitated for a moment and then said, "All right, son, but please be careful!"

Don't worry, Mom, I'll be OK." Those were my famous last words.

I started out before dark for Simple City, Southwest (around Third and R Streets SW). I passed Joseph Only's house but didn't stop. I was a block away from the community center when I saw this small group of guys standing between the center and me. They were a rough- and mean-looking bunch. I had to walk through them to get to my destination. I kept up my quick pace as I passed through them. They situated themselves so that I would have to walk past each one. They looked at me with a kind of puzzled amazement, as if to say, "Where in the world did he come from?" I avoided eye contact by looking straight ahead. They were all silent as I walked past. I did not falter, or alter my pace. I was nervous but tried hard not to show any fear. I tried to look like I knew *exactly* what I was doing! I reached the center. A big dude stopped me at the door, and I told him I was there to see Rosita. He said, "You must be Thomas Duball! Yeah, she has everybody expecting you. You will find her in the front row center. She is holding a seat for you. And that ain't an easy thing to do around here! But she is a determined person, and those who tried to take that empty seat had to deal with her first!"

I did not know what to say. Had she prepared everybody for me coming? Everybody seemed to know who I was! They pointed to me and said, "That's Dutny's boyfriend!"

"Who the hell is Dutny?" I asked her.

She said, "That's what they call me around here." She said it was a name her mother called her!

I felt safe in there, but the attention I was getting was unsettling, and I was not handling it too well. I didn't like being the center of attention. I asked her if she had told these people I was her boyfriend. She said she hadn't, but little good that did.

When the movie was over, I said good-night to Rosita and faced the return trip home. I looked down the street and noticed that it looked poorly lit, but I had to go that route. I soon found out that I had the streets to myself. I passed no one on the way home and arrived home to find Mama waiting up for me. I thanked her for her vigilance and kissed her good-night.

The following week, I did my Wednesday thing and headed for Simple City. I got to the spot where the gang hung out and continued my clip. This time, however, the last boy I was about to pass stepped out and blocked my way. My heart jumped into my mouth! I tried to walk around him, but he moved to block me. I stopped and looked at him. He was about my size, maybe a little taller. He said to me, "Don't you have any girls in your own neighborhood? You gotta come down here to *our* neighborhood?"

I decided to try to get around him. The other boys standing around started to yell, "Take him, take him!" I knew he couldn't back down now and braced myself for a fight.

He took a swing at me, and I ducked. He continued to try to connect, and I silently thanked God for the little boxing training I had acquired. I was able to dance around him and block his blows. He was getting frustrated, and I was not trying to hit back. I did not want to strike him because I did not want to draw this thing out. At the same time, I could not get myself to run away. He finally landed one on my head, and I retaliated. This slowed him down a little. I then backed off, because the other boys were beginning to encircle me. I decided to make a break for it and made a dash for the center's front door. I made it inside, and the big guy at the door said, "Don't worry, they know better than to come in here!" I thanked him, and he showed me where Rosita was saving my seat for me.

I didn't tell Rosita about the confrontation, but I did ask her if there was a boy in this neighborhood who had eyes for her. She said, "These boys are always saying things to me, but I ignore them. Why do you ask? Did you hear something about me?"

"No, but I thought I picked up a little jealous comment from one of the guys down here."

"What was his name?" she asked.

I told her I had no names. She said to please be careful because those boys were bad, and I told her I would be careful.

Every Wednesday after that, that gang waited for me to come walking by. And every Wednesday that I showed up, they would systematically kick my ass before I could get to the center's front door. This went on for months.

One Wednesday, as I tried to pass through their ranks, they all looked at me in astonishment. They said that they just could not *believe* that after all those ass kickings, I was *still* coming back there. They said to me, "Duball [somehow they had found out my name], we are *tired* of kicking your ass, so we are going to let you go on by from now on!"

I smiled, thanked them, and went inside to see Rosita and the movie *Abbott and Costello*. I never told Mama or Rosita about my experience with those boys. I was twelve years old.

Another summer passed, and I was back at St. Vincent de Paul to finish up the last two years of Catholic school. I was now in the seventh grade, and my teacher was the Mother Superior of the Nuns.

Her name was Mother Mary Pious. She had never really liked me, but I had no intention of getting on her bad side. She was a rather handsome woman. She was quite petite and had a little bit of a mustache, which did not detract from her femininity. She tried to be a disciplinarian to the nth degree. I could see on her face that she had learned that Thomas and Rosita were boyfriend and girlfriend. I could also detect that she intended to sever this relationship at all costs.

When one of the girls in the class dropped a piece of paper on the floor, Mother Pious called out Rosita's name to pick it up. Rosita tried to explain to Mother Pious that the girl standing next to the paper on the floor was the girl who had dropped the paper. Rosita was sitting at her desk and was nowhere near the paper on the floor. Mother Pious had not seen the girl drop the paper, but the girl knew she had dropped the paper and was deliberately waiting for Rosita to pick it up. This light-skinned, long-haired girl was standing there waiting for Rosita to bend over, pick up her paper, and put it into the trash.

Rosita refused to do that, so Mother Pious began to hit her on the legs with a ruler. Rosita cried out in pain and anger and ran out of the room. In disgust, I jumped up, picked up the paper, and threw it into the trash. I tried to make eye contact with this girl because I wanted to ask her why she hadn't picked up the paper. We could have heard a pin drop on cotton in the room. We were center stage now.

"Return to your seat!" Mother Pious said to me. I don't remember what else she said because I was thoroughly disgusted. That's how my year started in Mother Pious's class.

Regardless, I really did like Mother Pious, in spite of her ways. She had a sweet side and a dark side, but my love for her was unconditional. She was feminine even when she tried to hide it. *We "secretly" like each other,* I said to myself. Was I trying to psyche myself up for two years with the petite and gentle woman who was a bit twisted and wanted to be a Mother Superior?

Every day when I entered the classroom, she would call me to her desk, take a bucket of holy water, dip the pestle into the bucket, and splash me across the face with it in the sign of the Cross. I wanted to wipe my face but was afraid to do so because it was holy water! I sat there with water dripping off my face all winter. What a way to start the day that was.

Every day I was kept after school because of some abstract infraction of one of her rules! No rules were posted anywhere in the room, so I never knew from one moment to the next whether I was in violation or not. She would have me do menial tasks, like beating out the erasers, emptying her pencil sharpener, dusting off her desk, and so on. She would dismiss me after one hour of this puttering around. I would walk around the corner, and Rosita would be standing there waiting for me. I tried to tell her it was not cool to do that.

"Mother Pious is holding you after school so that we will not see each other on the way home!" she said. "I am not going to allow her to get away with that." So every day that I had to stay after school, she would faithfully wait for me, and I would walk her home.

One day while I was walking her home, the very guy who had blocked my path the night we traded blows appeared from out of nowhere, snatched my hat off my head, and dared me to come after it! I hesitated and looked at Rosita. "This is the guy I thought had eyes for you," I said. "Do you know him?"

She said, "Yes, and he always makes a nuisance of himself."

I went after him, and he took off running. This went on for a while, and I was getting frustrated. He then ran into a house and locked himself in it. I had to go around with no hat on and worried about what my mother would say. I went home without a hat and dared not tell Mama the truth.

A couple of days later, Rosita walked into the classroom and handed me my hat. I asked her how she had gotten the hat. She said she knew where he lived, so she and a few of her girlfriends had gone to his house and taken it back. "And by the way," she said, "you won't be having any more problems out of him when you come to our neighborhood again!"

Wow! *That* was a mouthful. I thought about my *Afro-American* newspaper robbery rescue, plus the escort home. Boy, the might of the sisters astounded me. God bless 'em!

Mother Pious was having us boys move some file cabinets into the classroom, and I noticed one of the file drawers was labeled SHIPS. So I said to one of the boys, "Ships?"

All of a sudden, Mother Pious spun around and said to me, "THOMAS DUVALL, you are PUNISHED! So march yourself into that closet and close the door behind you!"

"Mother, what did I do?"

"You know very well what you did! Now do as I say!"

I did as she said. I walked into the closet, and she LOCKED the door behind me! This closet had a window, I discovered, but it was a room not much larger than the window. There were books everywhere—on the shelves, on the chairs, and all over the floor. They were mostly discarded books and old textbooks. I decided to take a closer look at these books and found myself reading them as I sat by the window.

About three hours later, I heard someone trying to open the door. I was on my feet. It was the teacher's pet. She told me that I was to come out for lunch and recess. I came out to find the rest of the class had already been dismissed. I proceeded out of the classroom to the street. It seemed I was no sooner out there when the bell rang for me to return to class. I returned to class and was immediately sent to the closet to continue my punishment. I readily commenced reading more of the books spread about the room.

A couple of hours later, there was a rattle at the door; someone was unlocking it. It was Mother Pious, who told me the list of things I had to clean up before I was allowed to go home. I did the chores and got Mother Superior to inspect the work. She puttered around, inspected everything, and then dismissed me. I left the school, walked to the corner, found Rosita faithfully waiting there for me, and walked her home.

The next day I arrived at school to be splashed with holy water. I was then sent to the closet to spend the whole day again reading old dusty books. Shortly after three o'clock, I heard the rattle of keys at the door. The door was opened, and again Mother Pious gave me a list of chores to be done before I was allowed to leave. Rosita was there waiting for me, and I walked her home. All of these goings-on had me feeling like I was in some kind of twilight zone!

The next day (Wednesday), the same thing happened. I arrived at school, got splashed in the face, and was sent to the closet for more punishment. This time, when the door was locked behind me, I got a depressed feeling in my chest. Why was I being punished? I tried to find a book I had not yet read. I found an old geography book and began to read it. I was visiting all these wonderful faraway places, and the more I read, the more I wanted out of this room. I was also beginning to feel claustrophobic and anxious and I was breathing hard!

I tried to calm myself down, but something was overtaking me. I felt like I had to get out of that room. I ran to the door but could not open it. She really had me locked in! I rattled the doorknob hoping she would show some mercy and let me out of there! I waited in vain for a response. The next thing I knew, I was standing in front of Mother Superior. She had a shocked look on her face. It was as if she had just witnessed the stone being rolled back on the third day of the resurrection! I then realized that I must have broken through the door. I looked back over my shoulder, and sure enough the door was torn from one of its hinges and was hanging only by the bottom hinge. I could not believe my eyes! I didn't remember forcing that big heavy solid oak door open. Had I gone crazy and gotten superhuman strength for a split second?

Now that I had her undivided attention, I decided that this would be a good time to ask her what I was being punished for. She meekly said to me, "You know what you said. You used profanity in this class!"

"Profanity?" I said. I then walked over to the file cabinet and pulled out the drawer marked "SHIPS." I then said to her, "This is the word you heard me say! I am being punished for something you *thought* I said. I would never use profanity in class!" I told her.

"Well maybe you didn't, but you will still have to pay for that door!" she said.

I said nothing, as I knew she would have to explain why I was locked in that closet for three days straight if she reported this to my mother. I was praying for her to do so, but she didn't.

I could not help but look at that door again—the door that stood between me and freedom. I suddenly noticed the size of the door and the wood it was made of. It was a heavy oak schoolroom door! It was larger than the doors in private homes. I became unglued and was *stunned* by the reality of what had just occurred. How could a boy of twelve, who was small for his age, have done such damage? She never reported me, and the door remained broken. I also learned something about my mind and how it could play havoc with my brain. Was intensity a source of strength?

Word had gotten back to Mother Pious that Thomas and Rosita were *still* seeing each other. She used every trick she could think of to keep us from being within earshot of each other. I was seated right behind Rosita, and Mother Pious suddenly decided she would have me move to a desk in the back of the room and have Henry Skinner, a guy everybody knew was always playing with himself in class, take my desk. All day long he would have one hand in his pocket stroking his "joy stick."

Somebody in class made the comment, "Maybe Skinner will give his dong a rest, now that he is near the front of the class!" But Skinner got worse, it seemed. Every time Rosita or any other girl would rise to recite something in class or walk across the front of the class, he would immediately put one or both hands in his pockets and start squirming in his seat. NOBODY could believe the Nun didn't notice what was going on, but she acted as if she didn't see a thing!

I was upset that this Nun had put that "pocket pool-playing" so-and-so in my seat behind my lady friend. Every time Rosita stood up, his hands would find his pocket, *and* he was sitting in my seat. I must admit, Rosita had a substantial amount of behind, and every time she stood up, she had my attention too! Nonetheless, Henry was gloating. He knew doggone well that that Nun had put him in my seat to keep me upset. The whole classroom knew it! And she knew he was a pocket pooler!

This scene went on for weeks, and my patience with this was growing thin, but what could I do? I was only a kid, and the Nun had the power. I was finding it hard to concentrate on the subject matter at hand. Nothing was the same anymore. Everything seemed tainted with an evil underhandedness that smelled of decay. I had a flashback of that woman who had lied to my mother about that Army truck of mine belonging to her son. *Why are there people like that in existence and in positions of power and authority? Why are there adults who seem to enjoy keeping the children of others stressed out in some way?* I thought to myself. I decided to take it to Henry Skinner directly; I saw no other way.

We went on a field trip and had to pair off to walk together. Everybody scrambled around to be with their best friend so they could talk among themselves as they walked. Mother Pious looked at me with disdain and said, "Thomas, you walk with Skinner!" As soon as she said that, the whole class fell silent. They all looked at me as if to say, *Oh no! There is going to be a fight.* I was *crushed*! None of the boys wanted to be with Skinner, and she knew it. I was the only one in class who did not get to choose who he would spend the day with. Skinner looked at me, and I looked at him and suddenly felt pity for him! I was confused by this. I wondered, *Why in the world am I feeling pity for a dude I should be punching out?* We walked along in silence for a while, and I was perplexed about just how to approach this one.

I decided to just come on out with it and let the chips fall where they may. I said to Skinner, "*Say, Jim!* Everybody in class knows you are a pocket pooler, and the girls find it disgusting. Maybe you ought to check yourself out." He looked at me with great surprise! He even denied the charges. I told him that I liked Rosita and that I wished he would refrain from playing with himself around her so that I could enjoy my day as much as I could in this miserable situation. I told him that Mother Pious was constantly trying to keep me on one foot.

Skinner was not a handsome young man by any stretch of the imagination. He was short and had one eye and a breath problem. The girls didn't like him, but he was a pretty good student. He responded to me in a negative way, as if to say that the Nun seemed to be at ease with what was going on, so I shouldn't be complaining. When he said that, *I saw stars*! It was as if a thunderbolt had hit me. It was all I could do not to hit him in his mouth, but I had promised my mother that I would never strike first! Instead of striking, I said to him, "I just thought you should know how the class felt about what was going on. And now you know how I feel about it!"

Skinner got *worse* after that! The only one in class who did not seem to be bothered by Skinner sitting behind Rosita with one hand in his pocket all day was Mother Superior! Mother Superior was pleased and was satisfied that I seemed to have resigned myself to the situation. For the record, **boys were not allowed to put their hands in their pockets in Catholic school,** so why was she letting this boy get away with this violation of school policy?

A few days later, we were outside at recess when my friend Cookie Coates approached me, balled his fist up, and socked me in the jaw! I stepped back and asked him why he'd hit me. He said that I had a girlfriend and that she was taking my attention away from him! "I don't want you to have a girlfriend!" he said. I looked at him and said that I was sorry and that I wanted us to remain friends. He said to me, "You are not mad at me? You are not going to hit me back?"

"No," I said, "it's all right! I understand how you feel. I forgive you because I value our friendship!" He broke down and started to cry! I was surprised, as I had never seen him cry before. I put my arms around him, and we went off to play.

Cookie Coates was a funny guy; he kept me laughing all the time. Cookie Coates and his brother, Steve, were a comical pair. Those two guys, my two brothers, Roland and Herbert, and I were always together and always laughing at something. The Coates brothers had an older cousin named Baggy Leftridge. He was in charge of the altar boys at St. Vincent de Paul's Church. He came up with the idea that the altar boys should go on an overnight hike to commemorate the end of the school year. We all thought that was a good idea. We had never been on an overnight hike in the woods before.

The day of the hike arrived, and we were to meet at the Church at 7:00 a.m. to leave at 8:00 a.m. My brothers and I got there on time and saw the Coates brothers and Baggy arriving at about the same time. None of the other altar boys showed up, so we were only six out of maybe twenty-some altar boys. Baggy asked us if we wanted to go on, and we said, "Yeah!" We had to catch the Friendship Heights streetcar to the Chain Bridge station, walk across the Chain Bridge to Virginia, and then proceed up the forest path to a campsite predetermined by Baggy Leftridge.

The trail wound and turned and twisted and seemed to nearly go straight up and then straight down sometimes. We eventually reached a spot that leveled off near a creek that emptied into the Potomac River. It was an ideal spot to set up camp. We immediately went about clearing the area and began to pitch our tents. Baggy was a good leader; he kept us busy doing things that prepared us for the night. We spent the better part of the morning gathering wood.

Baggy said that we should take care of everything at the campsite before the sun went down. We hustled around all day and into the evening in preparation for the night. We started joking about how much work was involved in setting up camp for the night. We said that if we had known how much work was involved in camping out, we would have stayed home and spent the day playing! Baggy said a successful overnight hike depended on the preparations made the day before. He said the night should be worry-free!

We had worn ourselves out preparing for the night and were now preparing dinner. Dinner consisted of beans and hotdogs prepared on an open fire. It was a gas, *Jim*! (Jim was the word we used back then to signify an emphatic profundity. In my neighborhood, we used "Yeah, Jim" in lieu of "Yeah, man.") We dined elegantly! We now understood *why* we had had to work so hard before dinner. We were so full and tired that we only wanted to lie around the campfire!

> Softly falls the light of day
> While our campfire fades away.
> Silently each Scout should ask
> Have I done my daily tasks?
> Have I done and have I dared
> Everything to be prepared?[3]

Baggy called everybody to the campfire and lowered the boom on us. He made the announcement that he could not spend the night with us.

"What do you mean?" we asked.

"Well," he said, "I did not want to disappoint you guys, so I figured I would bring you this far and then you could decide among yourselves whether you were brave enough to spend the night on your own! I would love to stay, but I have an important appointment I must keep in town in the morning. Herbert DuVall will have to go back with

---

[3] A revised version of the *Original Scout Vespers*

me, though, because he is only eight. You other guys are ten and older, so you are old enough to spend the night."

Herbert was heartbroken but had known that rule before we'd left home. Herbert cried his little eyes out. But Baggy had promised my mother he would see Herbert home and was determined to keep his word. "So what do you say? Do you want to stay or go?" Baggy asked.

We looked at each other for a moment. We then looked at all the hard work that we had put into setting up the campsite. They looked at me to see what I had to say, so I said, "I am ready to spend the night!"

Cookie Coates said, "Yeah, me too!" Steve and Roland said they wanted to stay also. Baggy (I never knew why they called him Baggy; he was a tall, neat dude) gave us last-minute instructions and had us put all our food in a knapsack that we hung from a nearby tree limb. He said that would keep the food safe from animals that might roam through the area looking for food. With that done, he took Herbert by the hand and told us what time we were to meet him at the Church—the next evening at 6:00 p.m.—and left us standing there, *Jim*!

We stood looking at the trail for a long while. I guess we were waiting for Baggy Leftridge to reappear and say, "Just kidding!" The sun was setting, and the shadows were getting longer and longer. We were still standing in the same spot, and *nobody* was talking, *Jim*!

I finally broke the silence by saying, "We'd better put some more wood on the fire!"

"Yeah! Let's put some more wood on the fire," everybody said. We did that and then looked up the trail again to see if Baggy was coming back. It was getting darker, and the fire was the only noise we heard. We were now convinced that Baggy was not coming back. The fire was burning bright, and we were talking about sleeping arrangements. We had two pup tents, so we decided that Cookie and Steve would bed together and Roland and I would bed together.

We started cracking jokes loudly to scare off any evil spirit. Not only that, since we were all alone, we were also enjoying being loud and profane. When we had to pee, we would just pee. We were FREE, *Jim*! It was just us and the things that go bump in the night. It was our first night outside under the stars, and it was a GAS, *Jim*! We made wolf sounds and various other animal sounds, hoping we would get a response, but I guess they weren't fooled by us fools.

We were now undressed and in our respective tents, yelling at each other from tent to tent. Roland and I were laughing out loud at the Coates brothers for giving each other a hard time about where their feet should be in the tent. They both had big feet. Cookie was thirteen and wore a size thirteen double E shoe, and Steve was twelve and wore a size twelve shoe, so they had their hands *full*. Roland and I were telling them how we were going to have to pitch another tent just for their feet! (Oh, boy!)

We eventually laughed ourselves to sleep. Every now and then, we would hear Cookie telling Steve to move over. Other than that, it was a quiet, blissful night. Just us and the creepy crawlers. We also found out that we could see at night without a flashlight, as the moon was extremely bright. We hadn't experienced that living in the city. The night had its own light, thanks to the moon. Now that was what I called cool, *Jim*!

Morning was upon us, and we were completely at peace with ourselves and our surroundings. We lay around in the tents until about nine or nine thirty. Steve was the first one up and was talking about breakfast. We rekindled the fire and cooked bacon and eggs. We washed our utensils in the creek and started discussing how we were going to spend our day. We decided to do some trailblazing.

We found a trail that seemed to lead deeper into the forest, so we followed it. Cookie said he would lead because he was the oldest, and we agreed to follow. It was the lead trailblazer's responsibility to announce aloud any obstacle found on the trail, and the announcement had to be repeated by each person down the line until it reached the last person. Every time we would hear Cookie stumble or fall over something, we'd then hear him yell, "Stump in the road!"

It seemed that every few feet or so, his big feet were getting caught in something, and as he was falling, he would holler, "Ouuuch! Stump in the road!"

We were passing it back and laughing like hell, *Jim*! Not only that, but Steve (with his big feet) was the next in line and would stumble over the same obstacle! So I would yell, "Same stump, y'all!" That would kick off another round of laughter.

We found ourselves collecting things like discarded snake skins, frogs, beetles, unusual rocks, turtles, and other items. Each guy had his own little collection. We followed the trail until it ended at the edge of a high cliff. We looked down and saw the mighty Potomac. We were a good hundred feet above the river, and it was a majestic sight to us city boys. Cookie yelled, "Come on. Let's climb down to the river and try to catch some fish for dinner!" We all agreed, and down we went. It was a precarious thing to do, and the path was hazardous, but we pulled it off, *Jim*, and without loss of limb!

We got to the river's edge and tried our hand at fishing. We caught a few fish, and I spotted an old rowboat that had either washed up on the shore or been abandoned. There was one old oar in the boat, and the boat had water in it. It also needed a good paint job. We hung around for a few minutes to see whether anybody was going to return for it. Then we decided to turn the boat over and dump the water out. We sat the boat in the water to see whether it had any leaks. About an hour later, we checked the hull and found little or no water in it. It was then that we decided to look for the other oar but had no luck. Someone suggested that we find a good tree branch and try to use it as an oar.

Then there was talk about pushing off into the river. I was skeptical because none of us were swimmers, and I didn't want to put my brother Roland at risk. But Cookie tried to convince us that we could make it out and back. I looked at the river again. The water seemed to be moving faster, or perhaps my nerves were getting the best of me. The undercurrents near the Chain Bridge area were no joke, and the water was quite choppy near the center because of the jagged, rocky riverbed in the area. I felt that if we found ourselves caught in that rough area of the river, we would be swept away down the Potomac to heaven knows where.

I was outvoted, so I agreed to go along. I don't remember Roland saying anything, but he was willing to follow me into the boat. I made it a point to bring a tin can along, just in case the boat started to take in water. We all got in the boat, and Cookie pushed us off. Cookie had the oar, and Steve had the tree limb. Roland and Steve were in the middle, and I was at the back end of the boat. We were now about two-thirds of the way out into the river when I suddenly noticed there was more water in the boat than when we had started. I did not say anything because I didn't want anybody to panic. The water was coming in faster, so I reached for the can. Steve noticed me with the can and got nervous and dropped the tree limb in the river! The swift current immediately took the limb out of reach. We tried desperately to retrieve it, but to no avail.

In our vain attempt to retrieve the tree limb, we failed to notice that the boat was spinning clockwise on its own! Water was coming in faster than I was bailing. Steve looked down, saw his feet in water, and yelled, "Oh SHIT!" In an attempt to get his feet out of the water, Steve was rocking the boat! Roland's mouth was hanging open, but he was still. Cookie, seeing his brother Steve scrambling and the boat rocking, panicked! His face turned white as a ghost, and he leaped to his feet.

The boat was about to tip over because Cookie had started flailing his arms and yelling, "WE AIN'T GON' MAKE IT!" I was yelling at Cookie to please sit down before we all turned over, but he didn't pay me any mind.

All of a sudden, I recalled a similar scene in a movie I once saw in which the people were in this little lifeboat and a guy panicked and jumped up, threatening to tip the boat over. The captain (Humphrey Bogart) slapped the guy across the face and ordered him to sit down!

So I said to myself, *If this doesn't work, we are all going to drown! But I can sure try it!*

I slowly but steadily rose up, reached for Cookie, slapped him across the mouth, and told him to sit down! He was stunned but he *sat down* with a dazed look on his face. I was amazed that it had worked! I then turned to Roland, gave him the tin can, and told him to keep bailing and not to stop, no matter what. He immediately started bailing water. I took the oar from Cookie (who still looked stunned) and told him and Steve to clench their fingers together in a cuplike manner and paddle with their arms while I used the oar to steer toward shore. Everybody *silently and calmly* went about their assignments. I was impressed with the way the guys were applying themselves. Though I was able to get the boat to stop spinning and rocking, I was *not* getting closer to shore.

There were quite a few White folks on the shoreline fishing, and we had their undivided attention. They had all stopped fishing to watch some Black boys who were trying to be *adventuresome* foolishly drown. But it was my intention to cheat them and death, because I did not want Mama on my case about how I had jeopardized my brother's life. I was determined to return him and my friends home safely!

I then said to my crew, "We are in better control of the situation but must work faster and harder if we want to cheat this river, and those watching, of a fickle fate." It took us a little while, but we began moving toward shore. We were so focused that we did not have time to talk. We also did not notice that we were now close enough to shore to jump out, if need be, and not drown. We seemed to have a silent agreement to paddle right up to the shoreline and step out on dry land, as *true adventurers* would do.

When we were all back on dry land, we started talking and laughing again. We also noticed that our audience looked somewhat cheated. We reclaimed our two fish and headed back up the trail to our campsite *swaggerin' and singin'*, "Hup, two, three, four!"

Softly falls the light of day
While our campfire fades away.
Silently each Scout should ask
Have I done my daily tasks?
Have I done and have I dared
Everything to be prepared?
On my honor
I'll do my best
To help the GIRL SCOUTS
To undress!
You had a good home, but you Left!
You're right!
Sound off! One, two!
Sound off! Three, four, count cadence count!
One, two, three, four, one, two, three-four!

We returned to the campsite, built a fire, and tried in vain to cook the fish. Eventually we decided to eat it raw. We justified it by saying, "The Eskimos do it!" Then we started to strike camp. Our morale was running sky high. We had come through the middle passage and were now on our way to manhood. We had *braved* the night and *survived* the Potomac. We formed a bond that could never be broken (I thought). Roland and I returned home on time and decided not to tell anybody but Herbert about the boat ride. Our parents never knew what we had just gone through.

I did not hear or see the Coates brothers for the rest of the summer. I would go by their house, but their mother would always say, "They are not home!" The way she said it made me feel that I was no longer desirable!

Months later I ran into Baggy Leftridge in the neighborhood. I couldn't believe my eyes. I was surprised to see him so soon because my friends had said that if anybody could make it in the priesthood, he could. They said this because of his effeminate mannerisms. Was he back from the seminary school? Had he finished his studies? I caught up with him so that he could clue me in on the latest news about the priesthood. He looked at me and said, "I gave it my best try, Tom, but there were just too many gays for me, so I gave up on it." Baggy was effeminate only in his manner (as he'd been raised by his aunts), not in his behavior. (I had wondered if he would be successful at seminary school.) We embraced and shook hands, and he walked away. That was the last I ever saw of Baggy. I spread the word among the other fellows that I had seen and talked to Baggy and told them what he had said to me. Everybody seemed relieved. God bless you, Baggy Leftridge, wherever you are.

Summer was over, and I was back in school. I was now about twelve years old, and this was my *last year* at St. Vincent de Paul. I entered Mother Pious's class, and she immediately went for the bucket of holy water and gave me a good dousing. I made the sign of the cross (like a good Catholic) and sloshed off to my seat. As I was sitting down, I noticed that the seat directly behind me was now occupied by Puffy Coates, who was Cookie Coates's older brother! Cookie Coates was now sitting in the back of the class, and I couldn't figure out what was happening. Last year Puffy Coates had been in the fourth grade, so how could he be graduating this year?

Puffy Coates was a big, strong, gorilla-type bully. He was a dude with not much smarts. After keeping him in the fourth grade year after year, they had decided to advance him from the fourth grade to the eighth grade because he was having trouble getting in and out of his seat. He was the size of a senior high school student trying to sit at a fourth-grader's desk, so he was always breaking his desk. In the eighth grade, he still could not get his feet under the desk, so he straddled it with his legs in the aisle. But at least he didn't look so ridiculous now. I always thought he was as big as hell, but I'd been told I was small for my age. Now that I think about it, he was the tallest and the oldest guy in the whole school.

I was sitting there listening to Mother Pious speak to the class when Puffy Coates decided to grab a huge handful of my hair! He yanked my head back so far that my neck hurt. Everything was hurting, and my ears were ringing. I said, "Puffy, Puffy, please let me go!!"

Every time I would yell, he'd say, "SHUT UP!" and pull tighter. I figured I'd better not say anything else then. I didn't know how much tighter it could get. I could hear and feel hair tear from my head, and tears were rolling down my face. Mother Superior was standing right there, and I thought she would stop Puffy. Instead she stood there with her arms folded across the crucifix around her neck and didn't *open* her mouth!

Lord, I am calling on You, again, I said to myself. *Looks like I gotta make a decision fast; I may not have time to talk to you long because this hurts.* I saw a chair and thought that if I could get away from him, I was going to grab that chair. (It was one of those fold-up chairs that they use in the wrestling matches on TV.) I knew he'd come after me, so I pulled away. I had to leave the hair there, but who needed it? I was going for the chair!

When I went for the chair, that big bully stood there because he didn't think I'd hit him with it. He looked at me as if to say, "You'd better not try that!" But as far as I was concerned, that chair was coming down on his head. At first I had to really strain to get that chair in the air. I didn't know it would be so heavy! If I had known that, I wouldn't have picked it up. I wasn't sure if I could follow through. I had it over my shoulder, but it wasn't coming down. With all my might, I pulled that chair down and hit him with it—BLAM! That's when I found out why the chair was so heavy. The Nun had been holding onto it, but I hadn't noticed. Down went the chair and the Nun. That's also when I found out what they wore under those long skirts. Now all three of them were on the floor—the bully, the chair, and the Nun, one on top of the other.

The whole class burst out laughing, but I could not laugh because this meant that I would not be graduating this year as planned.

My school days were over, I was sure. She was the Mother Superior here. Sure enough, she expelled me and sent me home, all because of some hair. How could she have allowed Puffy to do that? That was way out to me. With God hanging on the cross on the classroom wall, what was going on? I hadn't done anything to Puffy! I always wondered if someone had told him to do that because that Nun was standing right there. As long as she didn't see me do anything, she wasn't going to do anything. Once I started to do something to help myself, she made a move!

That continues to puzzle me to this day. I didn't want to go back to school, but my mama insisted. She promised the Mother Superior that I would be a model student. I always tried to please my mama.

I had now reached my thirteenth birthday and asked Mama if I could have a birthday party. She said yes but said that I could invite eight to ten people only and that it must be by invitation only. This made things very tricky because it meant someone would not get invited. I hated picking and choosing because I knew somebody was going to be hurt or disappointed. I tried to be selective and discrete, but it made me feel awful. I passed out the invites to my friends at school and asked them to keep it a secret. Before I knew it, people were asking me why they weren't invited too. I told them I wanted to invite everybody but could invite only eight to ten people. (That went over like a fart in Church!) The day of the party, *nobody* from school showed up except Rosita Phifer. I was crushed!

Mama told me to go out into the neighborhood and round up some children to come by and eat the ice cream and cake so that they wouldn't go to waste. After I rounded up some stray kids to eat the cake and ice cream, my father walked into the house piss drunk, stood in the middle of the room, and said to me, "Thomas, you did not empty the slop bucket!" In those days (the thirties, forties, and even the fifties), the houses on Half Street SE still had outdoor toilets. People kept a pot in their bedroom to relieve themselves during the night. Our slop bucket was full, with big turds floating around, and I knew I was supposed to have disposed of it. But because it was my birthday and I was full of excitement, I thought I could put it off until after the party.

Well Daddy wanted it emptied *now*! He had me take that pot downstairs past that lovely birthday cake, and the slop pot did not have a lid on it! It smelled so bad I lost my appetite for cake and ice cream. Some of the kids came up to me and said that they were sorry for me and that I should try to enjoy myself because it was still my birthday.

The high point of the day was when Mama gave me a Red Ryder BB gun. It was a beauty! When the party was over and the houseful of kids I did not know went home, I turned to Mama, thanked her for the gift, and told her I never wanted to have another birthday party. I never have to this day, and neither have my two brothers, who were present at my party.

The next day at school, people who I hadn't given invitations to snarled at me and said, "You didn't give *me* an invitation to your party!" Those I had given invitations to never said one way or the other *why* they had not come, and I was determined not to ask them! What I learned was that if you can't invite *every*body, don't invite *any*body!

Immediately after the graduation exercises at St. Vincent, one of the girls approached me. She wanted to know why I was the only one in class to get "blessed" with holy water every morning when I arrived.

I said to her, "You mean nobody else ever got splashed?"

"No," she said, "just you!"

I decided to ask the Mother Superior why that was. Mother Pious responded, "Because I recognize the Devil when I see him!" I was *crushed*. I wondered, *Does Mother Pious see me as a "Purgatorian?"* We had all done the trick-or-treat thing, and at one time or another, we had all misbehaved, so I wondered why I was being singled out.

I told my buddy what she'd said, and he replied, "It's your name, Thomas Joseph DuVall; there are six letters in each name, which is six-six-six, the mark of the Devil."

"WOW! I didn't know that!" I said.

I told Mama what that Nun had said, and she was visibly *upset*. Mama just shook her head and said, "That Mother Superior is trying to make something *evil* out of a good intention."

My brother Herbert asked Mother Pious why his brother was always being accused and punished for things he did not do. Mother Pious said to him that no child could know all the things that I knew and not be the Devil in person. Then the Mother Superior broke down and started to cry, he said. Herbert said he thought the Mother Superior was secretly in love with me. So I said, "Well she sure has a peculiar way of showing it!"

It dawned on me that Cookie must have told his big brother Puffy about how I'd slapped him in the boat crisis and that Puffy had probably attacked me to compensate for his brother's weakness or something. Nonetheless, I had not slapped Cookie to hurt him, but to help him. Furthermore, when he'd hit me that time because I had a girlfriend, he'd made a fist and busted my lip. He'd drawn blood! But I had forgiven him! I had slapped him not to draw blood, but to calm him down. I know now it was wrong to try something I'd seen in a dumb movie. But Cookie could not forgive me. He let me know that he and Joseph Arguellas were bosom buddies and that I was out of a friend. I said to myself, *Well good riddance!*

Joseph Arguellas was a really light-skinned boy with naturally straight hair. He could almost pass for White. I had thought we were good friends until one day, while walking together down Seventh Street SW, Arguellas said he wanted to get a milk shake. I said, "Yeah, that sounds like a good idea!" So we walked into High's Ice Cream Parlor and sat down to a table.

The waiter walked over to us and said to Arguellas, "If you want to be served here, your friend will have to wait for you outside!"

Joe turned to me and said, "Wait outside. I'll be out in a minute."

I was dumbfounded! The waiter escorted me out and proceeded to take Joe's order. Joe sat there and took his time enjoying his milk shake. I waited patiently because I just knew he was going to order a milk shake for me on the way out. Joseph Arguellas got up, paid the man, and walked out.

He then walked up to me and said, "OK, we can go now!"

So I said, "You didn't order me a milk shake? You know I would have paid for it!"

He looked at me and said, "Sorry, Tom, but that's the way things are, OK?"

"Joseph, if you ever speak to me again, I will try to kill you. You are no friend at all," I replied. *SO this is Cookie's "new friend," and Cookie looks like Kwame Nkrumah!* I thought.

CHAPTER 23

The Summer of 1947: The New Neighborhood

We were on summer vacation, and Mama had found a house for us to move to. We were moving from 1218 Half Street SE to 1536 D Street SE. It was two blocks from Daddy's sister Lucille's and her husband William's house at Eighteenth and Potomac Avenue SE, which I now find to be ironic.

The day after we moved in, we found out that we were the only Black family on that block, as far as I can remember. It turned out to be quite an experience. Mama had to go in to work and told us to play in the front yard and not to leave the yard under any circumstances, so that was what we did. The front yard had a wrought-iron fence around it. White folks would come by and stare at us as if we were three little monkeys in a zoo cage! They would never say anything; they just stared. They looked like Zombies to us kids.

That evening we were all in the kitchen having dinner. Mama got up to go to the sink, and when she reached the sink, she let out a scream! We all jumped up to see what was the matter. Our kitchen window faced our neighbor's kitchen window, and our neighbor's family was standing at the window and staring at us while we were eating! They saw our startled reaction and showed no shame; they continued to stare. We did not have blinds in the kitchen, so Mama had to pull the shades all the way down so that we could eat in peace. This went on for weeks. It was a real *drag*, and they never would speak, just stare. It was the damndest thing! It was like being among the living dead. It was a bit unnerving.

Someone in our neighbor's house was ALWAYS at the window looking into our kitchen. The people who lived there even had chairs stationed at their window. Sometimes their kitchen would be full of people jockeying for a "peep" at what we monkeys were up to!

Mama would always jump up, pull the curtains closed, and say out of disgust, "Jesus, you can't even let a little sunlight in your kitchen for the buzzards on the perch!"

I had an idea. I decided to make myself a mask like the one the Lone Ranger wore, only I wanted a blue mask and a blue cape like the red cape Superman wore. I named myself *"The Blue Phantom."*

I would station myself just out of sight, and when I caught someone stationing themselves at their window, I would allow them to sit for a moment. Then I would *"suddenly appear"* and stare at them with my arms folded across my chest! They would look at me in complete *disbelief*, jump up, and walk out!

This went on for several weeks. Sometimes I would stand at the window just in case they walked by. Finally, when I put on my Blue Phantom hero costume one day and went to the window, I found their curtains closed! At last, the "final curtain call" on that little sideshow had come!

Mama soon noticed that they were keeping their curtains closed. We all said, "YEEEH!" I had to retire my Blue Phantom hero clothes. (But I did not discard them.)

My two brothers and I spent a lot of time in the front yard. We were true yard birds. We had hooked up the railing around the porch with make-believe horse reins and saddles and were having a ball riding the range and singing cowboy songs. That's when we got our first visit from the police. They pulled up to the yard, got out of the car, and yelled to us, "Y'all got to cut that noise out and be quiet, do you understand? Because the people in the neighborhood are complaining about the racket y'all are making, so cut it out!" They scared the hell out of us! They got back into their car, slammed the doors, and drove off. We were stunned and scared. We couldn't believe somebody had called the *cops* on us. We sat on the porch for a while in complete silence. We did not think we were being loud and unruly. We were visibly shaken and decided to go inside.

That evening we told Mama how the police had come to the house and told us we were too noisy. She flipped out! She told us that we were to go back out there in that yard the next day and play as usual. If the police came back, I was to tell them our mother had told us to play in the yard and not in the house. "And you let me know what he says to that!" she said.

"Yes, Ma'am," I said.

The next day we went out in the yard to play. The cops came by, and one of them yelled, "I thought I told y'all to stay inside that house!"

We yelled back, "Mama said we can play in our own yard!"

"I'm warning you; stay out of trouble, or we will be back!" They then drove off.

"Should we call Mama?" my brothers asked. I said, "No, why get Mama upset on her job? Let's just tell her when she gets home. In the meantime let's keep playing in the yard." Sure enough, they came back and began driving real slow and snarling at us. We were beginning to feel nervous and could no longer sing to each other. About an hour later, they drove by again! This time we decided we'd better go into the house.

That evening we told Mama what had happened. Poor Mama was so upset. She immediately went to the phone, called the precinct, and asked why they were harassing her children! I don't know what they said, but it made Mama hit the ceiling! She was yelling at them over the phone, "My children will be back outside tomorrow and every day after that, and if my children tell me you came by here again frightening them, I will have your badges! Now just try me!" she said.

Mama slammed the phone down, turned to us, and said, "I want you all out in that yard every day until I say differently. And if those policemen come by and say anything to you, call me immediately, do you understand?"

"Yes, Mama," we all said.

The next day we went out to play. The cops drove by but did not stop. They looked but did not speak! "It looks like Mama told them a thing or two," we said. Mama had removed our fear of them, and we began to play and sing our cowboy songs again.

After a few weeks went by, we began wondering if there were any other kids in the block besides us—White or Black! Then one day a little White boy came by and stopped at our yard. He stuck his dirty face between the wrought-iron bars and said, "Can I come in and play with y'all?" We looked at each other in surprise. We noticed that he was not the cleanest kid we had seen, but he wanted to play with us, so we let him come into the yard. We also found out that he was intellectually disabled. He said that his name was Lester and he lived near the corner of Fifteenth and D Streets SE. Lester was also tongue-tied (a speech impediment). We decided to let him into the yard (which was a mistake, we later found out).

The first thing he did was pick up one of our trucks and said, *"Tin ah HAW dit? Pyease le' me haw dit."* I couldn't understand him and had him repeat it several times. "He said, 'Can he have it?'" I told my brothers. We tried to tell him he could play with it, but he could not "HAW dit!"

Lester spent the rest of the day picking up all of our toys and asking us if he could "haw it." What made it even worse was that he was getting upset because we were constantly saying no! Eventually another little White boy showed up. He said he was Lester's cousin and wanted to know if he too could come into the yard and play with us. We paused and looked at him. He didn't sound disabled or tongue-tied, but his face was just as dirty as Lester's! I asked him his name, and he said, "Sonny-man! Lester lives with me." We let him in.

We all played for a while, and got along just fine, and then Sonny-man suddenly said, "We gotta go now. Come on, Lester." And they took off down the block. We trailed them with our eyes to see what house they went into. The state of their house matched the state of their faces.

At around seven o' clock the next morning, we had not yet gotten out of bed and there was a knock at the front door. Nobody moved. There was another knock, this time louder. I was now wide awake. The knocking got even louder and longer. I got dressed and went to the door. I opened the door and could not believe my eyes! It was Lester and Sonny-man! I saw on their faces the same dirt that I had seen the day before, plus a few new stains. I wanted to ask them if they had running water at home.

"What's going on?" I asked.

"We want to play with your toys!" they said.

"But we are still in bed."

"Can't we come in anyway?"

I wanted to say, "Go home, wash your faces, have some breakfast, and then come back!" But what I said was, "We are not allowed to have company when our mother is not home, so you will have to come back a little later." They wouldn't take *no* for an answer, so I closed the door, locked it, and went back to bed.

We got up, got dressed, ate breakfast cereal, and headed for the front room window to see if we saw Lester and Sonny-man. They were not in sight, so we gathered our toys, *eased* out into the front yard, and started *quietly* playing. We weren't out there a hot minute when we heard, "Can we come in to play now?" It was Lester and Sonny-man!

Roland said to me, "Were they hiding behind a tree or something?" We hadn't seen anyone come from the direction their house was in. Where had they popped up from? And their faces were even dirtier than before! I wanted to ask them if they had running water!

We had no choice but to let them in. Everything Lester picked up he wanted to "HAW," and Sonny-man was continuously trying to get our toys into his pockets. They were driving us *CRAZY*! Suddenly a police car pulled up in front of the house with the same two cops who had troubled us before.

They yelled at Lester and Sonny-man, "I'm telling your mother you're playing down here in this yard!"

Sonny-man yelled back, *"She knows it!"* The cops then pulled off toward Sonny-man's house.

Sonny-man then yelled to Lester, "Come on, Lester, let's go!" As Sonny-man headed for the gate, I grabbed him by the trousers, reached into his pocket, and retrieved one of our toys. Then I opened the gate to let him out. The appearance of those cops that day was a saving grace! Once that happened we did not see those two characters for several weeks.

We were heavy into reading comic books. I was into reading about Donald Duck and his Nephews, Archie and Jughead, and war stories. Roland and Herbert enjoyed Bugs Bunny, Elmer Fudd, and Daffy Duck, but we read them all!

A week or so later, we got a visitor—it was Sonny-man! He put his face against the wrought-iron fence and said, "Hey! Ya' wanna trade some comics?"

I said, "Go get them, and we'll talk!"

He took off down the street and came back later with a bunch of comic books that looked awful. *All* were missing their covers, some looked liked they had been rolled up to swat flies with, others were missing pages, and some had only half pages! We couldn't believe our eyes.

Sonny-man dropped his remnants on the porch and began to pick out the ones he was going to swap with us. Roland blurted out, "Sonny-man, you must be *crazy*! I'm not giving up my comics for something that looks like your dog's been chewing on it!"

I said, "He is right! Can't you see our comics are almost *new*? We can take these back to the store and sell 'em for half price!" Roland snatched his comics from Sonny-man, who acted like he didn't know what we were talking about. A trade was a trade, as far as Sonny-man was concerned! After all, we were *only* niggers (that was the look he had on his dirty face).

We unanimously decided not to trade and told him if he wanted to trade with us, his books would have to be at least as good as the ones he wanted. He did not look very happy. Rather than send him away empty-handed, I told him to pick out one comic that he could have. He picked out a good one and started to leave. He turned around and said to us, "Do y'all go scavenger hunting on Thursdays?"

We said no. Then he said, "Well if you change your mind, we can go out this Thursday, and I can show you where you can find comics that have been thrown out that are in good shape."

"OK!" we said. "Pick us up this Thursday."

Thursday came, and sure enough Sonny-man and Lester were at the door knocking. "Hey!" he said. "Come on, let's go! We got to get an early start to beat the trash collectors there!" We got dressed and went downstairs. Sonny-man turned to Lester and told him he couldn't come. Lester moaned and groaned and turned back home.

"Why can't Lester come?" I asked.

"My mother won't let him go out of the neighborhood," Sonny-man said. We didn't *need* to ask why!

It turned out to be a bonus day! We had armfuls of comics. We were amazed at the quality of things thrown out as trash in this neighborhood east of Seventeenth Street near East Capitol Street NE. A lot of the books were in mint condition. Maybe Sonny-man had felt guilty about what he'd attempted to pull on us and was returning a favor for the effort we'd made to accept him and his cousin Lester the Pester. We became heap big traders after that. We even let Lester the Pester "haw" some of our toys! Not only that, but Lester's phrase became the byword of the neighborhood! We had everybody saying, "Ooh, look! *Tin ah HAW dit?*"

The next time we went out, we took a wagon and decided to expand a little. There was another White boy who lived directly across from me named Joe Shelton. He was a year older than I was. Joe Shelton was a snob who was always sassing his mother. He was very girlish, and his mother had him wear his hair in bangs that hung down over his eyebrows. He was always running his fingers through his bangs. He was also extremely slue-footed.

When he saw that we were trading comics, he could not help but cross the street to visit us. He was arrogant, and the other White boys shunned him, so he had no real friends. He had a well-kept collection of comics and was willing to trade with us, though he would not scavenge.

One of the most popular comics among the White boys was the *Superman* comics, which I could not seem to accept as legitimate. This perplexed the White guys, and they always wanted an explanation! I explained that *I* just could not, for the life of me, sit down and read a comic about a White guy who flew around the world lifting ships out of the water and throwing locomotives around and was bulletproof *and* indestructible!

They would then ask, "Well why do you read *Batman* comics?"

I would reply, "At least Batman has a utility belt that he uses, and if he has to leap around buildings, he uses a rope!" That would shut 'em up.

There was another White boy who started coming by the house to read and trade. His name was Ray Gordon. He and I were the same age. He was heavyset with red hair and freckles. He was a happy-go-lucky kind of guy who always stood with his thumbs hooked in the pockets of his pants. He lived above the Pope Funeral Home, which at the time was located on Fifteenth Street near D Street SE. We would tease him about living above dead bodies and ask him if it affected his appetite. He replied, "Do I look like I have an appetite problem?" We all laughed. He indeed looked well fed.

Ray Gordon and I hit it off right away. He was manly in a boyish way and easy to get along with. He would come by with his comics and sit there for hours at a time reading. He read with such intensity that he would never answer to his name when called. We would even go over and tap him on the shoulder, and he would not respond. One day we even pushed him over on his side and he just lay there, his eyes glued to his comic. It was as if he was in a trance. We could get his attention only when he was in the process of looking for his next comic to read. Ray Gordon was a lot of fun to be around. He was also fast with the one-liners! He wasn't a big talker, but whenever he did say something, it was always profound, accurate, and funny!

Ray Gordon showed up one day with his little sister, Nancy. She was as sweet as could be. He said he was *stuck* with her because his mother had to go out. I told him to introduce her to my little sister, Jeanne, because they were about the same age.

Jeanne was my mother's brother's child. He had died, and my mother had adopted her. Mama said, "I always wanted a little girl, so could you all regard her as your little sister?" We all said yes.

Jeanne and Nancy hit it off right away! They spent many hours together playing with each other. That worked out fine, and we boys were left alone with our comics.

Joe Shelton's mother would come to the door and call him to come home, and he would yell back to her, "Shaddup, and leave me alone;

I'll come home when I'm ready!" We were all shocked at the way he talked to his mother!

One day I said to him, "You shouldn't talk to your mother that way!"

He said to me, "She gets on my nerves, and I hate her for it."

Wow! I couldn't believe it. My mother would have taken my head *off* if I had even looked like I was about to say something like that. I found it unacceptable that he treated his mother that way, but it didn't seem to bother Joe Shelton any.

I soon heard Sonny-man talk back to his mother in the same way and began to wonder if it was a White thing. I asked Ray Gordon if he did the same thing. He replied, "I may be crazy, but I ain't *that* crazy! My old man would kill me." I liked his response and told him so.

Ray Gordon came by the front yard one day and suggested that we plan a hike down behind the Gallinger Hospital (later known as DC General) so we could do some exploring near the train tracks and the eastern branch of the river. It was a brilliant idea! We all decided that everybody should bring something to cook for lunch.

We met at my house around nine o'clock and headed for the river behind Gallinger Hospital. About an hour or so later, we were talking about eating, so we picked a spot near the train trestle and started building a fire. We got the fire going, and I broke my frying pan out and propped it up on the burning fire. I smacked a little butter that I had in some wax paper into the pan and asked for the eggs. Everybody went gently for their precious cargo—eggs. After I had everybody's eggs in the pan, I broke out my beautiful ripe tomatoes.

Everybody screamed, "Tomatoes? You are not going to put those tomatoes in those eggs, are you? What in the world possessed you to bring tomatoes, Thomas? Are you crazy?"

So I said, "Yeah, man! Y'all never heard of tomatoes and eggs before?"

"No!" everybody said, all at once. They asked me if I had ever combined the two before.

I said, "No, but I was almost certain it would be just fine!"

"Almost?" they said. "We tiptoed all the way down here, through the woods, the bushes, the sand traps, and other obstacles, juggling and struggling to protect these eggs from breaking with our lives, just to have you ruin them by putting raw tomatoes in them? Why couldn't you just bring a piece of bacon or at least an egg like everyone else?" they kept saying.

The scrambled eggs were getting overcooked, so I quickly diced up the tomatoes, threw them into the pan, and stirred them into the eggs. People could have heard the moans and groans clear across the river! I stirred the eggs a little more and told everyone to hold their plates up.

"I'm not eating that!" they said.

"You eat it!" I said. "Allow me to demonstrate." I took a big mouthful, and that was enough for Ray Gordon (Ray loved to eat). He jumped right in and started putting it away. The others immediately followed suit. Then they started raving about how good it was. (Even I was amazed at how great it turned out.) It became the topic of discussion for weeks to come!

We were in the process of cleaning up when we saw a train coming across the trestle. When the train got alongside our little campsite, the Engineer leaned out the cab window and yelled to the White boys, with a snarl on his face, "Can't y'all find somebody else to play with?"

My brothers and I were shocked and frightened. This was a grown man upset because we were enjoying each other's company.

Joe Shelton yelled back, "Our mothers know we are here!"

Ray Gordon yelled, "Yeah, mind your own business!"

Roland, Herbert, and I just looked at each other. We had never been confronted with anything like that before! Our White friends saw we were shaken by the incident and tried in their own little way to apologize for the behavior of some of the grown-ups out here.

A few days later, there was a knock on the door. I answered the door, and it was Joe Shelton. He started telling us how he could no longer play with us, so we asked him why. He said, "I am now sixteen, and my mother told me I am not to be seen with you all again." He said it was all right if a White boy played with Blacks before his sixteenth birthday, but once a White boy became sixteen, he had to associate himself only with other Whites.

In response I said, "You have never paid any attention to anything your mother has said in the past, so why are you so obedient all of a sudden now?"

He looked at me and said, "My mother is preparing me for manhood, so I must take my rightful place in the world." He said goodbye, turned, showed me the back of his girlish head, and never looked back.

Even though I saw him every day, he never spoke to us again. It was as if we had suddenly become invisible. He actually did not see us! I couldn't believe people could act this way. Sonny-man also disappeared. One day he simply stopped looking at us when we'd pass him.

A week or so later, Ray Gordon came by to see us, and we were surprised. We told him about Joe Shelton and Sonny-man, and he could not believe it! I asked him if his parents had said the same thing to him. He said, "No, I can't picture my mother and father saying a thing like that to me!" He then said he had never liked Joe anyway because he was always acting like a sissy.

We were pleased to hear that because we liked Ray. He would always come by, which reassured us that all White people were not like Joe Shelton or Sonny-man. He was a good friend, and we were always together. He had a great sense of humor too!

One day Ray said to me, "Let's go on another hike! But this time let's go somewhere different."

I said, "I know a real good spot to hike to, but we would need permission from our parents to do it!"

"Where is it?" Ray asked.

I said, "It's in Virginia, just on the other side of Chain Bridge."

Ray said, "Hey! That sounds like a good idea! Let's do it! I can take my Red Ryder rifle with me!"

I said, "I have a Red Ryder rifle too!"

We decided to ask our parents. Mama said yes, but I would have to take my brothers with me, which I didn't mind doing. Ray's parents said yes also, so we planned to do it on the first Saturday of promised sunshine.

Saturday came, and Ray was at the front door with his knapsack and BB gun. I was still busy making sure my brothers were ready with the gear they would have to carry. A few minutes later, we headed down to Fifteenth and Pennsylvania Avenue to get the Friendship Heights Streetcar to take us to Chain Bridge.

It was early in the morning, and the streetcar was empty. I told everybody to take the last seat in the back so that we could rest our gear without being in the way of the passengers getting off and on as we traveled to our destination. We had quite a lot of gear too—two tents, shovels, rope, hunting knives, two BB rifles, three canteens, several blankets, two axes, four mess kits, first aid kits, two pocket knives, a change of clothes, four cans of beans, a dozen hotdogs, sardines, crackers, bacon, eggs, a skillet, and a pan for hot water.

About an hour later, we arrived at the Chain Bridge crossing. We always thought that it was the longest bridge in the world (little did we know)! There was a store in a little log cabin on the Virginia side where we stopped for a soda before we hit the trail that took us up to our old campsite. Ray Gordon was tickled pink at being out there with us and camping out. He was as happy as a punk in Boy's Town. He was not a bit of trouble, and we were enjoying each other's company. We cracked jokes and sang bawdy songs as we hiked up the winding trail to the top of the mountain.

We reached the campsite in the woods, pitched our tents, built a fire, made breakfast, washed the dishes in the creek, and started planning how we were going to spend the rest of the day. We had just decided to leave camp for a while to do some trailblazing when these four White guys appeared and began heading toward us. They all had these 30-30-caliber rifles (about the size of an Army 30-caliber Bolt action). The men were kind of wild-eyed looking, and I felt a bit unsettled as they approached our campsite. They were shooting birds out of the trees as they walked toward us.

They greeted us and wanted to know if we came there often. "Not too often," I said. "We are from DC." I looked at Ray Gordon, who did not look as concerned as I was, and relaxed a little more. Ray Gordon was fascinated with the 30-30s and asked if he could see one of the bullets. They passed one around, and we all held it in our hands.

Then one of them asked Ray if he would like to fire one off. Ray said sure, took aim at a tree, and fired (I was hoping they would ask me, but they never did). Ray picked up the spent shell and asked if he could keep it! "Sure, kid," one of the White guys said to him. They then turned and started walking away, shooting at everything that moved.

I was in a state of distress as I watched my feathered friends plummet to earth. "I caught tha' son of a bitch on the wing," one of them said as they walked away. I was visibly upset.

Ray Gordon looked at me and said, "I don't shoot birds and don't like what they did. I only shoot rodents, Tom." I was glad to hear that, I told him. We gave the birds we could find a decent burial.

We stood around for a moment, thinking about what we'd just witnessed and tried to do for the birds. We started talking about whether we should leave camp to do some more trailblazing. We were afraid those guys would come back, see us not there, and raid our supplies— at least that's what I was thinking. I suggested, "Let's disperse and each take a direction. Travel as far out as you can while still being able to see the camp, and if you find something of interest, call out and we will come to you." That idea didn't yield anything interesting, but we killed a lot of time farting around, which meant to us that we could now look at "stretching out" and do some trailblazing.

We had a lot of fun following new footpaths and gathering turtles, frogs, bottles, transparent quartz rocks, and a four-foot-long snake, which we killed and brought back to camp. Ray Gordon said he had heard that if you threw a dead snake in the fire, he would come back to life, so we built a fire, and when it got good and hot, we threw the snake on the fire. To our amazement, that dead snake started wiggling and squirming to beat the band! We could not believe our eyes! We decided to take the snake out of the fire and skin him so that we would have a souvenir of our adventures. Ray Gordon did that.

We then moved on to less exciting things, like setting up targets of cans and bottles and picking them off with our Red Ryder rifles. For some odd reason, Ray and I decided to switch rifles. His was practically brand new, and mine was about two years old. Nonetheless, we carried each other's rifle for the rest of the trip.

We looked at the time and decided to fix something to eat, clean up, pack, and head for Chain Bridge and the Friendship Heights Streetcar. We were halfway across the bridge when we had to stop to make an adjustment in Ray's backpack. I realized that I would need both hands to fix the problem, so I decided to lean his rifle against the guardrail of the bridge. *Boy*, what a mistake that was! The guardrail was taller than the rifle, so the rifle slipped through the railing.

As the rifle plummeted, Ray Gordon looked over the railing and humorously described how gracefully his rifle was tumbling as it sailed to its final resting place: 150 feet to the rocky water's edge. "Oh, what a wondrous sight to behold!" he said. I was *feeling really bad*. His brand-new rifle was now smashed to bits. He just stood there with my rifle in his hand. I told him to keep my rifle and that I would go down under the bridge to retrieve the broken one.

Ray's face lit up like a Christmas tree! He immediately said, "Thanks, Tom, that's mighty sporting of you." He looked relieved and said, "Now I won't have to worry about my Dad." His face also told me that he liked my rifle.

We reached the rifle and saw that the stock was completely broken off and the barrel was bent to the right. Ray Gordon jokingly said to me, "Well at least you'll be able to shoot around corners now." He also told me again how impressed he was that I had given up my rifle.

A few weeks later, my brother Roland ran up the steps to tell me that the police were downstairs in the dining room asking for me! I got dressed and went downstairs to see two red-faced, overfed-looking cops standing in our dining room with my broken Red Ryder BB gun in their hands.

They asked me if I was the owner of this gun. I said, "Yes!" They said that they were responding to complaints that someone was killing all the cats in the neighborhood. "Well as you can see, it couldn't have been me because that gun has been broken for some time," I said. That's when their faces got redder! I was afraid they were going to have a stroke! It was kind of frightening to see them swelling up like that. I didn't know what was going to happen next.

One of the red faces finally spoke: "Listen, we want you to take these pieces and throw them away! When we come back here, they had better be gone!" They then turned and stiffly swaggered out of the house.

I immediately called Mama and informed her of what had just taken place. She was infuriated! She asked me, "Did they show you a search warrant?"

I said that they only showed me my broken rifle, so Mama called the precinct and told them that if they ever entered her house again, she was suing the entire Metropolitan Police Department. And that this was her LAST WARNING! (Go, Mama!) From that day on, we did not hear another PEEP out of the Metropolitan Police Department!

That early morning visit by those two goons brought me out of my depression over my BB gun, as they were the ones who had made me decide to make an all-out effort to repair that gun! I looked at the bent barrel and realized that the outside barrel, which held all the BBs, was at least three-fourths of an inch in diameter. The inner barrel couldn't have been more than three-sixteenths of an inch in diameter. With this in mind, I went about taking the barrel assembly apart and saw that the dent did not touch the inner chamber! The rifle was repairable! I took that rifle completely apart—every bolt, nut, and spring. The very next day, I was off to the lumberyard to purchase a plank for the stock.

I laid the broken parts of the stock on the plank and took a pencil and traced around them. Then I grabbed an old rusty saw that Mr. Wal'er had left behind and tried to saw with it, but it was too rusty. I remembered that Mr. Wal'er used to put a little motor oil on each side of the blade and spread it out with a piece of newspaper. I tried it, and it worked! I found an old file and a piece of sandpaper and smoothed it out. Next I made some holes in the new stock and used the original screws to secure the stock to the housing. I then oiled and reassembled the trigger, its spring, and the firing pin. Last but not least, I inserted the rifling in the barrel and screwed it in nice and tight. I even found some brown paint, so I painted the stock with an old rag and then wiped it off to make it look like it was varnished. By about four o'clock that evening, I had remade that rifle! I couldn't believe it myself!

The next day I was ready to test my rebuilt, almost-new Red Ryder rifle, so off to the hobby shop I went to buy a box of BBs. I went to the backyard, aimed the rifle at a stack of old newspapers, and fired several rounds off. Well bust my britches, it worked! I could not wait to show it to Ray Gordon. But I had to be cool and wait until Ray came by the house, as I did not want it to be seen by those nosey neighbors, who would surely report it to the fuzz, so I had to be cool. My two brothers were certainly impressed with it. I knew that.

Ray Gordon showed up one day. I invited him in and showed him the rebuilt rifle. He couldn't believe his eyes! I took him out into the backyard and let him shoot it. He was surely impressed and happy for me!

I then asked him if the police had been around to see him about any cat killings or to tell him to destroy his rifle. He said no and could not believe the story I told him about the cops' walking into our house and ordering me to destroy the already-broken rifle! "Well you see how I replied to that," I said.

As I mentioned, Ray Gordon and I would shoot only at rodents. And speaking of rodents, we had a mouse in our house that had been driving my mother up the walls. She had been setting traps for the longest time, but that mouse had been taking the bait without setting off the trap. Mama was the only one who had seen him.

As luck would have it, I had a little ritual on Friday nights. I would stay up until midnight and then quietly go downstairs to the kitchen, fix myself a bowl of cereal, and eat it in the quiet of the night. I was sitting there eating my Wheaties and listening to the midnight noises of the street one night when I saw something moving across the kitchen floor. When it got to the middle of the floor, it stopped and stood up on its hind legs in a begging position. I saw the eyes looking at me and realized it was the little mouse Mama had been trying to catch. I couldn't believe my eyes! I never heard of a begging mouse! I immediately thought of my BB gun, but it was in the closet in the next room. I didn't want him to leave, so I decided to throw him a few flakes of my WHEATIES. He took the flakes and took off under the refrigerator. I told everybody what had happened that Friday night, and nobody believed me!

At midnight on the following Friday, I decided to do my midnight ritual, but this time I went to the closet first and got my Red Ryder, cocked it, laid it on the table, and *then* went to get the Wheaties and milk. I was munching away and tuned in to the philharmonic sounds of the night when suddenly I saw *two* little figures moving across the kitchen floor. The guy that had begged for my Wheaties the week before had returned with a friend! I said to myself, *If they did not believe the one-mouse story, how am I going to explain the two-mouse story?* I needed a witness!

I snapped out of my bewilderment and decided to shoot one of them, knowing the other would probably escape. I plucked one in the chest, and he fell over and didn't move. The other one, to my surprise, did not run; instead he stood his ground and was looking confusedly at his fallen friend. This act gave me the time I needed to reload and pluck him off too! I felt awful after that because they seemed like such a nice couple, but Mama was going crazy with concern. Now she did not have to worry.

I thought to myself, *I can easily get rid of the evidence and let them think I am a fabricator or save the evidence and prove I am tell-ing the truth.* I decided to scoop up the two remains and place them in a vase that was sitting on the buffet in the dining room until I had everybody's attention. Unfortunately Mom thought it was the most disgusting thing she'd ever seen and chastised me for using her Ming vase to put those nasty dead rodents in. My brothers were too scared to go near the murder scene, so I was left with my memories.

The only time it was ever discussed again was when they wanted something disgusting to say. I had merely been trying to clear my name but had made it worse. That was the first and last time I ever took a life. It was also the end of the "mouse-in-the-house" problem for good!

Ray Gordon came by, and I told him the mouse story. He was impressed. "That was some steady-handed shooting," he said.

"That target practice paid off," I said.

Ray suggested we walk over to the Congressional Cemetery at Seventeenth and Potomac Avenue SE. We jumped over the wall and proceeded to peep into the fantastic mausoleums that lined the streets. Some had little glass windows we could peer through to see the caskets. Others had visitors' chambers where people could sit and lounge and public facilities for those who would come to spend long visits with the deceased. Our minds were blown!

We eventually found ourselves at the east end of the cemetery and noticed all the fruit trees that were growing there. It looked like an orchard; there were apple trees, peach trees, pear trees, plum trees, and grapevines! We decided to taste a few of the fruits, and they were delicious! The next thing I knew, we had climbed a big peach tree and were eating peaches to beat the band. When we tired of peaches, we swung over to the apple tree. "These apples are out of sight," I said. Ray never said a word; he just kept picking and eating. We were there all day long. We witnessed people coming and going, but even the groundskeepers did not bother us. We were the last people to leave as the sun began to set. We returned many times to those trees over the summer.

My two brothers had made new friends their age among the Black families moving to the area, but I spent some days in the cemetery by myself.

A couple of the guys my age asked me where I disappeared to during the day. I told them where I went to be alone. They wanted to know if they could go with me the next time I went. I said OK and took them where I hung out. They had quite a different experience that day. They said that they couldn't play games in the cemetery, and I had to agree with that. Not only that, but these guys were Black and had a different slant on things. We needed to be playing some games. Before there were any Blacks in the neighborhood, everything had been based around White boys and what they would allow themselves to do with us. When the White boys wanted to play sports or other games, they had only to say they were going to the *club* and would see us later. They never said, *"Let's* go to the club!"* The club was the Metropolitan Police Boys Club of Greater Washington, which was located at Seventeenth and Massachusetts Avenue NE. Black kids were not allowed there! We couldn't even think about it!

The big blow below the belt came the night of the big Joe Louis vs. Jersey Joe Walcott fight. All the White kids on the block said their so-longs and took off for the club to enjoy watching these two Black boxers knock each other around on a giant television screen. All the Black kids had to go to their homes and hope that they could hear something on the radio about their hero, Joe "The Brown Bomber" Louis. I found that to be insulting. How could grown-ups hurt children like that? And it didn't seem to bother them! "Do unto others as you would have others do unto you and keep holy the Sabbath day. Love thy neighbor as thyself!" These words kept ringing in my head. *How dare they break God's commandments!* I thought. *Why, they must think God is on their side. They must really believe that God is White, not universal, and that therefore it's all right to hurt those who are non-White.*

Why didn't God show himself and correct those dastardly things they did to us darker children? What was the message here? Why were the wrongdoers going unchecked? Where was *our* Almighty God? We needed a Supreme Being too. Joe Louis was our hero, but he could not be everywhere at once, like God could. We needed an *Omnipresent* Black hero to champion our cause. *I will do everything in my power to fight against this wickedness and its wicked worship*, I thought. *I am determined to champion "our" cause, dear God.*

Ray Gordon was standing there staring at me because he knew I could not accompany him to the club. He was wonderful and we enjoyed each other's company, but he was not going to deny himself the privilege to see that fight. He wanted a nod from me, so I gave him the nod, and he said he would report back to me with the details of the fight. I said OK, and he split. I couldn't blame him. He tried to be a decent White boy. He did report back to me, and I appreciated his effort to bring me up to date with details.

About a week later, Ray Gordon showed up at the house to announce that his family was moving out of town. His father had found a better job in another state. We shook hands, said our good-byes, and he was gone.

CHAPTER 24

The Piper Cub Contest and Other Fun and Games

When I was between thirteen and fourteen years old, I was eating my cornflakes and noticed a contest on the back of the cereal box. I read, "Learn how to fly! Win free Piper Cub flying lessons! Just send a box top with our name and address, and we will send you what you need to enter!" *Wow! All contest winners will receive free flying lessons, offered by Kellogg's!* I thought. I immediately tore off the box top and asked Mama for a stamp to mail it off with. She went immediately into, "Boy, why did you tear off the top of that box? Now how am I supposed to close the box up with no top? Can't you use your head for something besides a hat rack? What is the matter with you?"

She took the top, taped it back on the box, and said, "Now you wait until that box is empty before you tear any more tops off around here!"

"Yes, Ma'am!" I said.

She walked away. Suddenly I wanted to eat more cornflakes! I ate two more bowlfuls and was stuffed. I tried to recruit my brothers and sister to help me, but they were quite blasé about it. I was eating cornflakes for breakfast and lunch. I would even come down at night and eat while the house slept. I also put some in a plastic bag and carried them in my coat pocket.

About a week or so later, I got to the bottom of the box. I went to Mama with the box top and asked her for a stamp, and she gave it to me! I was out the door and down the street to the mailbox. I opened the mail-drop door, slammed it a few times to make sure it was in there good, and returned home. I waited and waited for what seemed like years!

Finally, about three months after I had long given up on watching the mailbox, I heard a knock at the door. It was the mailman, and he had something that wouldn't fit through the mail slot. I saw that it was a parcel from Kellogg's! My kit had arrived!

I tore it open to find a Piper Cub single-engine model kit. *I felt like I was in heaven!* I had been heading outside to play, but now there was no time for outside 'cause I had work to do and books to read! I carefully removed each and every item. Then I sat down to read the instruction manual on how to assemble the thing so that I could learn how to fly it. Oh, boy, oh, boy!!

One glance inside the instruction manual gave me the feeling that I had bitten off more than I could chew. I thought, *Whoa, they must think I'm an engineer or something!* I sat there for a few minutes. Then I remembered there was an old plane in the Acme junkyard behind the house on Half Street. I went out back to see if I could scale the fence, but it must have been eleven feet high. No way could I go over it, but my dog, Daisy, started digging a hole under the fence, so I decided to help her. We got in. (I had a smart dog!)

Lo and behold! The plane was an old Piper Cub! I could not believe my eyes! I climbed into the cockpit and just sat there with my hands on the joy stick for what seemed like hours. I said to myself, *God must be helping me.*

A little voice in the back of my head said, "Just study one page at a time, and don't look at the next step until you have a good understanding of what is going on." I jumped out of the cockpit and headed for the worktable (dining room table).

I gathered the tools I needed—scissors, glue, ruler, a pocket knife, and plenty of strong thread. After I gathered the tools, I went to the next step, which was punching out all the parts. Then I assembled the control panel, the console, and the right and left rudder pedals. I attached the joy stick to the console. The next step was to assemble the parts of the plane. I started with the fuselage, being very careful not to cut or crease the material in any way other than instructed. I then assembled and attached the stabilizer to the fuselage and assembled the rudders and attached them to the fuselage. Next I attached the wheel mounts to the fuselage and then attached the wheels. I assembled the right and left wings and attached them to the fuselage. Last but not least, I assembled the engine housing and propeller mount, attached them to the body of the plane, and added the wing struts. I had been working for weeks, it seemed, and I was only halfway finished.

I decided to take a break for a few days and check out the neighborhood, to see what was going on on the block, since I hadn't seen the gang in a while. Everybody wanted to know what had I been doing. I told them the story, and they said, "Good luck, and if anybody can do it, Duball, you can!"

A few days later, I went back to the worktable and came face-to-face with the engineering task of having to wire all the movable parts in the joy stick to the corresponding moving parts of the plane. I thought, *So that's where the strong cotton thread comes into play.* The directions referred to the thread as "wire."

I ran wire from the left rudder to the left rudder pedal, which allowed the left foot to bank the plane left on application. The same thing had to be done to the right rudder and pedal. Next I ran the wires for the left and right wings and the joy stick for ascending and descending. Finally I ran an inspection check to make sure all moving parts were correctly connected. This required me to know the nomenclature of each and every part in that plane.

With all that done, I was ready to study the next chapter, which included topics on how to fly the aircraft, how to take off and land, and how to survive a crash landing, if necessary. One method of surviving a plane crash landing was to dump the fuel, aim the plane between two trees so that the wings would be torn off by the trees, thus slowing the forward momentum down, and keeping the NOSE UP!

After taking a few days off to run through the 'hood, checking out my running buddies, I was back at the worktable to tackle the last phase of the project: the written test! There were about twenty-five questions that had to be answered in detail. That took up the better part of the evening. I was ready for bed when I finally finished. I hit the sack and was up early to check and recheck my answers. Everything was ready to be mailed. I asked Mama for enough money to mail my papers off to Kellogg's Cornflakes Company.

Mama looked at me really hard like and said, "Son, I watched how diligently and earnestly you worked on your project. I admire you for that and I hate to tell you this, but winners generally are picked from certain postal zones. They all know when they see your postal zone that you are in a Black neighborhood. I pray they won't do that but feel I must warn you so that you won't be too upset when they let you down."

"Yes, Ma'am," was all I could say.

About six weeks later, I received a letter from the Kellogg people. I hesitated to open it, as I heard my mother's words in my head. I sat there for a moment or so and then opened it.

It read, "Dear Thomas, we regret that you were not chosen as a winner for the 'Learn How to Fly' contest. However, we thought you would be interested in knowing who the winners are, so we have enclosed a list of names from the Washington, DC, area. They are as follows…" They also said if I was still interested in flying lessons, I could report to the airfield and pay an Instructor a hundred dollars a lesson for eight lessons. If I successfully completed all the requirements, I would be given a certificate. I immediately got out our map of the city of Washington, DC, and checked out the addresses of each winner in the DC area. They were *all* from the White neighborhoods! Mama had been right. She'd tried to warn me, but I was glad she had not tried to stop me! Thanks, Mom! Lord knows I tried. And with the knowledge I learned about flying, I am certain I can fly on my own, if and when I ever get my hands on a Piper Cub!

I began building model airplanes and was doing a fairly good job, I thought. One day a couple of White guys approached me and said they were also model plane builders. They invited me to come by their place to spend some time with them and asked me to bring my equipment with me. I said OK and stopped by their place a few days later. They invited me in, and we sat around and talked for a while. I looked around the room and saw many model planes, but not one of them was completed. Most had the understructure and frame built, but none had been covered with the paper material that's used for the skin of the wings and fuselage. I figured they had waited for this day to do the covering of the frames, which required coating the paper skins with a substance called "dope." This dope was a volatile substance that required proper air ventilation, like an open window. It was used to shrink the paper on the frame to make the paper skin tight and smooth.

Suddenly one of the White guys got up and said, "Let's get the dope out and get started!

I yelled out, "OK!" I took out my dope and began painting my paper. But the White guys all picked up their dope and started pouring it into paper bags. I was confused, as the dope was supposed to go on the paper skin! Why were they pouring good dope into paper bags? Everybody had a paper bag except me; I was the only one in the room with a paintbrush in his hand. They all lifted the bags to their faces and buried their faces in the bags. I watched in disbelief.

Suddenly they all looked at me looking at them. "Hey, that stuff can mess your brain up!" I said.

They looked at me with their faces *flushed* and said, "Yeah! What are you waiting for? Aren't you going to join us?"

The smell of the dope was permeating the enclosed room, and I was beginning to feel sick. I quickly gathered my belongings and made a beeline for the door and some fresh air! I looked back over my shoulder as I left the room. I don't think they even noticed me leaving. So much for that scene. (Great day in the morning!)

A few days later, I decided to walk around the block to see if more Blacks were moving into the neighborhood, as I was looking to hang out. When I got to Fifteenth and C Streets, I was stopped by three Black boys who informed me that I would have to beat all three of them if I wanted to get past them! I asked if they meant all together or one at a time. They agreed to one at a time, so I squared off with the first one, and he eventually said he'd had enough. The second guy stepped forward, and in a little while he said he'd had enough. The third guy stepped forward. I was beginning to run out of steam, but my adrenaline was up, so I pushed on. I was getting some good licks in, and the third boy was beginning to stagger. I was tired but was winning. He eventually gave in, and I was pleased.

As I started to proceed down the block, a fourth boy, who had been standing on the sidelines, said to me, "Hold it! You got to fight me now."

The other three boys chimed in, "Yeah! He's with us."

I said, "I don't want to fight anymore." But they said if I didn't, they would all jump me together!

This fourth boy, I noticed, was as raggedy as a jaybird. *Everything* he had on was filthy and full of holes. He stammered badly and seemed to be severely intellectually disabled. I told him I was through fighting.

The other boys egged him on, "Yeah, Tommy, kick his ass!"

Tommy looked at me and slurring his words said, "Yyyyyyyeeahh, ah aah I'm ggggggooooonnna kkkkkkiiiiiiiick yyyyyyyo aaaaaaaaa aaaaaasss ggggggooood!"

And kick my ass he did! I didn't know where he had learned to fight like that, but he was opening everything I had closed and closing everything I had open! He was blocking *all* my punches and *hitting* me all at the same time. He was as strong as a bull.

I hastily said, "OK, OK, enough!"

"Ssssssee, ah ah ah *told you* ah ah ah ah was goooonna kkkkkkkkkick yo ass *ggggggood*!" Tommy said. They told me to turn around and go back to my own block. I obeyed.

The next day a guy named Possum (who wore football shoulder pads all day long, whether he was playing or not) knocked on the door and wanted to know if I wanted to play some football with him and some guys he had gotten together to choose up sides, so I said OK. They called him Possum because he was extremely small for his age. Though he had small hands, he could throw a perfect spiral past a city block with pinpoint accuracy. He was a phenomenon. He had gotten all the Black guys in the area together—Joe Bug Douglas (a strong runner), Benny Moore (a good lineman), June Bug (a good center), The Nose (a good catcher), Crip (though one of his legs was shorter than the other, he was a good scrapper), Billy "Kawoogi" Wiggins (a good lineman), Cigar Green (a good catcher), Ralph "The Shank" (on line), and me, "Hatchet Face," which was my nickname because of my nose. These guys became regulars, and we called ourselves the Ragaleers because not one of us had a whole uniform of any kind!

The White boys in the neighborhood played on the Metropolitan Police Boys Club of Greater Washington team. We played on the "street-between-traffic" team! The White boys from the club decided to challenge us to a game, and we accepted their challenge. We met on the triangle in front of the club at Seventeenth and Massachusetts Avenue SE at around two o'clock that Saturday afternoon. The club boys were there with full equipment and were ready to *ROMP* us. We fell out there with no equipment at all, except for Possum, who had his usual everyday shoulder pads on. He was so small that he looked ridiculous in those oversized shoulder pads. Nonetheless, Possum could throw that ball the length of that field and put it right in his teammate's hands (as he looked in the opposite direction to confuse the opposition). He was small but *mighty*!

They won the coin flip, and the game was on! They kicked off to us, Bug caught the ball, and we ran it back for a touchdown. From that moment on we scored touchdown after touchdown. The White boys were too proud to quit, so they started playing dirty by clipping and so forth. Some of us wanted to play rougher and dirtier, but Possum made us realize that we didn't need to do that. We decided to play fair and kick their butt at the same time. They never asked us to play with them again; so be it! We continued to play in the streets, dodging cars as we ran for Possum's passes, and so went the summer of '47.

CHAPTER 25

St. Cyprians: 1947 to 1948

St. Cyprians, a Catholic school for Black kids, was located at Eighth and C Streets SE, right across the street from Hines Junior High School. Of course, Hines is still there, but St. Cyprians has been demolished, and there is now a town house in its spot. Except for the wall that is still there, you would never believe a school had once existed there. We Blacks who had attended St. Vincent de Paul in Southwest Washington had to go to St. Cyprians because St. Vincent had no eighth grade, but St. Cyprians did. We finished the ninth grade at St. Cyprians in order to get into a Black senior high school in Washington, DC.

After entering the school, I was directed to my classroom by a Nun named Sister Mary Angela (a Nun with a peculiar body odor). I entered the classroom, and another older Nun introduced herself as Mother Berchman (pronounced Berkman), the Mother Superior. She had a hard, severe look about her, and I recognized her face. I remembered that Mother Berchman had been leaving St. Vincent as the Mother Superior when I started kindergarten there. The students there had named her "Bulldog Berchman," and here at St. Cyprians she was referred to as "Big John." They both suited her well.

Right off the bat, she started laying the laws of the school down to us and telling us what we had to do if we wanted to graduate. She was very intimidating. The students in the class immediately started referring to her as Big John! She walked with a swagger; it was amazing to me. The White Nuns I encountered seemed to glide across the floor, and the Black Nuns swaggered!

I began looking around the classroom, sizing up my fellow students. I can see their faces now—Anita Mayo, Joan Savoy, Rebecca Dorsey, Fred Thomas, James Murphy, Benjamin Thompson, Joseph A. Walker, Robert Young, Agnes Brown, James Young, and Walter (Dusty) Bowman.

Big John ran down the subjects we had to tackle: religion, mathematics, Spanish, French, history, and so on. Lunchtime finally came, and we were shown the boys' playground. We could not believe our eyes! The boys' playground was what was on the other side of that wall we could see when we were on the Eighth Street side with Hines Junior High behind us. The wall was as high as we were tall, so we could not see the White kids at play, and the White kids at Hines could not see our playground. We were given two balls to play with, a football and a basketball, and sent out to the YARD.

The YARD was approximately thirty feet by thirty feet and completely walled off. The turf was covered with burnt cinder ashes, and it reminded me of a prison yard. We could not see the outside world, and the outside world could not see us. If we didn't play with the ball and get our hands dirty black from the cinder ashes of the turf, then we just stood around until the bell rang for us to go back to our cell (I mean class). It was like being in one of those black-and-white Humphrey Bogart and Jimmy Cagney prison movies. It was very depressing. Three o'clock coming around was like getting a parole to be with my family before having to report back in the morning. I passed that wall recently and saw that they had sandblasted the bricks, torn the convent down, and built a town house that adjoins the wall.

Big John loved to play the complexion game. This was her theory: the lighter we were, the smarter we were. She had the light-skinned girls playing together, the brown-skinned girls playing together, and the dark-skinned girls playing among themselves. What was interesting and disconcerting to me was the fact that the girls seemed to *accept* this hierarchy.

One day we got a new girl in the class, and she was very light-skinned with hazel eyes and reddish hair. I thought Big John Bulldog was going to pee in her pants! She was so excited by the presence of Alice that she continuously called on her during class to stand up and recite the answers. The girl was not the smartest and kept giving nonsensical replies to whatever questions were asked. Mother Berchman would just go off! "Oh, isn't she an ANGEL?" Mother Berchman would say. Nobody replied.

One of the smarter girls in the class, if not the smartest, was a dark-skinned girl named Rebecca Dorsey. Rebecca was rarely called on to recite in class, but she was a straight A student. Alice (the perfect angel) would get up and rattle on for hours, it seemed, and we would just look at each and wonder what in the world was going on. All the boys were disgusted with this scene, but the girls just seemed to go along with the wickedness. Was Big John a stud or just color struck?

All the boys hated her, and she hated all the boys. There was nothing we did right! She was particularly disgusted with me because I was light-skinned and didn't try to hide my disgust for her behavior, so I was just a *cur* to her!

One day she sent two of the darker girls (Rebecca and Cecelia) on an errand (probably just to get them out of class), and they got lost and returned to class without completing the mission. Bulldog jumped on their case in a flash! She ended up saying to them that if she had sent Anita and Alice (two light-skinned girls), they would have found it! I felt so sorry for those sisters; they were almost in tears. Such was life with Big John Bulldog Berchman.

When the weather was bad, we remained inside and were allowed to play cards during our lunch hour. I noticed that the girls had three card tables and that at each table were seated girls of a different complexion. The first table was occupied by the light-skinned girls, the second was occupied by the brown-skinned girls, and the third table was occupied by the dark-skinned girls. And that's the way it was. The boys didn't play that shit, so we all sat at random tables. On one rainy day, the darker sisters were coincidentally absent from school, so Cecilia, one of the darker sisters, sat by herself while the other girls played cards with each other. The lighter-skinned girls never looked at her, and there was no invitation to join them.

Cecelia sat there for almost half her lunch hour. She eventually approached the "high-yellow" table and asked them if they would please let her join in. We could have heard a pin drop in that room at that moment! One of the light-skinned sisters, Anita Mayo, broke the ice and said, "Sure, Cecelia, have a seat." Anita told them to start a new game and deal Cecelia a hand. Anita was the only one who spoke up. Anita and Cecelia were honor roll students.

I did not interact with the boys in my class much after school because they all lived outside my neighborhood. Joe A. Walker (the author of *The River Niger* in later years) was the closest to my area, and he lived at Seventh and Massachusetts Avenue SE. We would visit each other now and then.

When I was at his house and Joe left the room, his mother came over to me and said, "Thomas, do you have any brothers and sisters?"

I looked at her face and saw this handsome woman looking into my eyes. I was taken aback because I had never really looked at her up close until then. I immediately saw myself married to her and living happily ever after (I was embarrassed for myself).

I eventually spoke and said, "I have two brothers."

"No sisters?" she asked.

"Not yet," I said. She then asked me if I was the youngest or the oldest, and I told her I was the oldest.

Mrs. Walker paused for a moment and then asked me if I looked out for my younger brothers. I said, "Yes, Ma'am, I do!"

She said, "I believe you do." She looked at me (I know I was blushing) and asked me if I would do her a great big favor.

"Sure," I said. I was mesmerized by the beauty of my buddy's mother. Her voice was velvety and rich, and my head was spinning!

Then she said, "Would you look after Joseph for me? Now you don't have to if you don't want to. I know you have two brothers to look after, and if you think you already have your hands full, I will understand!"

"No, Ma'am, I can do that for you!" In a cracking voice, I asked, "Mrs. Walker, why do you feel Joe needs looking after?"

She said, "He sometimes speaks in a way that might get him in difficulty with some of those boys at school, and I would feel so much better if I knew you would be watching his back, since I can't be everywhere."

"I understand," I said. "Don't worry, Mrs. Walker, I'll keep an eye out for any trouble, and if I don't say anything to you, then you know everything is OK!"

She smiled, put her warm, soft hand on my cheek, and said, "God bless you. You are a nice boy."

I never mentioned the conversation to Joe because she had approached me in confidence, but I was curious about *who* could have it in for Joe at school. I thought we all were getting along pretty well.

I found myself monitoring everything the guys said to Joseph, and everybody seemed to be cool. But I was talking to Walter "Dusty" Bowman once, and he started telling me that he wanted to kick Joe's ass. Dusty was a big, heavy dude with lumberjack hands. He wasn't the smartest guy I had ever met, and I could see in his eyes that he just didn't like Joe. I also saw in his eyes that he was not "wrapped too tight" either. There was some kind of deficiency present, but I couldn't define it.

We were leaving the classroom one day, and when we got to the exit door, Dusty made a smart remark to Joe, and Joe came back with a smart remark of his own. Dusty then took a poke at Joe. Joe moved his head, and Dusty *smashed* his hand into the very edge of the door. Joe laughed and walked away! Dusty's hand swelled up to the size of a basketball and he couldn't hold his pencil to write without great pain! I decided not to tell Mrs. Walker about this because I thought Joe handled the situation quite maturely. *Why worry her?*

As luck would have it, Joe invited me by his house that coming Saturday, and I said OK. A few minutes later, Dusty approached me and wanted to come by my house on Saturday. I told him I had already promised Joe I would hang out at his house that Saturday. I watched Dusty bristle up. He said to me, "How can you hang out with him? Can't you see he's crazy?"

I wanted to say, "He is not as crazy as you!" But I was cool and he was almost twice my size, so I said, "A promise is a promise!"

Dusty looked at me, grimaced, and said with a snarl, "Well you will find out soon enough!"

He turned and walked away. I said to myself, *Wow, we are barely into October of this school year, and I've got to go through this until I graduate in June?* I was not a happy camper.

While I was walking home from school one Friday afternoon, Dusty caught up with me and wanted to know what I was doing on Saturday. I dared not tell him I was hooking up with Joe Walker;

instead I said I had to run some errands for my mom and that I would be gone for most of the day. We split and went in different directions.

Saturday came, and I readied my bike for the trip to Joe's house. He lived at Seventh and Massachusetts Avenue SE, and I lived at Sixteenth and D Streets SE, so it was not a long ride—twenty minutes, at the most. Joe lived on the fourth floor, so I had to carry my bike up.

He let me in, and we sat around the kitchen table trying to think of something to do. He started talking about food, and the next thing I knew, we were planning a trip to the wharf to buy some live crabs to cook for ourselves. Way Out? No, not really, because we had seen our parents do it many times but had never done it on our own before, so this was *"High Adventure"* to us kids. We were only fourteen years old then.

Joe said, "Let's get started so that we can eat early. I'm already hungry!"

"Me too!" I said.

We got the bikes down the four flights of stairs, and straight down Eighth Street we went, past the Marine Barracks and down to the main gate of the Navy Yard, where we made a right turn on M Street. The next stop was the wharf at the end of M Street.

We scouted around a bit until we saw the ones we thought were the best buy. We had about fifteen dollars between us, so we asked the man how many we could get for that. He said he would give us two dozen crabs. When we saw how many crabs there were, we knew we had a new problem. How were we going to get all those crabs back home? The man saw the look on our faces and gave us a bushel basket with a fastened top on it.

All we had to do was put one hand on the handlebars and hold onto the basket of crabs with the other hand. The trick was not to run into each other with our front wheel. We found out this was harder than it looked as we snaked along. We ignored the horns blowing at us as we went about our mission on one of the busiest traffic routes in DC.

We had to navigate a turn at Eighth Street to make it back up to Massachusetts Avenue and then make another two-wheel turn at Massachusetts Avenue to Seventh Street. When we finally made it to the curb and out of the road, we relaxed a bit. I guessed the crabs felt some relief too!

We had to decide what to do with two bikes, one bushel of crabs, and four flights of stairs. It was a busy neighborhood. "OK," Joe said, "I'll go up with my bike, open the door, and come back to help you." That was cool, so I said, *"Mission accomplished."* We put all the crabs into a tub of water to see if it was true that crabs would pull another crab down if they saw it trying to escape. We also spent a lot of time trying to figure out which were the females and which were the males. I don't think we ever reached a conclusion.

We found his mother's big pot, filled it with water, and brought it to a boil. Then we bent two wire coat hangers into tongs and began taking the crabs from the bathtub and putting them into the big pot of boiling hot water. That became a bizarre undertaking because the crabs fought back ferociously. Some of them even jumped out of the pot after we threw them into the hot water.

Pandemonium broke out as we chased crabs around the kitchen. It seemed to be an impossible situation. We even got bitten a few times trying to retrieve the horrified, panic-stricken crabs. We finally decided that one of us would station himself at the pot to hold the lid on while the other one would retrieve the crabs. We eventually were able, after a lot of hollering and running around, to get all twenty-four crabs into that boiling pot of water.

About an hour later, we were able to sit down and eat twelve boiled crabs apiece. We parted that evening with full bellies and a high sense of accomplishment, but we never did that again. To this day, I can't forget how those crabs were struggling for their lives. I would never again take a life to eat.

I found myself juggling my time between Joe and Dusty and trying to keep them away from each other. Dusty was becoming more and more of a nuisance. He started coming by my house unannounced. He even started hanging out with the guys on my block! He was a good ballplayer, and the brothers in the 'hood didn't seem to mind him coming around.

Dusty eventually rented a room in the neighborhood so that he could be on the scene *all the time!* I asked Dusty what the hell was going on, and he said that he wasn't getting along with his family, so he moved out. He said he liked my friends better than he liked the guys in *his* neighborhood. (We all thought that Dusty was a bit unusual!)

April came, and I had a birthday. My mom brought me a nice three-speed Red Racer bike. I was tickled pink! I was all over town with that bike! Now who showed up one day but Dusty. He said he had heard that I had a new bike. He then asked me to find the receipt for the bike and let him borrow it. He asked me what store the bike had been purchased from, and I, like a dummy, told him. He said, "I'll be right back!"

A few hours later, Dusty showed up at my house with a new bike that was just like mine! I was flabbergasted! He said, "Now we can ride together!"

"How did you manage to pull that off?" I asked.

He replied that he had walked into the store, selected the bike, and headed for the door. He said, "When I got to the door, I flashed your receipt at the man at the door and walked out!" (I then had to take a good hard look at this dude!) *Wow!* This cat had a criminal mind! I was afraid to ask him anything else!

Once I realized Dusty was *really* in left field, I became concerned about the safety of my friend, Joseph A. Walker, and about my own safety as well! He was capable of skullduggery, dry-gulching, and just plain meanness! But he thought I was OK and had decided that I was the guy he was going to hang with. When I left the neighborhood, he remained behind and was friends with my friends right into adulthood. Even to this day, when I run into an old neighborhood buddy, we talk about the way-out moves that Dusty made as a teenager and wonder if he is still alive somewhere.

We were nearing the end of the school year at St. Cyprians, and I had not decided who I wanted to escort to the prom. I had a crush on Rebecca Dorsey (the smartest, the darkest, and the prettiest to me). But she had eyes for Joe Walker. Joe Walker had eyes for Joan Savoy. Joan Savoy had eyes for me. I tried to tell Joe how Rebecca stared at him and how I wanted to move on her, but she didn't see me! Joe told me she was too dark for him; he wanted to take Joan Savoy!

I looked around for alternatives. My attention stopped at Anita Mayo or Cecilia Howell. I finally mustered up the nerve to ask the prettiest, smartest, light-skinned sister in the class, Anita Mayo. I asked her who was taking her to the prom. She said nobody had asked her. I could not believe my ears!

"Nobody?" I said.

"Nobody," she said.

"Anita Mayo," I asked, "may I have the honor of escorting you to the prom?"

She smiled and said, "Certainly," and I was on cloud nine!

To save money, I walked to her house, picked her up, and hailed a cab from there, and we were off to the races. My next-door neighbor had cut some roses from her rose bed and given them to me. I presented them to Anita, and she pinned them on.

Everyone at the prom had a look of surprise and disbelief when we walked in arm in arm. The guys and the girls couldn't take their eyes off of us! I told Anita how uncomfortable I was feeling. She was very reassuring and suggested we pay the others no mind. It was then that the petals began to fall off the roses I had given her, one after the other. I was gravely embarrassed. Every girl there had flowers on, and their flowers lasted through the evening. I told Anita that my next-door neighbor had given them to me to give to her. She thought that was very nice.

When the roses were down to the last few petals, she removed the stems and placed them on the table. She was now the only girl there who had no flowers. The girls were giggling among themselves, and the guys were looking amused. I was too embarrassed to stand up. I said to her that maybe we should just leave and I could find more flowers somewhere. She looked me square in the eyes and said, "We don't need any flowers; come on, let's dance!" From that moment on, nothing mattered anymore, and we had a wonderful time in each other's company, whereas all the rest of the students seemed aloof and confused. I fell in love with Anita Mayo at that moment; she made me feel at ease. She was full of self-confidence and pride and she let it hang out. Bless her soul!

I even tried to keep the relationship going by seeing her from time to time, but I guess it wasn't meant to be. I understand she married a doctor and moved to Africa. The last I heard was that she had since passed on. Her brother, James Mayo, who has also passed on, was one of the directors of the Anacostia Museum in DC.

CHAPTER 26

The Winter Overnight Hike

Things were quiet in the neighborhood. School was out, and a lot of the cats and kiddies were sleeping later. I liked getting up early; it was like being ahead of the sounds and noise of the day. I got to set the noise level for myself. Then I could sit and think or just look stupid. One morning I woke up thinking about all this camping equipment I had and was not using. The brothers in the 'hood didn't camp out, they hung out! I missed being in the woods, ever since Ray Gordon moved away.

I suddenly got the brainy idea to join the Boy Scouts. I had heard they hung out in the woods a lot. The nearest Scout Troop for Colored guys was at the Southeast House at Fourth and Virginia Avenue SE— Troop 512, I think it was. I was told I could tell if it was a White or Black troop by the first digit "5." I jumped on my bike and rode down to talk to the Scoutmaster to see what he had to say. The troop met at the same building where I used to get my *Afro-American* newspapers to sell, but I was too young to be a scout back then. I spoke to the Scoutmaster, Mr. Tyler. He asked me if I had any experience camping. I said yes and told him my story. He gave me a handbook to read. He marked pages of stuff for me to memorize and told me to come to the next meeting and recite what I had memorized. "If you pass, you get your Tenderfoot badge and you can wear your uniform," he said.

I said I didn't own a uniform, and he said, "You don't have to buy a uniform right away. So come on back when you are ready."

When I got back to the house, I told Mama what the Scoutmaster had said. Mama said, "Son, you know I don't have the money to buy you a uniform. Maybe you can find your father and make him do something. Lord knows he needs to do *something!*"

Mr. Tyler had said I wouldn't need a uniform right away, so I decided to study for the Tenderfoot badge anyway. In the meantime I would try to find my father. I went back to the Southeast House for the next meeting and passed the Tenderfoot test. Mr. Tyler gave me my badge and saluted me. He then asked me how old I was. I told him I had just turned fifteen. He said that I needed to be a Patrol Leader and gave me more pages to memorize.

I went back to the next meeting and passed the test. He pinned a Patrol Leader pin on my shirt and said, "Since you are fifteen, you also need to be an Explorer Scout so that you can reach the next step and become an Eagle Scout for life. Here is the handbook for that."

Mr. Tyler showed me a picture of the Explorer uniform. It was a different color (dark green) and included a cocoa brown necktie, rather than a kerchief. The cap looked like the Army service cap, rather than a campaign hat. I took the manual, studied it, returned, and passed the Explorer test.

Scoutmaster Tyler then said, "Congratulations, now you must be a Patrol Leader and start a Boy Scout Patrol!" This meant I had to start my own patrol by recruiting boys in my neighborhood, so I recruited my brother Herbert, twelve, his friend Barrington Williams, my brother Roland, thirteen, and his friend Ira Austin. None of the other brothers on the block were interested. Then I had to come up with a name. We went through the pack of names that everybody had already. All of a sudden it came to me; if I was an Explorer, then I was also a Pioneer. "Let's call ourselves the Pioneer Patrol," I said.

"Yeaaah!" they all agreed.

I had to create a patrol flag with our logo on it. The logo was a raccoon hat (like the ones Jackie Gleason and Art Carney wore to their lodge meetings, with the tail attached to the back). I placed it inside a circle of red and centered it on a white field. Every patrol had to have its own flag, which was taken on all hikes, camping trips, and activities when the patrol was together.

To make everything official, we had to go on a hike so that the Pioneer Patrol members could pass their Tenderfoot requirements. It took us the better part of the summer to pull all that off. We were steadfast and pulled off the hike, passed all the skills, and built and maintained a safe fireplace. I then had to write a report on everything we had done and submit it to the Scoutmaster at the next meeting. The Scoutmaster said that we had done a nice job. He said, "*Now* a good Patrol Leader must take his patrol on a winter overnight hike before they can call themselves a *true* patrol."

"A *winter* overnight hike?" I said.

"That's right, a winter overnight hike!"

"Have all the patrols present here tonight done this?" I asked.

He said, "*Nobody* has done this yet! I have been trying for years to get them to do this, but they all shy away from doing it. You *can't* call yourself a *true woodsman* if you can't survive in the woods in winter. That is the ultimate test."

We all stood there in silence. Nobody was speaking. I felt sorry for the Scoutmaster; I could see the disappointment on his face.

Somebody just had to help this man. A Black Scoutmaster with an all-Black troop, Scoutmaster Tyler could not call the Organization of the Boy Scouts of America and tell them that his boys had been on a winter overnight hike.

I finally broke the silence in the room by saying, "The Pioneer Patrol will go on a *winter overnight hike* for the troop!"

My boys looked at me and said, "Yeah, we can do it!" I couldn't believe my ears! I had not discussed it with them; they had come to that decision on their own!

The Scoutmaster's face lit up like a Christmas tree! Though he was in his fifties, he looked like a little boy again. The Scoutmaster tried to contain himself when he said, "OK, but you must get permission slips to me from everybody's parents before I can approve the move."

I could see on the faces of everybody there that they doubted very seriously if we would attempt it. Even the Scoutmaster didn't think we were really going to try it, but I could see in his eyes that he had been praying for *somebody* to step forward for a long time. I figured we could at least try. It was for just one winter's night.

As always, we walked from Fifth Street and Virginia Avenue SE to Sixteenth and D Streets SE. We talked about the winter hike all the way home. We agreed to ask our parents. I was not optimistic about getting the parents' approval though. The next day Barrington Williams (in a brand-new Boy Scout uniform) knocked on my front door. "Hey, Thomas, my parents said I can go on this winter overnight hike," he said. I was stunned because Barrington had just moved into the neighborhood and I still had not really met his parents.

I mentioned it to Mama, and she said, "They must have a lot of respect for you, Thomas. They are entrusting you with their *only* son to sleep out in the woods on a cold winter's night. I am giving you permission to take your two brothers, so go do what you have to do, son!"

"Well if I don't hear from Ira Austin soon, I guess it will be the four of us. Ira is a nice boy but doesn't attend meetings regularly, and

I don't think he is much of an outdoors person. I decided to conduct an equipment check. We have two tents, so that's two to a tent. Four guys is a good even number anyway," I said. My brothers and I had no uniforms but were serious Scouts, and Barrington was too!

It was now shortly after Christmas 1948, and we were steadily making our plans for a January or early February (1949) hike across Chain Bridge, Virginia, to our established campground. Our spirits were running high!

January brought some very bad weekend weather conditions, so we had to postpone things until the weather broke. During the first week in February, things started looking up with some sunshine, so we decided to go camping the next weekend to pull this off. I spent the next few days checking and packing our equipment. On Friday night we met and packed up the two-day food supplies and extra clothes we might need. We were careful to pack extra socks, as we knew it was very important to keep our feet dry. We put all of our personal items, like eating utensils, clothes, and toothpaste, into our knapsacks. Eggs, meats, and other foodstuffs were put into a separate knapsack, which we would hang from a tree limb when we got to the campsite. That would help safeguard our food. I would carry the heaviest knapsack because I was the oldest. I showed the others how to roll their blankets up in their shelter and attach it to their knapsack in a bedroll style. Around 10:00 or 11:00 p.m., we were done. We planned to meet at 6:00 a.m. Barrington said good-night and headed home. He lived only a block away on D Street, near Sixteenth.

At 6:00 a.m. Barrington was at the front door. I let him in, and he, my brothers, and I immediately did an equipment check. Everything checked out, so we all strapped on our gear and headed out. The rest of the house was still asleep, so we slipped out quietly.

We headed down Fifteenth Street to Pennsylvania Avenue. Our mess kit gear and eating utensils rattling around in our knapsacks and our boots hitting the pavement were the only sounds to be heard on the streets, except for an occasional passing truck. We reached Fifteenth and Penn to see the sun breaking on the horizon. It was a cold, clear, blustery morning. The weatherman was saying it was twenty degrees outside and clear. The four of us were standing there huddled up, and nobody was talking! Barrington was the only one who had a (brand-new) pair of gloves, so he volunteered to carry our patrol flag. The rest of us had our hands jammed into our mackinaw pockets. I could see on their faces that they were questioning the *wisdom* of this whole idea! I was trying to look like I was not sharing their thoughts.

The streetcar came, and we struggled to get on board. We made a lot of noise as we moved to the rear of the streetcar, as our gear kept hitting against the poles and handles on the aisles. The Conductor was looking at us in sheer disbelief but didn't say anything.

We offloaded our gear on the wide rear seat of the streetcar and unbuttoned our coats. None of us had spoken a *word* since we left home. It was a long ride to Chain Bridge, and we seemed to be relishing that fact because the streetcar was quite warm and cozy.

We had been riding along for a little while when I decided to break the silence by saying something like, "When we get to the campsite, the first thing we gotta do is make a fire and put some bacon on!" I wanted to know how they felt about pushing on. Everybody spoke in agreement, and that started us talking again, which made me feel better. It was as if they had needed to hear that.

We were nearing the end of our streetcar ride, so we began strapping on our gear again. We moved toward the exit and stood ready to alight. The Conductor took one long, last, look at us, as if to say, "Where in the *world* do they think they are going?" He opened up the doors, and the cold outside air hit us smack in the face. We had forgotten how cold it was. We faltered for a moment but managed to all get off. The streetcar pulled off, and we caught ourselves watching it disappear into the distance. After the streetcar was out of sight, it was unnervingly quiet. There was *nobody* around anywhere! It was an eerie feeling. I looked at these daring young guys and asked, "Shall we go on?"

They all said, "Yeah, let's do it!"

"OK, follow me then!" I said.

It was around 7:30 or 8:00 a.m., and the sun was brighter. We crossed the Chain Bridge and stopped at the trading post for some refreshments before starting the long climb up to the top of the mountain to our favorite campsite.

After a hike of a few hours, we arrived at our campsite. The climb up the mountain had warmed us considerably, and we were buzzing around like beavers. We offloaded our gear and started immediately looking for firewood, only to discover the wood was all quite damp! We looked high and low for dry leaves and twigs to start a fire. We found a few pieces that were not as damp, but it was *all* a bit damp. It then dawned on me that the night air had caused the ground to be moist and that later, as the sun rose, things would be dryer—at least that's what I wanted to believe. We had exhausted about a third of our matches, so I suggested we put the fire aside for a while and concentrate on getting the two tents up and cutting up a stockpile of wood.

Herbert began to complain about his hands getting cold. I was about to tell him to keep his hands in his pockets when Barrington offered Herbert one of his new gloves. Herbert accepted and joined the search for firewood. I could not let them see my grave concern about not getting that fire started as I had planned. Everybody still seemed in high spirits, even though it was still cold. Roland and I didn't seem to have much trouble with our hands getting cold, and I was too preoccupied with the *nighttime* camp preparations to be concerned about my hands. I was also beginning to feel the awesome responsibility I had put on myself concerning the safety and well-being of the guys who had been foolish enough to follow me up there in the dead of winter.

What had the parents been thinking when they allowed me to bring these boys up here? Weren't they aware of the dangers of overexposure and the fact that no one was around for miles? They could never find us up here. We could be frozen stiff and dead for weeks before they would find us. I prayed to myself, *Oh, dear God! Don't let us freeze to death up here. I am sorry I dragged everybody into this.* I looked at them and was relieved they hadn't seen me fretting.

I was just finishing up digging the trenches around the tents when I heard Barrington screaming at the top of his lungs, "Hey, look, I got the fire started!" I could not believe my eyes! Barrington had started a fire, and I saw smoke! "Fan the fire! Fan the fire! Keep fanning until I get there!" I yelled. I took off like a bat out of hell for the campfire. The smoke was getting heavier. I yelled, "That's good, just keep on fanning! The heat will dry the leaves out, and we can lay on a twig at a time." The twigs started to burn. We added a few heavier twigs. I had one of them take a few twigs, shave them with a knife, and throw the shavings still attached to the twigs into the smoldering leaves until the fire was burning brighter. We had it going so well that we were then able to throw on a few small logs.

I grabbed Barrington and told him how he had made my day by starting that fire and how much better I felt now that I could feel the warmth of those flames! We all stood around the fire talking about how we now knew how the first man had felt when he built his first fire and felt that warmth.

We were in the midst of cracking a few jokes when Herbert screamed out, "Roland, your pants leg is on fire!" I looked at Roland's pants leg, and sure enough his pants at the knee were aflame! Roland was astounded. I smothered the flame with a towel and looked to see how much damage had been done. Roland's knee, just that fast, had swollen up into a big blister the size of a grapefruit!

Oh, Lord! I said to myself. It was our first casualty. I ran for the first aid kit and smacked some burn ointment on the knee. The blister got bigger. I hesitated and said we might have to strike camp and take Roland home. He needed to see a doctor. Roland had been quiet up until I said that. Roland said to me, "I'm not going home! I came to spend the night, and that's what I'm going to do!" We were all silent for a minute. I broke the silence by saying that maybe I could wrap it to keep it clean. I wrapped it with some gauze and tied a knot in it. I then asked Roland to walk around some to see if he had good knee movement without a lot of pain. I watched him walk. If he was in pain, he hid it from me.

I looked at everybody, and nobody was smiling!

There was a long pause, and all of a sudden, I heard all the creature sounds of the forest as the animals went about their morning. I looked at Roland; he still had a look of determination on his face. I looked at Herbert, and he was looking at me. I looked at Barrington, and he was staring straight at me. I read their faces. They were *totally* prepared to stay the course! I finally said, "Herbert, put some more wood on the fire! Barrington, do a search for more dry wood, and Roland, get the bacon an' eggs from the food stash. I'll prepare the skillet for breakfast."

Everybody broke out in big smiles and took off to do their duty. Breakfast was a gas! Everything was back on track. We went to the creek and used the sand to wash out our mess gear and the water to rinse it off. We had a good stash of firewood. The tents were all squared away, ready for whatever Mother Nature was going to throw at us. Our esprit de corps was bursting at the seams. We were completely on our own out there.

We had generated enough warmth in ourselves that we had to shed our mackinaws. We were cutting down trees and building monkey bridges across creeks. We even built a bridge where we didn't need a bridge. We blazed new trails, and I was able to have everybody pass all their Tenderfoot requirements in one day. We had a *ball*, Jim! We had completely forgotten it was winter until the sun started to set and things started getting a little chilly. At that point we headed back to the campsite.

The campfire had long gone out, so we started building another campfire. This time around it was a snap because we had stashed the stockpile near the fire so that everything was nice and dry. The sun was just below the horizon. We began preparing dinner, which consisted of baked beans, toasted frankfurters, rolls, toasted marshmallows, and hot chocolate. We pigged out!

The sunlight was just about gone, and the cold of the night was beginning to set in. We cleaned up the dishes and threw more wood on the fire. Barrington dug a hole to bury the garbage in. The rest of us ran around looking for more firewood. We had to try to keep the fire going all night, if possible! We had no radio or communication with the civilized world, so we had to follow our best judgment. We figured that since it was the middle of February and would be a long, cold night without firewood, we had to stock up or freeze our butts off!

By the time it was dark, we had a good fire going. We stood around the fire cracking on each other and wondering what was going through our parents' minds right about then. That kind of jazz went on for a couple of hours. We finally agreed to bed down for the night. Those were the days before the sleeping bag had been invented, so all we had were our little wool blankets and a cold February night.

Somebody asked if he should take off his clothes, and I suggested he sleep with his clothes on because his blanket would feel mighty thin as the night wore on. I said that everybody should take their shoes off, and when they asked why, I told them that feet needed to have plenty of space to circulate the blood and couldn't do that with boots on. We all took our boots off. I didn't really know if that was a good and wise decision, but it sounded OK! I did know that if our feet got cold with our boots on, they would never warm up. If we took off our shoes, we could warm our toes with our hands. I had had to do that already!

I could not sleep. I was worried the fire would go out and we'd wake up with frostbitten feet. I knew that I would never be able to forgive myself for dragging them out there if that happened, nor would I ever be able to explain it to anybody.

I lay there until everybody was sound asleep. I then stepped out of the tent and walked around the campsite to check on things. I went over to the fire and stoked the flames a little.

When the flames got a bit higher, I selected a log that I figured was good for two to three hours of fuel and gently laid it across the fire. I went back into my tent, wrapped myself in my blanket, and decided to lie awake for a few more hours and then throw another log on the fire.

I fell asleep before I was able to do that. When I opened my eyes again, it was dawn and the birds were chirping. I jumped up and ran out of the tent to check the fire. It was out! The ashes were cold. I panicked. I feared the worst and was afraid to look in on the others. Then I suddenly realized my feet were not frozen! It was definitely a cold winter morning. So I knew I had to get another fire started right away. Luckily the twigs we had stashed near the fire were still dry. I immediately went about getting a flame started. When the shavings and twigs began to smolder a little, I gently fanned the fire until it broke into a flame. I then looked back at the tents and listened for any movement.

They were all still asleep. I was almost afraid to look in on them but knew I needed to do it. I went to my tent first and woke up Roland. The first thing I said to him was, "Roland, check your feet!" He did and he said they were OK. I immediately went to Herbert and Barrington's tent to check on them while Roland was putting on his shoes. They were both OK and in good spirits!

WE HAD MADE IT THROUGH THE NIGHT! We all paused and gave thanks to the Creator for protecting us fools out there in the cold. The worst was over, and it was just a matter of time before we returned home triumphant!

"Let's fix breakfast!" I yelled, and everyone went for their stash. We had scrambled eggs and bacon with hot biscuits and hot chocolate. Everything tasted new and different. Our spirits were running so high

that we forgot to put our jackets on! We were running hot. We ran to the creek, scrubbed our utensils and mess gear in the sand, rinsed them off in the creek, and ran back to camp to take down our tents.

While we were packing, we talked about how shocked and surprised they were all going to be when we got back to the Boy Scout club meeting. We just couldn't wait to see the expressions on their faces as we swaggered down the center aisle with our patrol flag held high. Yeah, Jim, we were the only ones who had dared to camp in the winter! We were the Pioneer Patrol!

After everything was packed, Barrington discovered that Herbert had lost the brand-new glove his mother had given him, so he threw the other one away and said, "We don't need gloves; we are the Pioneer Patrol!" We collected the garbage and buried it. We put out the fire and buried the charred pieces. We were leaving the campsite in better shape than we had found it. It was our way of showing nature our appreciation.

I announced, "Pioneer Scout Barrington shall lead us out to the main road and call out aloud any obstacles in the trail as we proceed to the bridge." Barrington was tickled pink when I said that. And I let him carry the patrol flag because he was the only one who had on a Scout uniform. That made his day. He had earned it, as not once had he complained or hesitated to do anything I had asked. He was a model Scout, and we all dug him for it! God bless you, Barrington, wherever you are.

We crossed the bridge and waited for the Friendship Heights streetcar to DC and home. We arrived back in the neighborhood a little before sunset. We said good-bye to Barrington and watched him walk down D Street to his house. He looked back, waved, and went inside. We then turned and went inside.

Mama saw us straggling in and dropping sand all over her floor as we offloaded our gear. She asked us how it went, and we all said, "FINE!" Then she noticed the big hole in Roland's pants leg. "What happened there?" Mama said in alarm. I had forgotten about the leg! Roland and Herbert fell silent. I said, "We were all standing around the fire when a spark fell on Roland's pants leg and began to burn his knee—"

Before I could say more, she grabbed his pants leg and pulled it up to see this burned knee. "There is no burn here," she said. We all looked down at the same time. Sure enough, the burn was gone! We were dumbfounded. "Well I guess we will have to throw those pants away, but at least you were not injured," she said.

She smiled and asked if we wanted some dinner. We all said yes, so she said, "Then go clean up, and it will be ready by the time you are done." I don't remember what it was we ate, but it was a meal "f'real"!

Before I turned in that night, I decided to write out my report in the logbook while things were fresh in my head. I described in detail everything we had done from the time we hit the trail until the time we got back home. I particularly gave note to Scout Barrington for getting the campfire going. I reported how each Scout had been able to pass all his requirements to be a Tenderfoot, and they were now all qualified to wear their Tenderfoot badge and their overnight winter hike's merit badge. I felt we had accomplished a lot. I fell asleep smiling.

Wednesday finally arrived. There was a knock at the door. It was Barrington, on time and in his cleaned and pressed uniform, campaign hat on, with the string tightened under his chin and all. On his face was the biggest, broadest smile I have ever seen on a twelve-year-old. I called to Roland and Herbert, and we left for the meeting.

As we were walking away from the house, Barrington came to me and said, "What did your mother say when she saw Roland's burned knee? I bet she flipped out then!"

I giggled and said, "When I showed her the knee, the burn was gone."

"Wha'd you say?" he asked.

I said, "The burn was not there."

"Wait a minute," said Barrington, "that burn was the size of a tennis ball. What do you mean it wasn't there?"

"It disappeared," I said.

Barrington was in complete disbelief. He went over to Roland and made Roland pull up his pants leg. Barrington's mouth dropped as he looked at the spot where the nasty burn had been. In amazement he said, "What about the hole in the pants leg?"

"The hole in the pants leg was still there," I said, "but the burn was gone." Barrington straightened up and was silent for a while. We all just stood there for a moment, looking at Barrington. The look on his face was one of, "I have just seen a miracle!"

"Thomas, how can that be? We treated that wound!" he said.

"Yeah, and I worried myself to death about infection. I guess the Good Lord saw we could use a little help," I said, "so he helped a little. So let's give thanks to God for helping us pull this off."

"Yeah right!" everybody said.

I said, "Now let's move on before we are late for our grand entrance with Troop Five Twelve."

It was the day of the monthly Scout meeting. It was the day all the Scouts in Troop 512 put on their uniforms and neckerchiefs and pranced around the Southeast House, fronting for the girls. What a handsome sight they thought they were. These dudes had been going to these gatherings for years and had never been on a winter hike, let alone an overnight winter hike. But they had the cleanest uniforms around and the shiniest shoes. They even cracked on our homemade patrol flag. Everybody else had professionally made official patrol flags, such as the Fox Patrol, the Wolf Patrol, the Raccoons, and so forth. We'd wanted something outside the standard stuff, so we'd come up with the Pioneer Patrol. The Boy Scouts of America had no Pioneer Patrol, so there was no official flag for us. Scoutmaster Tyler said we should make our own, so that's what we did. To Troop 512, we were a rag-tag oddity. But to the Scoutmaster, we were his hope.

We had to walk from Sixteenth and D Streets SE to the Southeast House at Fifth and Virginia Avenue SE, which was about a twenty-block walk. When we got to Fifth and Virginia Avenue, we paused to compose ourselves for the grand entrance. I gave Barrington the Pioneer flag, because he had a uniform on and he made the flag look more dressed and official. We formed a single line, and Barrington led us in down the center aisle. We could not help but notice that all the seats were taken except for those in the front row. Barrington did not look right or left. He went straight for the chairs in the front row. I was proud of him. We followed him to the chairs and all sat down in unison.

For the first time *ever*, there was complete silence in that hall. You could have heard a pin drop. We were sitting right in front of the Scoutmaster. He looked at us and smiled. We all stood up on his command, said the oath of allegiance, and then sat back down. He called the meeting to order. The Scoutmaster called out to each Patrol Leader to give his report. They all had nothing of any real significance to report. He then called out to the Pioneer Patrol. "Pioneer Patrol, do you have anything to report?"

I stood up and said, "Yes, sir! The Pioneer Patrol went on a winter overnight hike this past weekend."

MR. TYLER JUMPED TO HIS FEET. "What did you say?"

"I said the Pioneer Patrol has just returned from a winter's overnight hike."

For a moment everything stood still. Then Mr. Tyler said in a loud and gleeful voice, "Did you really do it?"

"Yes, sir," I said. He wanted to hear all the details! We had his attention for the rest of the meeting. Mr. Tyler, a man of middle age, was acting like a twelve-year-old. We gave him all the details. He asked me if I had kept a log. I said yes and gave it to him.

He looked at me and said, "Now I can finally send something to those Whites up at Headquarters in Bethesda. This report will be recorded in the logs of Troop Five Twelve as having met the requirements for knowing how to survive in the wilderness in winter. I have been trying to impress upon these so-called Scouts here that you can't call yourself a 'woodsman' until you have spent at least one winter night in the wilderness. *Anybody* can take a hike in the summertime. At last, after years of trying to qualify this troop, somebody has done it."

Scoutmaster Tyler called us up and pinned the Tenderfoot badge on Roland, Herbert, and Barrington. He then turned to me, promoted me to "Explorer Scout," and said, "Now you will have to buy a uniform and prepare yourself to be an Eagle Scout." *Wow!* I thought. *Now where am I going to get money for a uniform?*

CHAPTER 27

Life after the Hike

I know what, I'll get me a paper route! I thought. If I could make ten bucks a week, I could have uniform money in a couple of weeks. The first thing Monday morning, I went around to the neighborhood newspaper stations—the *Evening Star, The Washington Post,* and the *Times Herald.* They all told me they did not hire Colored boys. I was crushed. I didn't want to ask Mama because she was struggling just to put food on the table. However, I guess she knew that I would eventually ask.

I tried to pick the right time and the right place. There was no such thing. I eventually came out with it one day when my brothers were not present. She said exactly what I had heard in my mind: "Son, you know I have lost my job and they are only giving a small benefit check, which barely pays for the telephone bill. If I buy you one, your two brothers will want theirs. Maybe you can find your father or something; surely he could do *something*!"

"OK, Mom." I replied. Mama had had a pretty good job working at the Bureau of Engraving as a Press Supervisor. Her job was to see to it that the money-making machines did not stop printing that money. She eventually developed asthma from the paper dust in the place. When it became chronic, they laid her off. Even though she had been there for some years, they said she did not qualify for any retirement benefits. They could give her only what she had put into the plan, which didn't amount to much.

Mama, trying to think creatively, came up with the idea that maybe she could open up a coffee and sandwich shop! She found a place over on New York Avenue NE. It was located on the corner across from a large Greyhound Bus garage on New York Avenue NE. She made a deposit on the place and renamed it "Connie's Cozy Corner." Shortly after her grand opening, Mama's condition worsened, and she could no longer run the shop. She tried to hire help, and the help stole supplies. She tried to use relatives who were unemployed. They couldn't keep their hands out of the cash register, so she gave up on it.

I did find my father, and he did help, eventually. I was even able to unite Mom and Dad for a short spell. He was a kind, gentle, and loving father. But he just could not stay on the wagon for more than a week or so. It was like watching Dr. Jekyll and Mr. Hyde! The more he drank, the worse the rage. He drove everybody crazy. He would spend his whole paycheck on drinks and cards. Mama begged him to leave, so he did. Poor Daddy was a prime example of that old American saying, "Don't give an Indian firewater!" I think it made everybody crazy. It set your brain aflame! It was great seeing Dad for a couple of weeks though. We all regretted that he could not turn his life around.

Life had to go on, and things around here slowly got back to normal. There was no more camping or playing Scout for me; I was back on the block hanging out.

Somebody said they saw a Colored guy delivering the *Times Herald* newspaper door to door. "They are hiring the brothers now?" I asked. "That's what I heard," somebody said.

Well, the next day I decided to check it out. I visited the paper station and spoke with the Manager. He was about to tell me there were no routes available when one of the boys there said, "He can take over my route because I'm leaving in two weeks."

"How lucky you are!" the Manager said. "OK, Tom, you meet Mike here Monday morning, and he will take you around and show you the ropes. You also must meet Mike here on Thursday through Saturday nights so that you can meet all the customers face-to-face."

Mike took me around to introduce me to his customers, most of whom were Black. I asked Mike if he had had any trouble with collecting. He said all the customers paid their bills and some of them tipped. Mike said that he had built the route from just seventy-five customers to now ninety-eight customers. He added, "I can guarantee that you will be able to pay your bill on your first night of collecting and never later than Saturday. I always pay my bill on Thursday. You will have no problem."

"Thanks, Mike," I said. *Wow! What a stroke of luck,* I said to myself. "By the way," I asked Mike, "why are you quitting such a nice route?"

"Because I am going to work for the *Evening Star* newspaper. I'll be making more money there."

"Oh, I see," I said. The *Evening Star* was the paper that had stated it had no intentions of hiring Black delivery boys now or ever. The conversation got a little strained after that.

On Sunday morning at 5:00 a.m., I had to pick up my Sunday papers. I had to lug ninety-eight Sunday papers without a wagon, as Mike had taken his wagon with him. When stacked on top of each other, the papers stood eight feet off the floor. I knew I couldn't deliver them without a wagon and asked the Manager if there was a wagon I could use. He said, "No. You can order one if you have the money. Otherwise, take as many as you can carry and make several trips back and forth." I had to make three trips to the route area, which meant I had to walk from Sixteenth and E to Twelfth and C, where the route began. Then I had to walk up Twelfth Street to the park and down Twelfth Street into Walter Street, doing both sides of the street. Finally I had to walk around C Street to Fifteenth Street. If I had had a wagon, I could have completed the job in about forty-five minutes; instead it took me more than three hours! My back was killing me, and my legs ached. If I was going to do this thing, it was going to be in a wagon.

It was Thursday evening, which was Collection Day. At seven thirty I was out the door. I started on C Street, where there were mostly Black customers. I went to each house on the block, on both sides of the street. They all told me the same thing: "Come back next week!" I turned the corner and worked my way up Twelfth Street and down the other side. Most of those customers were White, and they had their money ready when I rang the bell. Blacks lived on the block too; they were more middle class and paid on time. I arrived back at the station with just enough money to pay half my bill. This was not good. Most of the Blacks told me to come back next week. I went to the homes of those who had not answered the door on Thursday. Those who answered the door said, "Come back next week." I was able to scrounge together enough money to pay my weekly bill but was not able to collect money for myself.

This routine went on week after week for several months. The majority of my customers were Black, and they did not seem to be willing to pay a Black paper boy.

I registered complaints to the Manager and asked him to please contact these customers and speak on my behalf. He wouldn't do it and kept saying for me to keep trying. After about six months of this, I decided to take matters into my own hands. I threatened my customers that I would cut off the paper if they did not pay me. They just looked at me and said, "So cut it off then!" I started cutting them off. My route went from ninety-eight papers to seventy-five papers in about six months' time.

Now I had the Manager's attention. "Thomas, what's going on here?" he asked.

I said to him, "I asked you to help me by calling these people and asking them about the money they refused to pay me, and nothing happened. So I decided to take matters into my own hands. I have been serving this route more than six months and have yet to collect my share of the money. I don't mind getting up at five in the morning to serve someone who respects what I'm trying to do. Everybody who works all week gets paid at the end of that week but me, the Black paper boy."

"Well, you've got to pay your bill first, Tom. That's the rule," he said.

I decided to come up with my own plan. If I collected $20, I would give them $15 and myself $5. They said that I was stealing money from the paper company and if I persisted in doing so, I would be fired for embezzlement. I told them I was not going to work week after week and not have a dollar in my pocket for myself. Then I just quit!

I decided to make a poem up about being a paper boy:

> Now I need not set my clock.
> There's no more "paper route."
> Now I'm back on the block
> And just "hanging out."

Even though things were getting rough at home and Mom was not doing well, she was able to scrounge up enough money for me to finally buy an Explorer Scout uniform. I couldn't seem to find gainful employment, and school was about to start. I was not mentally or financially prepared to go back. I hadn't even chosen a school.

One day a friend of mine came by the house to talk to me about high school. His name was Alexander Jones, and he was a tall, slender, dark-brown-skinned, intelligent, good-looking dude. I decided to ask Mama what high school she had attended. She said she had wanted to go to Dunbar, but because she was dark-complexioned, she had had to go to Cardoza. (DC had four Black co-ed high schools with all-Black teachers: Cardozo, Dunbar, Armstrong, and Phelps.) "Is that the truth, Ma?" I asked. She said, "Would I lie to my children?"

Alexander came back to see me that night to talk me into going to Dunbar with him. Alex was as Black as an ace of spade. I told him the story my mother had just told me, and he replied, "Yeah, but they can't get away with that anymore! That's why I am going there. I want you to be with me when I go. Plus, they have a swimming pool there, and I want to be a swimmer!"

"Yeah," I said, "I got a good reason to go there too. I want to go out for football."

"Football?" Alex said. "Man, you don't want to do that! As skinny as you are, you don't need to be in any contact sport. In swimming you have your own lane, and if anybody crosses into your lane, that person is immediately disqualified. Nobody touches anybody," he said.

"Yeah, you've got a good point there," I replied. Off we went to enroll. God bless your soul, Alex, wherever you are.

We had plenty to talk about every day after school, as the complexion thing was still alive and well, though not so much among the boys as it was among the girls. The light-skinned sisters greatly outnumbered the darker sisters and seemed to be running things. But the darker sisters were smart and focused on their books. I saw my mother in their faces and was bursting with pride.

It was HOMECOMING time, and all the light-skinned girls were campaigning to be the "Queen of Dunbar." From what I was told, there had never been a dark-skinned Queen in Dunbar's history. I was "boiling" inside. I kept seeing my poor mother in this environment. My heart was hurting. I started talking to the boys in school to find out who the "smartest" girl scholastically was. A few days later, word got back to me that it was Betty Armstrong, a straight-A+ student all her life. I was pleased. I took a class with her. She was a chubby, girlish, extremely pleasant, pretty, dark-brown-skinned sister who was always smiling. She also had short hair, which I loved.

As God is looking down, this sister will be Queen, I said to myself. I was so pleased with this sister that I immediately launched a campaign to promote the fact that a queen should be selected on her scholastic achievements and personality, in that order! It caught on like wildfire among the male students. And the girls (at least those who looked like Betty Armstrong) were pleased to hear this from the male student body.

Because of my instigating, Betty Armstrong won hands down. She was beaming! Not in her "wildest dreams" was the expression she had on her face as she took her position in front of everyone. My heart soared.

Things got worse for me at school. The light-skinned girls found out who had instigated this upset. I was feeling the pressure. I couldn't get a girlfriend but didn't care at the moment, because I felt my mother had been vindicated through me. Perhaps that was the *"Divine Providence"* I'd heard older people talk about.

Alex Jones and I were lucky enough to land in Mr. Penderhughes's class together. He taught physical hygiene and was the Coach of the swimming team. Twice a week we got swimming lessons, naked. That's right, we were not allowed to wear trunks. Mr. Penderhughes said swimming trunks carried germs. Friday was co-ed day at the pool, so we had to put on our trunks on Fridays. Fridays were a gas, because no other sport that I know of had a co-ed day in swimsuits!

Mr. Penderhughes announced that he was taking applications for the swim team. Our big day had finally arrived. Alex and I jumped right on it. The day of the tryouts came, and we were told what it was we must do. We first had to tread water for three minutes. The Coach looked at me as I stepped forward and said to me, "DuVall, are you sure you can do this?"

"Oh, sure," I said. He knew that I had just barely learned to swim but that I wanted to be on the team.

"OK, DuVall, in the water. You must tread water for three minutes, nothing less."

I jumped into the pool. I decided to tread water for at least ten minutes, just to really impress him. When I started to tire, I figured I must have been treading for a good ten minutes but decided to tough it out for a few more minutes just for the hell of it. When I could no longer go on, I painfully pulled myself out of the pool and lay there for a while, trying to catch my wind. Mr. Penderhughes walked up and said to me, "Why did you get out of the pool?"

I looked up at him and said, "You only wanted three minutes, right?"

Mr. Penderhughes looked at his watch and said, "According to my watch, you were only in the water for forty-five seconds. So you can get back in there or come back in two days and try again."

"I'll be back in two days," I said, panting. I struggled to my feet and staggered away. I met up with Alex and told him I hadn't passed the test. Alex had passed and was to do the laps test next. He was really elated, as he truly wanted to be on that swim team.

Two days later I was back at the pool. I reported to the Coach, who looked at his watch and said, "OK! Jump in, DuVall." I jumped in, determined to tread water for at least fifteen minutes. That way I knew I would have cleared the three-minute minimum. I treaded and treaded. I was committed to ensuring I would not have to do the test again. I had been out there for a while and my arms were beginning to tire, but I was going to stay there until I couldn't tread another stroke. After what seemed like several hours in the water, I could no longer tread, so I desperately reached for the edge of the pool and tried to pull myself up. My arms wouldn't allow me to lift myself, so I clung to the side of the pool and rested for a moment.

I eventually pulled myself out and stumbled over to where the Coach was standing. He looked at me, looked at his watch, and said,

"Well, DuVall, you are improving; you were in the water a full minute." I was blown away! I couldn't believe I had not even been in the water for five minutes, let alone fifteen.

Mr. Penderhughes said, "Next test will be in two days, DuVall, if you want to try again." Then he turned and walked away. I had to find a seat somewhere and think about what had just happened. It was like a bad dream!

Two days later I was back in front of the Coach. Mr. Penderhughes said, "DuVall, you are back? OK, jump in when you are ready." I jumped in. My attitude was one of ambivalence because I had already flunked twice in attempting to increase my speed and couldn't seem to get past the one-minute mark, let alone three minutes. I figured I would just stay out there as long as I could, and that was it.

While I was treading water, I was looking at all the other guys doing laps around the pool. I saw Alex, and he gave me the high five as he came past me. He knew I was having difficulties but pretended that he didn't know, so I pretended too. I pretended I was going to stay out there for at least half an hour.

Some time had passed, and the team members began leaving for the day. The pool was almost deserted, and the only sound I heard was me splashing around. The Coach had not looked at me once all evening. I was moving slower, the water was up to my lips, and I was spitting water and gasping. I decided that that was it. There was no way he was going to tell me I had not been in the water for more than three minutes. I laboriously pulled myself out of the pool and stumbled up to the Coach. I was too tired to stand still and panting like hell. The Coach looked at me with a straight face and said, "Well, DuVall, you are improving. You were in the water exactly one minute and twelve seconds!" (This may be a perfect example of how anxiety can warp real time.) He looked at me and his face took on a fatherly look.

"Tell you what, DuVall, because you have shown such determination, I will allow you to move on to the next test, which is that you must be able to swim twenty-five laps around the pool," said the Coach. I looked at the pool, and all of a sudden, it seemed like it was a mile long and half a mile wide! Twenty-five laps seemed like twenty-five miles to me right. I swallowed hard and said in a cracking voice, "Gee, thanks, Coach, I won't let you down!"

The following week I was there to start those laps. Alex was there; he was shaking my hand when the Coach yelled, "Everybody in the water." We all took off in a counterclockwise circle around the pool. There was a blind student who also was trying out for the team; his name was James Green. Mr. Penderhughes believed in equal opportunity. It was Tuesday, the swim team and tryouts were meeting tonight. The grind was on. We met twice a week. I began to notice some of the guys faltering. Alex Jones and James Green were both having problems. Green was having a serious problem staying in his lane as he swam. Because he was blind, he could not tell when he drifted out of his lane. Mr. Penderhughes was a clever person. He gave Green all the time in the world to get it together. My friend Alex had a different problem. His problem seemed to be one of speed. He had the strokes and the rhythm, but everything seemed to be in slow motion!

The day arrived when the Coach called Jones and Green out of the lineup. I felt bad. They had tried so hard. I did not see Alex much after that; he just sort of faded away.

Alex's reason for coming to Dunbar had been to swim, but he hadn't made the team. I had come to be with Alex and was on the team! Life certainly was contrary. I couldn't believe that I was standing there with such heavies as the Featherstone Brothers, freestyler Jim Cook, and Tatum. Wow, I wish I could remember everybody's name! In one year I went from learning how to swim to coming in fourth in a city competition. We were only allowed to compete with each other, not against the White high schools.

Mr. Penderhughes was the only male teacher I got along with. I was having problems with all the other male teachers. They didn't like me, and I didn't like them. I tried to set up my classes with female teachers. They didn't exude this EGO thing in my face and seemed to be more caring.

Shortly after I made the team, I was called into the office of the Commander of the Cadet Corps. He told me that I had to buy a cadet uniform and take a year of military training if I expected to graduate. I asked if I had a choice in the matter, and the Captain said, "NO!" But I didn't need military training. I owned an FM 22-5 (Army field manual). I had memorized the entire book. The Commanding Officer looked at me and said, "If you don't buy a uniform and report for military training Monday morning at 7:00 a.m., you will never graduate from here. Now dismiss yourself."

I went home and told Mama what had just been said to me. She said I should talk to some of the boys in the neighborhood who might have a uniform and see if they would be willing to sell their uniform to me. I did that and found somebody who was about my size. The uniform had been sold and resold so much that it was a bit frayed around the edges. I priced a new uniform and found out a new one cost as much as a silk tuxedo. It did not make sense to buy a new one for just one year of this foolishness, so Mama bought the hand-me-down.

I reported to duty at 7:00 a.m. Monday morning. The Lieutenant was a brash senior whom they had promoted. He was entitled to wear a saber, which he used to *whack* guys across the ass if they made a mistake or misinterpreted a command he had given. I was of special interest to him because I was *new* in his company, yet I seemed to know all the drill commands and was able to execute them. This pissed him off, as it gave him no reason to *whack* me with his saber.

One day I misunderstood something he said. His face lit up like a Christmas tree. He immediately drew his long shiny saber and headed for me. When he reached me, I was holding my ten-pound Springfield .003 rifle as if it were a baseball bat. He stopped dead in his tracks and said to me, "What do you think you are doing?"

I said to him, "If you whack me with that saber, I'm whacking you with the butt of this weapon."

"I'm reporting you to the Commanding Officer!" he said.

I said, "You do that." He did that, and I was called before a review board on charges of insubordination. When I told them I had only been trying to defend myself, they said I was guilty as charged and they were going to write up charges on me that would prevent me from graduating on time. I was then dismissed with a warning.

The only *good* thing that came out of the incident was the fact that I had at least thirty or so witnesses to his behavior, and some of these cadets *eventually* came forward and started registering their complaints. However, my charges were dated before the barrage of complaints, so the charges against me *stood.* (If they were rescinded, they did not notify me of it.)

I was getting sick of that school. I'd never liked Dunbar's colors (red and black) anyway. I refused to wear color combinations that upset my stomach, like purple and yellow or red and black. Armstrong High School colors were easy on my stomach, so while everybody at school was wearing their Dunbar sweaters, I was wearing BLUE AND ORANGE. For years everybody thought I was an Armstrong student (Dunbar's rival).

I also had a problem with my two electives. I was told I was free to choose two courses I'd like to take. "OK," I said, "I would like to take Spanish and Typing." The student interviewer looked at me and said, "You cannot take Typing, because we know you just want to get in there with those *girls!* I have seen your *type* before!" I could not convince her that I really wanted to learn how to type. She refused to admit me. She looked at my record and saw that I was from a Catholic school, so she decided that I needed *more* Latin, not Spanish. But nobody I knew spoke Latin.

"I can't communicate with anybody I know in Latin," I said. "I have a minimum of *nine years* of Latin already; I need a change." She mumbled something about how they knew what was best for me, so I never got to *"elect"* anything.

I managed to finish my second year with an F in Latin. I wanted no more Latin, so I taught *myself* to speak Spanish just so I could feel better about myself.

And for the record, Dunbar lost the drill team competition to Armstrong High. I was so tickled that I shed my cadet uniform and put on my beautiful blue and orange sweater.

I want to thank Ms. Whitehead, my Chemistry Teacher; Ms. Brown, my English Teacher; Ms. Williams, my Geometry Teacher; Mr. Penderhughes, my Swimming Teacher; and last but not least, Ms. Cunningham, my Art Teacher, for making me understand what I still practice today. God bless all of you, wherever you all are.

CHAPTER 28

Back on the Block

Summer came, and I was back on the block and hanging out. My seatless Red Racer bike had been stolen. Funny, when the neighborhood had been predominantly White, there had been no stealing going on that I can remember. Now everything had to be kept under *lock and key*.

One of the guys we called "Nose" (because he had a big nose) said to me, "Hey, Hatchet Face, do you still have your camping equipment?"

"Yeah, why?" I said.

"Well maybe you could take us out on a hike one day?"

"It's OK by me, if you want to do it," I said. Nose said he would find out who would be interested and get back to me.

A few hours later, Nose was back with a list of names. "Hey, Hatchet Face, I got some guys ready to go!"

"Who are they?" I asked.

He named himself, Kawoogi Williams, Bug Douglas, Crip Hopkins, the Shank, and June Bug. *That's the whole gang,* I said to myself, except for lover boy Linwood, the neighborhood Casanova. "OK, set up a Saturday morning, and I'll ready up the gear," Nose said. We agreed on the next Saturday. At the last minute, Linwood threw in his hat.

The guys I hung out with were between the ages of fifteen and eighteen and had never spent any time in the woods at all; they were strictly neighborhood dudes who had never been off the block except to go to a movies or something. I had to show them everything from how to pack and carry a knapsack to how to start a fire. They were thrilled to death. We had a ball, and they did everything I instructed them to do.

We had some time to explore our surroundings, and Linwood suggested that we try to scale the side of the cliff that was above the campsite overlooking the Potomac River. We were about a good fifty to sixty feet above the river on the face of the cliff when Linwood grabbed hold of a large rock and the thing gave way and started a landslide. Everybody below him started getting hit with rocks. They were crying out in pain, and some were bleeding from the head. I was becoming unnerved because of what was happening and began to fart like crazy each time I started to speak. I did manage to say, "Nobody move until we find a secure foothold." Everybody stood still. It seemed like everything we touched was loose soil. We could not go up and we could not go down.

I looked down at the river below and saw a gathering of White folks looking up at these crazy monkeys clinging to the side of a cliff for dear life. I think a few of them were even taking bets on whether we would all fall into the river or not.

By the grace of God, we were able to ease our way down to the river's edge slowly and carefully, but not without more casualties.

We kept getting hit on the head and shoulders by rocks that had been loosened by the person above us. It took us the better part of the afternoon to get down. We could tell from the faces of some of the Whites looking on that they were disappointed that we'd been able to escape disaster and embarrassment.

All and all the guys had a great time and were soon able to laugh at what we had just come through. That evening we packed up our gear and headed back to civilization. The next day they were already planning the next hike.

They had decided on the Saturday two weeks from then. I said OK and went home. The next message I got was that the guys wanted to take some girls on the next hike. I told them I was against taking girls on a camping trip for fun. They were all taken aback by this statement! Everybody wanted to know why. I told them that being in the woods was not the same as a picnic. I told them there were chores that must be taken care of and that girls were not trained for such work. There was a lot of manual labor involved—pitching tents, cutting down trees, building fires, and so on. "Hey man, are you gay or something?" someone said. "What have you got against taking girls to the woods?"

"OK, bring your girlfriends, if you wish; maybe I'm wrong," I said.

Two Saturdays later the guys showed up ready to go with their girlfriends. I distributed the gear to the guys, they strapped on their gear, and we headed for the Chain Bridge area. We arrived at the campsite, and I assigned chores to the guys. In the meantime I told two guys to put up one tent while I put up the other. I asked Nose to help me with the other tent. I asked two others to gather firewood and start the campfire.

The guys with girlfriends decided that they were going to take their girls with them as they looked for wood. I started clearing the area and putting my tent up. I threw my gear into the tent and dug a

ditch around it in case of rain. I got to where the campfire was supposed to be and saw that there was no campfire. I looked around for
some wood to start a fire with, but there was no wood to be found.
I decided to go on my own search for wood because I was getting
hungry and wanted to start a fire. I finally got a fire going and figured
that the guys and the girls who'd gone on the wood detail would soon
show up with a bundle of wood.

They were gone a long time, and when they did come back to
the campsite, the only thing they had in their hands was each other's
hands. "Where's the firewood I sent you after?" I asked. They just
laughed and said, "Oh, we forgot the wood!"

I looked around for June Bug and realized he had jumped into *my*
tent with his girl. He never did put *his* tent up. I asked him again if he
would please put up his tent so that I could get into my tent. His answer
was that he would be out in a minute. The fire was beginning to die,
and there was no wood. Everybody was paired off but me. I knew that
if I wanted a fire going I would have to find some firewood. After all,
the fire was my idea; they had their love to keep them warm. I was
gone for a spell, gathering wood and rebuilding a fire. I looked over to
where June Bug was supposed to pitch the other tent and saw the tent
still lying on the ground. June Bug was still in *my* tent with his girl.

It was now well into the afternoon, and the sun was getting lower
in the sky. I had been gathering firewood all day and trying to cook the
meals. They came over, ate, and walked away, leaving dirty dishes and
trash all about the area. Because the eating utensils were mine, I was
expected to clean them, so I did. The girls had done positively nothing
all day except enjoy all the attention their boyfriends were showering
on them. I was getting tired of trying to keep things going and wanted
to take a break.

I went over to my tent to stretch out for a minute. I opened the
tent to crawl in and couldn't get in. Now there were *two* guys and
two girls in my tent hugging and kissing. I was losing my cool. I

started taking down my tent with them still inside! I took the tent, rolled it up, and started packing my gear. June Bug, who was lying on the ground with the sun shining in his face, said, "Hey, man, why are you doing this?"

"I have decided to pack up and go home. You all can stay here as long as you wish, but I am going home." With that said, I shouldered my gear and headed for the trail back home. I glanced back at the campsite and saw everybody grabbing their stuff and struggling to catch up with me.

I didn't look back again until I heard all this *screaming* and name calling. I could not help but look back. I could not believe my eyes! Two of the girls were fighting like cats and dogs! The guys were just standing there, watching and looking dumbfounded. I was so upset that all I wanted to do was continue on my way, but things were getting worse, and nobody seemed to be able to do anything to stop them. I turned around and went back to the trouble spot. They were pulling hair and scratching to beat the band! I stepped between the two girls and pushed them apart. I then turned to the men and said, "I am embarrassed by this behavior. We are on private land, and we are the guests of the people who own this land. I have been coming out here for the past four or five years with no problem. Now I've got more than I can deal with."

I asked Nose what in the world had happened. Nose said that one of the guys, June Bug, had been caught kissing the wrong girlfriend! I approached June Bug for an explanation. He said, "Aw, man, I broke up with that chick before the hike, and my new girlfriend didn't believe me. So she started calling the old girlfriend names, and so forth and so on." I turned and walked away. This time I didn't care what was going on back there; I was not looking back again.

I had reached the streetcar line when they caught up with me. There was complete silence as we waited for the streetcar. As a matter of fact, they were quiet all the way back home. They realized that what

I had predicted would happen had happened, so nothing could be said. But what they should've said was that they were sorry they had made things hard for me.

That ended the hiking and camping with the gang and their girl-friends. But we did everything else together, so things were back to normal.

I was back on the block and just hanging out!

PART II

CHAPTER 1

Got t' Git a Job

Things were getting worse at home, and poor Mama was beginning to show signs of wear and tear. I decided that I must find a way to bring some money in to help Mama and my brothers and little sister. The better paper routes still were not hiring Colored guys as delivery boys, so I figured maybe I could join the Army. All I needed was Mama's signature.

That night I approached Mama with my plan. I said, "Mom, I got a great idea! I want to enlist in the Army. Yeah, Ma! I already know how to pass Basic Training. I have it all memorized."

Mama had to sit down. She said, "Son, you mean to say to me that you want to drop out of high school?"

I said, "Mom, you know and I know that I have just lost interest in Dunbar. You can finish high school in the military now, and the biggest plus is that you need my help. I am the oldest of your sons. Mama, just think, there would be an allotment for you. That alone can pay the house rent for you, Mama."

Mama looked at me hard and tried to hold back the tears I saw in her eyes. She said she was still against the idea of my dropping out of school. "But it sounds like your mind is made up," she said.

The Recruiting Officer said I should bring my birth certificate and health papers. I was concerned because I would be turning only sixteen soon, and the minimum age to join the Army was seventeen. I mentioned all of this to my mother. Mama paused, took a deep breath, exhaled, and said, "There is no birth certificate, son."

"No birth certificate? Wow! What do I do now?" I said. "What happened? Why don't I have a birth certificate?"

There was a long pause, and then she said, "The doctor I was seeing was killed in an automobile accident and never made it to the board of health. I did not know about this until years later," she said.

The room was quiet. I spoke first. "How can a guy go through life without a birth certificate? What do I do now, Ma?"

She said, "We will have to get a lawyer to draft an affidavit stating that I am your mother and that you're seventeen years old."

A week after my sixteenth birthday, I had an affidavit stating that I was seventeen. I put on my Explorer Scout uniform and caught the trolley car over to Ninth and Pennsylvania Avenue NW to the Armed Forces Recruiting Station with my affidavit and health papers in hand. They gave me a physical, and I flunked it. They said I had alum in my urine, so I needed to see a doctor. When I got back home, I told Mama what had happened, and she said, "Just drink a can of beer tonight, and go back there tomorrow. You just need to flush your kidneys before you take the urine test."

I did that and the next day I was back. I passed the physical and the mental test. I was sitting there waiting for the other shoe to fall when a guy came into the room with this highly impressive-looking version of the Army uniform and started talking about how great it was to be a Paratrooper. He had a white scarf around his neck and white laces in his boots (which were so shiny I could see my reflection in them). Then he said something that caught my attention. He said he got paid extra money for jumping! I asked him how much extra, and he said fifty dollars a month. The Army base pay was only seventy-five dollars a month, so that would almost doubling my salary! "Where do I sign up for this?" I asked.

The Recruiting Officer said, "First you must go through thirteen regular weeks of Basic Training, then we send you to Fort Benning, Georgia, to Jump School for another eight weeks of training. Then you will be assigned to an Airborne Unit." I said, "OK!"

Basic Training was at Fort Knox, Kentucky, which was just outside Louisville, Kentucky (Cassius Clay's hometown). We all went down to Fort Knox together, but after we arrived there, we were separated by race, and the Colored guys were sent to a different part of the base. We were known as Company B and were like a bunch of misfits. Basic Training was both boring and fun in a fatal sort of way.

We were, it seemed, isolated from the main camp, which was somewhat beautified with shrubbery and green, manicured grass. I didn't see any grass at all where we were—just rocks! Some were painted, and some were not. The barrack doors did not close properly. We used to wish for a breezeless night so that we could sleep without the doors flapping and banging against the walls throughout the night. The barracks had been "abandoned" since *World War I*, I was told.

CHAPTER 2

The Red Ball
(Circa Summer 1950)

Basic Training, Fort Knox, Kentucky
June 1950

My Uncle Ricky was drafted into the Army during World War II. He did not want to go. They made him a truck driver, and he sent us a picture of himself with his truck. He said he was a member of "The Red Ball Express." He never said what that meant, and I could never figure out why Blacks would call themselves "RED." I wondered why they didn't call it the "Black Ball Express." I was about twelve years old, and it never crossed my mind to ask Uncle Ricky about it any further.

It was not until I joined the Army myself four years later that I learned exactly what that "Red Ball" meant. I was about six weeks into Basic Training in an all-Black unit when I was told we all had to give a pint of blood to the Army Emergency Blood Bank. I soon found myself standing in line to give a pint of blood for the first time in my life. They called out my name and sent me to a line with all White soldiers. I was confused but said nothing. All two hundred of the Black soldiers I trained with were sent to a different room. They sent a doctor to take my tags and a sample of my blood. They brought my dog tags back, which now had my blood type stamped on it: "Blood Type: A." This meant nothing to me, so I stayed on line.

When it came time for me to sit in the chair to give the pint of blood, the White nurse looked at me and said, "Just a minute, I have to go find a red pencil!" As she searched, I said to myself, *She didn't need a red pencil for all those White guys in front of me, so why is she now running amok looking for a red pencil?* I was just sitting there, holding up the line.

She eventually came back with a look of accomplishment on her face. She picked up the empty jar assigned to me and drew a red ball on the label of the jar. I asked her what the red ball was for. In a smug, don't-you-know kind of way, she said, "This RED BALL means it's Black blood and has to be kept separate from all the other types of blood!"

All of a sudden, I got this flashback of my Uncle Ricky telling us about his Red Ball Express experiences, and everything started making sense to me. Wow, what he'd said was really true! I was surprised and infuriated at the same time. She stuck the needle in my arm, and a calmness swept over me. A voice in the back of my head said, *Say these words to her:* "Oh, that's a great idea. At least this way, I can be assured that my blood will only be used to save the life of another Black!" She looked at me with disdain, and the big smile she had on her face as she was drawing the "red ball blood" abruptly disappeared.

She went about her work without saying another word. When I arrived back at the barracks, a lot of the brothers were visibly upset with this "Red Ball" idea. When it became my turn to speak, I just told them what I had said back at the hospital. The response from the brothers was one of surprise and satisfaction.

"Duball, you were right on the money! At least our blood will be waiting for us when we need it," they said.

"Yeah!" I responded.

What I am about to say next I can't prove, but I truly believe that the Whites rethought their dastardly plan when their blood bank ran dry in Korea and decided that the White soldiers would accept Black blood. That means a lot of White veterans were our blood brothers! "Welcome to the tribe," as my folks would say.

Can you imagine spending most of your life thinking that you are Black after having been raised by a Black mother, grown up with two Black brothers, and sent to a Black school? *Who am I, and why?* I wondered. Did my mother know I had type A blood, which most Black people don't have? Was she hiding something from me? Who could have been White in our family? I say this because White people have more type A blood than any other race.

A Sergeant picked me and another brother out to spend the day at the shooting range. I thought we were being sent to run targets up and down for the White soldiers, but we were sent to a spot where we were left alone. A little while later, a truck pulled up and dropped off four White soldiers. They were on one side of the road, and we were on the opposite side. We were looking at each other from across the road. They didn't speak, nor did we. The sun was high in the sky, and it was getting hotter and hotter. We saw a truck coming toward us and figured maybe they were coming to pick us up.

The truck stopped in front of us. Two guys got out, walked to the rear of the truck, and unhooked what looked like a canvas water tank. They placed a ladle on top of the water cooler, jumped back into the truck, and drove off. Not a word was spoken. The truck disappeared down the road. We were all getting thirsty, and the sun was even hotter. We looked across the road at the four White guys looking at us. We all had rifles, but they were empty. I wanted a drink of water but was skeptical about using the dipper because it probably was meant for the White soldiers. The White soldiers were still watching us.

My friend said to me, "Duball, I want a drink of that water!"

"I do too," I said.

"Come on," he said, "let's go get some water."

We headed for the water bag and the ladle. I held the bag while he filled the cup and drank his fill. He then held the bag steady for me while I filled the cup and drank. We placed the ladle on top of the water bag, walked back across the road, and sat down.

The four White soldiers seemed a bit unnerved by the fact that they had not gotten to drink first. Now they had to drink behind us. (Hee-hee!) Our germs were on the cup, and we were in the middle of the desert with one water bag.

This was a hot Kentucky sun beaming down on us, and the four White soldiers had not touched that ladle. All of a sudden, one of the White soldiers got up and headed for the water bag! We were practically sitting in the shade of the water bag, so he had to excuse himself to get the ladle. But he got that ladle and drank until he could drink no more. Without a word to anyone, he turned and walked away. That was all the other White soldiers needed to see; they *all* broke for the water bag and drank their fill. We spent the rest of the day sitting around the water bag Indian fashion and cracking jokes. Self-preservation is the first law of nature, I guess.

Basic Training was tough, but we made it through. My orders were ready, and they included the *delayed route* method of traveling. This meant I had fifteen days to reach Fort Benning, Georgia, from Kentucky and a ticket to go from fort to fort. If I paid my own way, I could stop off in DC for a few weeks.

They dropped us off in Louisville, Kentucky, at the train station. I found out that the train from Louisville cost $50 more than I had in my pocket, so I hiked over to Greyhound. Greyhound wanted $22, and I had $25. Needless to say, I had no money for meals, but I was headed home. The trip took a total of twenty-four hours. When I got home, I was famished and ten pounds lighter.

Paratroopers doing training jumps from 250-foot towers.
(Photo by Joseph P. Wolfe)

CHAPTER 3

Headed for Jump School

I was home for a week, which gave me time to see all of my friends and hang out in the 'hood for a while. On the other side, things had not improved. I told Mama that getting the allotment might take several months, but in the meantime I would send as much as possible from my pay. (I did not tell her I was on my way to jump school. She would have balked at the idea of me jumping out of airplanes just to get a few more bucks in my paycheck.) I told her I was on my way to Fort Benning, Georgia, for a few more weeks of Basic Training.

I kissed everybody, said my good-byes, and headed for the Greyhound Bus terminal. I was headed for another experience in the Southland.

Everything was pretty quiet until I got to Columbus, Georgia. I had a bus layover there because I had to catch another bus that would take me into Fort Benning. I decided to walk around the block to stretch my legs a little. I walked out of the bus terminal and headed down the street. After having walked about a block or so, I noticed the people on the other side of the street were stopping and staring at me. *Gee!* I said to myself. *I guess they must not see many soldiers around here!*

Out of nowhere a police car pulled up next to me, and a White cop leaned out the window and said to me, "Where you from?"

"I beg your pardon?" I said.

"I said where you from?"

"Washington, DC," I replied.

He said, "I figured you weren't from 'round here 'cause you on the <u>wrong side</u> of the street!"

"I am? But how could that be?" (I had never heard of a wrong side of a sidewalk!)

"You are walking on the paved side," he said.

"Are you trying to say that I belong on the unpaved side of the street?" I asked.

"That's right," he said.

It was then that I realized that the people who had been staring at me were all Black and on the unpaved side of the street. They'd been staring at me because I was breaking the law!

To add insult to injury, it had just stopped raining, and the other side of the street was a mud hole. I had on a starched and ironed khaki uniform and spit-shined boots, and this cop was telling me I needed to get on the other side of the street, where there was no sidewalk? I could not, for the life of me, get myself to do that. I just stood there looking at my people looking at me, their faces sympathetic and fearful about what was coming next.

That cop said, "Get in the car!"

I said, "For what? I didn't do anything." I just stood there frozen in disbelief. The people on the other side had gathered into a crowd and were looking on.

The cop looked at me and said in a softer voice, "For your own safety, just get in the car."

I stiffened again. "Am I under arrest?" I said.

"Look," he said, "I am going to take you back to the bus station and see that you get out of here safely, OK?"

I looked in his eyes for some kind of hate or malice but saw nothing of the sort, so I said OK. Though I still felt like I had been defrocked, I cooperated. I climbed into the back, and as we drove off, I looked into the faces of my people standing in the mud and saw the pain they felt having to live in this town. My only solace was that those people knew that this little sixteen-year-old soldier did not go stand in the mud. He chose to be arrested.

We arrived back at the Greyhound bus station, and that cop stayed with me until the bus came to take me out of there. Every time I moved, he moved too. Was he my guardian angel? The bus came, and he walked me to the gate, escorted me to the bus, and watched me pull off. I watched him droop a little in the shoulders as I pulled off. I guess he felt relieved to get rid of this soldier. I guess if I were a *decent* White cop in an *indecent* White town I would have done the same thing.

Paratroopers jumping from a carrier plane.
(Photo by Joseph P. Wolfe)

CHAPTER 4

Jump School

I spent the next few weeks at Fort Benning, Georgia, trying to find *somebody* I could tell this story to. I saw a Black soldier in the chow line and made it a point to sit with him in the mess hall. I introduced myself, and he said his name was Bastian and he was from Barbados. He had a heavy West Indian accent and a good sense of humor. I enjoyed listening to his Barbadian jokes. We became the best of friends.

One day, while Bastian and I were hanging out, I remembered the "sidewalk" incident. "Hey, Bastian," I said. "Let me tell you about something that happened to me in Columbus, Georgia." I told him the story about me being on the wrong side of the street.

He let me finish telling the story and said, "Wow! *You were LUCKY!*"

"LUCKY? What do you mean? I was pissed off!" I said.

Bastian replied, "Yeah, I made that same mistake, and when the White people saw me walking on the paved side of the street, they chased my Black ass all the way to Fort Benning, Georgia—a good ten or fifteen miles."

"You're pulling my leg?"

Without a smile, he said, "I kid you not!"

"Were you in uniform? I asked.

"Yes, I was," Bastian said. "The only reason they couldn't catch me was I knew I was running for my *LIFE!"* We stood there looking at each other for a moment. Then we both decided to go get drunk!

Bastian and I got separated when jump school started because everything in the Army was in alphabetical order. There were a lot of guys with last names between Bastian and DuVall, so we wound up in different barracks. We saw each other on evenings and weekends.

Interestingly enough, jump school was not segregated. We all sat together and sweated together. There were little telltale incidents from time to time, like a fistfight or two, but all in all it went better than I had expected (being in Georgia and all).

On our first day out we had to fall out with these heavy-ass steel helmets on our heads. It was at least one hundred degrees at only seven o'clock in the morning. I knew I was in for a hell of a headache. The first thing on the list was PT, which entailed a five-mile run around the campgrounds while counting cadence as loud as we possibly could. It was awful, with guys falling out in the dust and dirt flying. I was determined not to be a straggler.

By the time we got back to the beginning, the Instructor was standing there on a high platform with his demonstrator. (A demonstrator is the person who actually does the exercise as the Sergeant talks.) The Sergeant said, "And now we will begin today's exercise with ten repetitions of squat jumps, ten repetitions of push-ups," and so forth and so on. This went on for the first two hours, and then we took a ten-minute break. Then the two hundred of us lined up single file to take our daily salt pill. The pill was about the size of a nickel and was three times as thick. We were directed to a water fountain, where we took this humongous salt pill. Then we double-timed to where we'd left our steel helmets and began another two hours of PT. We did this until we broke for lunch at noon.

Exactly one hour later, whistles started to blow. The Sergeant said, "FALL IN!" We scampered like maggots for our place in line. He said, "'Ention [Attention]! Rrrrigh' hace [right face] on the double, fooord harch [forward march]! Hup, two, 'reep, 'hor, hup, two, 'reep, 'hor, hup, two, 'reep, 'hor [one, two, three, four]. Companyyyy, hal' [company halt], one-two!"

His routine continued, "All right now, on my command, we are gonna do ten repetitions of push-ups, ten repetitions of...," and so forth and so on. This time I got sick as a dog. Everything was spinning and had turned blood red, but I was determined not to pass out. This routine went on for another two weeks. Every day that I took the pill, I got sick. On weekends I didn't take the pill and felt good, so I figured it must be the pill. I told the Sergeant I didn't need the pill. He told me to either take the pill or go to jail. That was an order. I pretended to take the pill and later on threw it away. I stopped getting sick and hearing bells ringing in my ears. I just felt sweat in my eyes and sand in my mouth; how sweet it was. I was told twenty years later that they had stopped giving salt pills.

We started learning how to hit the ground to prevent breaking our bones. We learned about landing on the balls of our feet and twisting our bodies in midair to make sure we hit the fleshy parts of our limbs and torso. At the same time, we'd put our elbows together in front of our faces for protection. This technique was called a PLF (parachute landing fall). This fall had to be practiced daily, over and over again. Then we were marched to a platform approximately three feet high. We'd jump off and go into the PLF. Those who were afraid were washed out.

Once we got the hang of it, we wore our canteens on our waists to practice our PLFs after jumping off a platform that was four feet. Some cats were already having problems and could not keep their eyes open at four feet off the ground. What had they been thinking when they signed up for this? The interesting thing was that nobody laughed at anybody; as a matter of fact, we tried to encourage each other. Nonetheless, some guys became washouts. "You must keep your *eyes open* at all times," the Instructors said. (I can dig it!)

After perfecting the four-foot jump, we went on the "Nut Cracker," which involved being suspended by a harness with no parachute attached to it. The harness had two straps that ran through our legs on both sides of our family jewels, as the Instructors called them. After hanging there for a few minutes, we began to realize why they called it the Nut Cracker. Oh boy! The longer we hung there, the closer and closer those two straps tried to come together.

An Instructor told us we were about to learn how to guide our 'chute as we descended toward Earth. I just knew he had come over to say, "You can't get down now! We haven't even started!" I could hear groans from behind me as the Sergeant yelled commands like, "To glide left, pull down on your left risers as hard as you can and hold it! Now release. Now let's go to the right, so pull all the way down on your right risers. Hold it! Now release." The Instructor had to go help some guy who didn't know his right from his left, and we got to hang there while this guy was told how his left risers were over his left shoulder and so forth. My harness straps had "met" in the middle, and I didn't want to hang anymore. But we all hung because we loved our country. When I got out of that Nut Cracker, it took a while before that discomfort left—f'real.

This went on for one week. Believe me, I didn't like it. They told us we would be jumping from a thirty-four-foot-high tower, "So keep your harness on," they said. They marched us over to a tower. It looked like it was fifty feet off the ground to me.

The object was to stand in line, climb up four flights of stairs, and jump off this so-called thirty-four-foot tower platform as if we were jumping from an airplane. As we dropped through space, we were expected to be seen *placing* our hands on our reserve 'chute and making sure our knees and toes were together. And our EYES HAD TO BE OPEN! All this had to be done before the cables we were harnessed to snapped us up before we hit the ground. The cables took us for a ride to a sawdust mound, where we were unharnessed. There was a man sitting in a chair at a field desk on the ground below watching us. If we were not doing these things as we fell freely, then the jump didn't count and we had to climb up the stairs and do it again. I ran over to the Sergeant sitting there and gave him my last initial and number. He glanced down at his sheet and said, "DuVall, you had your eyes closed, so go up there and try it again!" Wow, I thought it was a *big deal* I had jumped off the thing at all!

While standing in line for my repeat performance, I noticed the size of my company was getting smaller. Where had everybody gone? We'd started out two hundred strong; now it looked like half had washed out already. I asked around and was told that this thirty-four-foot tower was washing out a lot of guys. *I could dig it!* I was into my third day of trying to figure out how I could I keep my eyes *open*.

The guy sleeping next to me was getting good marks on his exit positions. His name was Dombrosky. I asked how or what he was doing to help him keep his eyes open. He said, "I keep my eyes open by looking at my toes as I fall."

"Yeah, I need to find my toes," I said. The next day at the tower, I jumped, and the first thing I looked for were my toes as I was falling. I kicked my feet out in front of me and looked down, and *there they were*! I placed my toes together and stared at them. I then placed my hands on my reserve and waited for the jerk of the cable line. They unhooked me, and I ran straight for the man at the field desk. He looked at me and said, "DuVall, now that was a perfect body position.

You are now ready for the two-hundred-fifty-foot free-fall tower." That night I thanked Dombrosky for his tip, and we started talking about this 250-foot tower.

We were into the seventh week of jump school and were being marched to the famous 250-foot towers. If you have ever been to the Coney Island Amusement Park, you have seen these towers. The big difference is that the towers at jump school did not have cable wires attached to the 'chutes. The towers were made to hoist us up and then let us free fall. (No cables.) Okay! All weekend long, I had to listen to horror stories about guys who had found themselves on the "Dirty Arm" and had to be "scraped" from the steel girders because they had been blown into the steel beams of the towers. The towers had four Arms—north, east, south, and west. The Arm with the wind blowing into the direction of the tower was known as the **Dirty Arm**.

Monday was my first day on the tower, and as luck would have it, it was a gusty, windy day. "ALL RIGHT! Company B! [My heart skipped a beat.] Faaaall in! Righ' hace! On the double, foooooord-harch! Hup, two, 'reep, 'hor. Hup, two, 'reep, 'hor. Companyyyyyb! Halt, one-two!"

The Sergeant said, "All right, fall out and get your harness on. Then form a line, and you will be assigned to an Arm. I fell in line and was assigned to the west Arm. Dombrosky was on the south Arm. They hoisted us up. The guys on the ground looked smaller and smaller. Clang! I finally reached the top. The other three Arms had been released; I was still hanging there, and there was nobody I could talk to.

About ten minutes later, the Sergeant got on the loud speaker and said, "DuVall, you are on a Dirty Arm! You are to listen *very* carefully to everything I say. IMMEDIATELY UPON RELEASE, you are to reach way up on your 'front risers' and pull those front risers all the way down as far as you possibly can! You got that DuVall? All the way down to your knees if you can!" The wind was blowing harder and steadier. I could feel the force of the wind against my body, and it was pushing me in the direction of the steel girders. I glanced over my shoulder to see just where those steel girders were. Wow, they looked closer than I had expected. It was a scary situation. Everything was noticeably quiet on the ground because everybody's eyes were on me.

I reached up on my front risers as far as I could and waited for the next command. My heart was in my mouth. Why had I gotten myself into this? I needed to say a prayer. I said the Our Father and two Hail Marys and waited for the next command. "All right, DUVALL, we are going to release you! Remember what I said, OK?" said the Sergeant. I waved my hand to let him know I had not fainted. I was so scared that I was breaking wind like crazy.

CLANG! I was falling! I tell you, I pulled those risers as far down as I could. I pulled down so hard that I emptied most of the air from the 'chute and was falling faster and faster. "DUVALL, release those risers NOW!" said the Sergeant. I released the risers and hit the ground so hard the medics came running to take me away in the ambulance. "You all right, soldier?" the medics asked. I did not know whether I was or not. I only remember that they tried to get the helmet off my head and couldn't do it. I was eventually able to get it off but had one hell of a headache! I must have fallen on my head. The next four days were without incident, thank goodness. I passed my tower training, and the next week we jumped from a plane in flight. We needed to do five jumps in five days. Then we graduated!

Monday morning was upon us, and we lay in our bunks waiting to hear our Sergeant's sweet voice. "All right! Company B, faaaall in! Atteeeenhut! Riiiigh' hace, on the double, foooord harch! Hup, two, 'reep, 'hor. Hup, two, 'reep, 'hor!" We double-timed (at a running pace) to the airfield. The planes were revving their engines for take-off. The planes were C-82s, or Flying Boxcars, as they were called. A truck loaded with parachutes pulled up, and they issued us these 'chutes called T-7s, which we strapped on. There was a "spot" equipment check, and then they loaded us on the planes.

It was very noisy on the planes because they had taken the doors off. We wouldn't be in there long anyway. I understood the whole operation wouldn't last more than a few minutes. They loaded up and took off, and fifteen minutes later the red light came on. The jumpmaster was now on his feet shouting, "GET READY!" We all grasped our static line in our right hand and waited for the next command. "STAND UP!" he shouted. "HOOK UP!" We all snapped our static line buckle to the cable in the plane. The jumpmaster then shouted at the top of his voice, "Each man check the man's equipment in front of you!" Then he shouted, "Sound off for equipment check!" We all had a number. We started at the back and worked forward: "Twelve, OK," "Eleven, OK," "Ten, OK," and so on down the line. Then there was a pause. "Is everybody HAPPY?" said the Sergeant.

We all answered feebly, "Yes!"

"ALL RIGHT then!" he shouted as our knees shook. "Shuffle down and stand in the door," he said. We shuffled to the door in a skip step, meaning we always kept our right foot in front of the left. We could bring our left foot up, but never in front of or beside our right foot. This was done so that when the next man stood at the door, he could pivot on his right foot and place his left foot on the threshold of the door and his hands outside the door. When he felt "a tap on his behind," he would push himself out the door and instinctively go into his body position—that is, eyes open, toes together, hands gently placed on his reserve 'chute. He had to do all this while falling and waiting for the "OPENING SHOCK!" He would fall about one hundred and fifty miles an hour and then be ABRUPTLY snatched to twenty-five miles an hour. It was enough to make our brains crash into the front of our skulls and cause our eyeballs to pop out! We didn't know whether to curse or say, "Thank you, Jesus!"

For about thirty seconds, we'd be floating gently down to Earth, but just as we would be about to enjoy such a lofty position, we'd suddenly realize that the ground was coming at us faster and FASTER.

At that point I usually recalled my training to look straight out at the horizon, slightly bend my knees while keeping my toes together and pointed, reach well up on my risers, and relax.

On my first jump, my toes touched down, I hit and rolled into my PLF, and it was over. When the dust cleared, I got up, gathered my 'chute, and marched out of the DZ (Drop Zone) area. As I was walking, I suddenly found myself dodging steel helmets that were falling from the sky. I realized that lots of guys hadn't tightened their chin straps enough, so the opening shock was knocking their helmets off. One of these things could *kill* a man if it hit him on the head; it was just another concern in the day of a jumper.

On Tuesday morning we did our second jump, and it was no problem. On Wednesday morning things begin to change. I felt nervous and unsure. I thought, *Maybe I don't want to jump today.* The Sergeant shouted, "Tweeeeeet! AAHRIGHT! Company B, FALL IN! Companyyyyb, ateehn' shun! Righ' hace! On the double, Forwaaaaard harch! Rup, two, 'reep, 'hor! Rup, two, 'reep, 'hor! To the airfield and pick up your 'chute."

I was fumbling at putting my 'chute on. I did not want to jump; I felt I was pressing my luck a little. Were things going to go all right for the third time? The Sergeant called my name, and I was not ready. I was a nervous wreck. I was all thumbs!

"DUVALL, why aren't you ready?" the Sergeant asked.

I answered, "I have to go to the latrine." By the time I double-timed back to my position, I had to go worse than before! I said I had to go again.

He said, "DuVall, you just came back from the latrine. There's no time for that now; go when you get back. Now get on that plane!"

"Yes, Sergeant," I said.

I jumped, but it was hard. However, *I no longer had to go to the latrine!* My nerves were shot; that's all. The next two jumps went well, and I was on my way to graduation.

On graduation day, the Sergeant said, "Tweeeeeet! Aaaaall righ'. Company B, fall in, in full dress, class A uniform. Companyyyyb! Ateeenshun! Righ' hace! Forwaaaaaard *harch!* Hup, two, 'reep, 'hor! Hup, two, 'reep, 'hor!" For the first time in two months, we were walking, not running! We were marched to the main Post Parade field. "Companyyyyyyyb! Halt! One-two." I glanced around me and saw we looked more like a Platoon (thirty-six men) rather than a Company (two hundred strong). A lot of men hadn't made it.

The band was playing its little heart out, and the Commanding Officer came by and pinned our wings on our chest and saluted us. We took the rest of the day off. We were now full-fledged first-class U.S. Paratroopers ready for assignment to another outfit. I was assigned to the Eighty-Second Airborne Division, Fort Bragg, North Carolina. I said to myself, *I'm still in the Southland.*

I found my friend Bastian, and he was going to the same outfit that I was, the 505th Airborne Infantry Regiment. My friend Dombrosky was being sent to the 101st Airborne in Kentucky. I definitely didn't want to go back there. Bastian and I got on the train headed for Fayetteville, North Carolina. We arrived in Fayetteville at around five o'clock in the evening and had a half-hour layover for the bus to Fort Bragg. The first things we saw when we got off the train were the "White" and "Colored" signs on the restrooms and the White and Colored drinking fountains. There was even a Coke machine that had separate slots for the Coloreds and Whites to put their money in (so help me GOD)!

We decided to walk down the main street to stretch our legs a little. The main street was named "Market" Street. After we had walked about three or four blocks, we came upon a round, one-story, well-maintained brick building called The Slave Market of Fayetteville. We could not believe our eyes! Our mouths were wide open!

Bastian said in a soft calm voice, "Well I'll be damned!"

A cop stepped up, grabbed Bastian by the arm, and said, "YOU ARE UNDER ARREST!"

My friend said, "For what?"

The cop said, "For using profanity while standing in the presence of a Historical Site!"

Bastian said, "What?" And I unintentionally said, "Well I'll be damned!"

The cop said, "You are BOTH under arrest." He grabbed us under the armpits and roughly marched us across the street, booked us, and locked us up!

The fine was $25 apiece, and we both refused to pay, so they marched us upstairs and locked us up "until somebody comes up with $50," they said. There were no meals served. We were determined not to pay the fine. (Twenty-five dollars was like a hundred dollars back then.) We didn't make but $60 a month. They wanted us to wire home for the money. We told them we had no homes to wire to. (Unbelievable! Right?)

The next day we still had not been given any meals. At about four o'clock that afternoon, a cop came, opened our cell door, and told us our fine had been paid and our "escort" out of town was waiting for us. We got downstairs and saw two White military police waiting to escort us to Fort Bragg. We climbed into their jeep, and off we went. There was no conversation the whole time we were traveling. We got to the Army Post and were sent before the Provost Marshall, who was White also! He said, "I'm getting sick and tired of spending my time and money to get you all [Blacks] out of jail." He said the Army did not reimburse him for the fines he paid out of his own pocket, so he expected us to reimburse him when we got our pay. "Yes, sir!" we said. When we got outside, we agreed that we had no intention of paying that fine! Let the Whites pay the Whites for their own wrongdoing! That was what my West Indian friend and I staunchly agreed on. We even talked about how we were going to blow that place up on our discharge date.

We had to catch a bus that would take us to our assigned out-fit. The bus took us to all the division outfits, and as we went along, we saw no Black soldiers. We began to wonder where they would be dropping us off. The bus had stopped at all the regiments, including the 505th First and Second Battalions. We needed the 505th Third Battalion (the Third Battalion was always Black) and figured our stop was next, but the bus did not stop. Only a few other Black soldiers were on the bus. We *left* the main post area and headed for what looked like an off-site area away from the main roads. We finally arrived at a place about thirty minutes from all the other barracks that the Whites called "Smoke Bomb Hill." It was where the Black soldiers' barracks were. "LAST STOP!" the driver said. We all got off. The Company clerk called my name and told me I had been assigned to Headquarters Company. Bastian was sent to M Company. We said good-bye to each other, and that was the last I saw of my good buddy.

The next morning I fell out (or got into formation) with the rest of the Company. I was introduced to the men in my barracks and discovered that quite a few were from the DC area. The Officers were White, and the enlisted men were Black. I was at home with my fellow soldiers. It was like being back on the block and hanging out.

Allow me to introduce some of the guys in the First Platoon of Headquarters Company. Staff Sergeant Smith, a.k.a. Smitty (a mousy little guy from DC with a John Wayne walk), gave me a hard time because I was from DC too. Smitty was my Platoon Leader and said he didn't want the others to think he would show favoritism. Corporal Claude Jerome Myers was also from DC, and he became my closest friend. Private Emanuel Logan was from DC. Sergeant William Smith was the Coach of the boxing team. Corporal Andrew Poole was from DC. Corporal Barber was from Philadelphia, Pennsylvania. Private Abner, also from Philadelphia, was my jump school buddy. Also part of the Company were Private Sam Kilpatrick, Private J. P. Banks, Private C. Davis (from Philadelphia), and practical jokers Coy C. Cunningham, James Adkins, James E. Jones, C. Lombard, Sergeant Wakefield, Sergeant Scott, B. C. Pitt, Corporal James Travers, and

Sergeant Lawrence Brown, to name a few. It was as fine a group as you could find anywhere. We were ALWAYS cracking on each other and cracking up, and we all had a story to tell about the Fayetteville slave market. EVERYBODY swore they were going to blow that place up on their way home after being discharged. I am sure it is still there!

About a week after I arrived, we had to arise earlier than usual because we had to complete a parachute jump. They had to call the roll for the manifest, and when the Sergeant got to my name, he stopped and just stared at my name and my vital statistics. With a confused look on his face, he said, "DuVall!"

"Yes, Sergeant," I said.

"DuVall, I think they sent you to the wrong outfit! What kind of blood is 'A' blood? Nobody here has 'A' blood. Are you *sure* they didn't send you to the *wrong* outfit?"

"I don't think so," I said.

"Duball, you *cannot* afford to get hurt, OK? Because if you do, we won't be able to *save* your ass!"

"OK," I said.

The Sergeant said, "Blacks have 'O' blood! Are you Italian or something?"

"Not to my knowledge," I replied.

The whole time I was in the "all-Black outfit," I was not *allowed* to take any unnecessary risks! (Hee-hee!)

Young Paratroopers Abner and DuVall.

CHAPTER 5

The Boxing Team

I was standing in formation for roll call while a young Greek Officer, Lieutenant Landis, was inspecting the ranks. When he saw me, he stopped suddenly and said, "We need a representative for the boxing team. I would like to see you volunteer, Private DuVall."

I said, "No thank you, sir."

He stood there for a few seconds, then turned and marched away. This went on for several weeks. One day one of the soldiers from my barrack came up to me on the chow line and said, "One of the guys in your barrack is a faggot, you know."

I said, "Oh, yeah, who?"

He said, "You'll find out!"

He smiled impishly and walked away. *Is he trying to tell me something?* I said to myself. One of the Sergeants came up to me with the same impish smile and said, "I bet you would make a nice Homo!" I told him he'd better not try anything with me! He smiled and said, "Well you got nice curly hair, and you are a nice-looking guy. Yeah, you would make a handsome Homo." He then turned and walked away.

My friend from DC started calling me Duvy Doll because I looked so young, and everybody chimed in, "Hey, Duvy Doll!"

I said to Myers, "Hey, man, you started this, and now it's catching on."

"Well you got to expect that because you look so young!" Myers said.

Another soldier walked up to me and said, "Hey, Duvy Doll! I hear somebody in your barrack is a Homo. Is that right?"

I answered, "If there is, he hasn't made himself known to me!"

The next morning Lieutenant Landris stopped in front of me again and said, "DuVall, I still think you should go out for the boxing team! Guys on the boxing team don't have to do daily chores or pull KP (Kitchen Police)! And they get three-day passes on weekends!"

I said, "OK, who do I report to?"

"Report to Sergeant Smith, and tell him I sent you!"

"Yes, sir," I said. I went looking for Sergeant Smith, who said, "The team is not fully ready to go into training yet, OK?"

"OK, Sarge, call me when you are ready." When I got back to the barracks everyone had already left for the morning training, so I decided to lie across my sack and fell asleep.

"Hey, soldier! What are you doing on your bunk?" I looked up and it was the First Sergeant!

"Oh, I'm waiting for Sergeant Smith to call me out for the boxing team."

"BOXING TEAM!" the First Sergeant hollered. "The boxing team will just have to wait! You are on your way to the mess hall. You are now on KP! The pot and pan man didn't show up for duty, so you're going to take his place. Move it, soldier, on the double! And tell the cook I sent you."

"Yes, Sergeant!"

The next day Sergeant Smith wanted to know what had happened to me. I told him Sergeant Robinson had put me on KP and that I was still tired from washing those two-hundred-man gallon pots all day and half the night. "Well, DuVall," he said, "I guess you don't know that the fight is tomorrow night! Are you sure you are up to this?"

I said yes. I was more than ready to get out of KP business.

Sergeant Smith said, "Put the gloves on, and get in the ring. Let's go over some tactics." He started testing my reflexes and discovered that I was dropping my guard and leaving myself open for a good left jab to the right eye. As he was trying to demonstrate what could happen to me if I did not cover up properly, he accidentally punched me in the right eye without any gloves on. His bare knuckles hit me square in the right eyeball. I could see with my left eye that he was sorry, and he felt bad about the eye. My eye swelled up and turned black and blue. What a shiner it was!

The following day I got up, shaved, showered, and headed for the fight arena. I found the locker room and suited up. They put my gloves on me, and I sat down and waited for my name to be announced. I could hear the crowd cheering and screaming for their teammates.

"OK, DuVall! You are on!" I jumped up, knocked my gloves together, and trotted out to the ring. I climbed into the ring and saw my opponent already sitting in his corner. He was smaller than I was, and his arms were shorter. The referee came to my corner to see if I was ready. When he looked at me, he blinked, did a double take, and said, "You have a black eye? Were you in another fight?" I told him I'd had an accident earlier. He took a good look at the eye and said, "Let's see what the ring doctor has to say."

The doctor came over, looked at the eye, and said, "Are you sure you want to do this?"

I said yes, so he said to the referee, "I guess he'll be OK!"

I knocked my gloves together and saw Sergeant Smith come to my corner from ringside. The Sergeant said, "DuVall, remember what I told you. If it gets bad, just look at me, and I will throw in the towel!"

The bell rang, and I got off my stool and headed for the center of the ring, where my opponent was waiting. We threw a few feelers out, and then he started pounding away at me. This guy was so fast that I didn't see him throwing any punches, but I could certainly feel the stinging blows! It was as if I had no guard up at all. Every time I would go to hit him back, he would hit me three or four more times—boom-boom-boom-BOOM. I did hear the bell, though, and I staggered back to my corner. Sergeant Smith asked me if he should throw in the towel. I said no; I wanted to go back out there. I figured it was only a three-round bout, and three rounds were nothing. (Poor me!) The bell rang for me to come out fighting, and I, like a fool, went back out there! (Lord, have mercy!)

That little guy closed everything I had that was open and opened everything I had that was closed! I mean he put a hurting on me in this round. And poor me, I was trying my best to get a punch or two in there in the meantime. Then the bell rang, ending round two. I staggered to my corner and plopped down on my stool. Sergeant Smith looked at me and threw in the towel! He lifted poor me off the stool, and I stumbled out of the ring and headed to the dressing room. They took my gloves off for the last time, as far as I was concerned. (I was finished with the ring forever.)

The next day on the chow line, all the guys started calling me "CHAMP!"

"What are you calling me champ for? I lost that fight," I said.

"Yeah, but you got *guts,* Duball. Nobody in boxing history ever went in the ring with a black eye! But you just kept on going, even though you were hurting. You are the talk of Fort Bragg!"

Needless to say, thanks to their efforts, my esteem was restored. And I liked "Champ," as it was certainly better than "Duvy Doll."

CHAPTER 6

Driving While Black (1951)

My friend Claude (Jerry) Myers, who was also from DC, went out for the boxing team too. He went on to be not only division champion, but champion of the whole Third Army! I asked him how a guy of average size (he was about five feet, eight inches tall) did it. He said to me, "I knew I was too small to reach their chin, but I could reach their heart. So I would hit them in the heart. And when they tried to cover their heart, I would work on their kidneys. Then they didn't know what to cover, so I started hitting them in the arms. Once their arms were hurting, they couldn't punch effectively. Then I went to work on their chin with uppercuts, and before you knew it, they were out for the count."

"Wow! I should have talked to you *before* I went into the ring," I said.

He had just bought a car, was going to DC for the weekend, and wanted to know if I wanted to go with him. I said sure, and we picked up two more soldiers in the barracks and were off to DC—the four of us. We all had a great time. On our way back to Fort Bragg, we began talking about the things we'd done while in town. It was early December, and the heat in the car was kicking. We were all in good spirits!

When we got down near the North Carolina-Virginia border, a scout car jumped out of nowhere and followed us for several miles. I asked Myers if he had been speeding. He said no, he was doing fifty-five! The cop finally flagged us over. It was about midnight, and the highway was quiet. The cop got out of his car and said we were speeding. He said we had to turn the car "around" and follow him back to the town we had just left to stand trial! (He kept his hand on his gun while he talked.)

Myers turned the car around and got behind the scout car. We drove for miles and miles, back over the road we had just covered, for what seemed like an eternity! About forty-five minutes later, the scout car finally turned up what looked to us like an abandoned road. It was rough going now with the dust blowing in our faces. We eventually stopped at what looked like an abandoned filling station; there were no lights on anywhere. The cop got out of his car and said, "Y'all wait rat-cher!" He walked around to the back of the abandoned-looking shack and disappeared out of sight. We sat in silence. There we were, God knows where, and nobody knew what was going to happen to us. (I envisioned a group of Klansmen in white robes coming back to teach us a lesson by lynching us all.)

The Sheriff came back and said, "Ah-rat', all y'all git out duh car an' folla' me!" We all got out and followed him. He led us to a shack behind the abandoned structure. He opened the door and said, "All o' y'all step inside."

We stepped inside the kerosene lantern-lit room and saw a man sitting behind a badly mauled desk wearing a black Judge's robe. He put his dirty shoeless feet on the desk and said, "My Sher'ff hea' tells me y'all was speed'n. So y'all owe me thirty-five dollars apiece! Now that's thirty-five times five, which equals a hun'ert 'n seb'ny fi'e dollah's. CASH, if you please!"

We all stood there in shock. I spoke first: "Those who were not driving have to pay too?"

The Judge looked at me in a scornful way and said, *"That's wrat, all o'ya!* And I only 'cept CASH! So pay up so I can git back to bed!" The four other soldiers collected $165. When they turned to me, I had only $5 dollars and change! We asked the Judge for mercy and asked that he let us go for $170 because we were soldiers and had to be back at camp or be marked AWOL. He hatefully said, "If you don't have the full amount, you will spend your time in jail until somebody shows up with the money."

One soldier spoke up, "I have a war bond in my pocket. Will you accept that if I sign the back of it?"

The Judge answered, "I said CASH! So you will spend the night in jail! And since we don't have a jail, you will have to sleep in your impounded car. Case closed!"

The Sheriff marched us out to the car. I said to myself, *At least we will be able to turn the motor on in the car and be kept warm.* The Sheriff then said, "Since the car is impounded, I need the keys!" He took the KEYS, turned, and walked away, leaving us to freeze to death.

We came up with a strategy to stay warm for a spell at a time by lying on top of each other. One guy in the back would lie on top of two guys until the top guy could take it no longer; then we would rotate the warm bodies to accommodate the cold bodies. The two guys in the front had to hug each other all night. It was the longest, coldest night of my life.

The sun finally broke over the horizon but did not warm us. We were thoroughly frozen to the bone! We were so cold that we spoke not a word as we waited for somebody to come and get us so we could be taken to a town. Once there we would find someone to cash the war bond we had to pay our bail.

The Sheriff finally arrived and said to us, "There is a town straight down the road, and you can walk there. They got a general store and a bank there. Come back here when you get the money." We had been hoping for a ride to town but dared not say anything. We headed down the road to find this town of which he spoke. We walked and we walked. Finally a town came into view, but nothing was open. We looked at the time. It was seven thirty in the morning. The general store had a sign in the window that said, "Open at 8:00 a.m." We stood there and waited, hugging ourselves and stomping our feet on the ground to get some kind of circulation going.

The man came and opened the store. We said good morning and walked in behind him. We presented him with the war bond and asked him if he would cash it. He looked at it and said, "I don't cash bonds here. You boys will have to wait 'til the bank opens for that. They open at nine a.m., down the street there."

The bank was a block or so away, so we went straight there and waited. The sun was getting higher, and someone suggested we try to call camp and tell them where we were. We agreed, and my change came in handy.

At nine fifteen the bank opened, and we went in and did a lot of explaining about why we needed to do this. Despite the fact that we were all in uniform, we had to show our IDs. While we waited for the teller to decide whether he was going to cash the bond, my mind was racing. *What kind of people are these? They can unjustly take your money, make you sleep out of doors on a cold winter night, and it doesn't seem to bother them one bit. This whole stinking country needs to go back to Europe! But the Europeans don't want them back either! That's why they were sent here in the first place, to get this scurvy lot out of Europe.* There was something inhumane about the situation to me.

We got back and gave the Sheriff the $5. He gave us the keys with a warning: "If y'all evah come back through these parts ag'in, you better go real slow, or we'll ketch you ag'in!" We said we understood and drove off. We were starved to death when we finally arrived at camp and were able to scrounge a meal at the mess hall that night. We told our story to the fellows, and to our surprise, they knew exactly where we had been stopped and the whole nine yards. They even knew the Judge's name. Payday came, and I had to give up $35 of my $65-a-month pay, and for what? God bless America!

CHAPTER 7

Willie B.
(Circa 1951)

About two months later, we got a new guy in the barracks. His name was William B. Harris, but nobody called him that. They all called him "HOG HEAD" because his head was so large. He must have worn a size ten hat. Not only was his head BIG, but it was larger on one side than the other. It made him look slightly cross-eyed. He was also UGLY! He was only about five feet, ten inches tall, and everybody seemed to be afraid of him.

I went into town one day and headed for the USO club, which was way up on the second floor. I saw HOG HEAD throwing two soldiers simultaneously down that flight of stairs. He was BAD! I pretended that I didn't see a thing as I maneuvered myself around them trying to get back on their feet. When I got inside, I asked Willie B. (I didn't dare call him HOG HEAD to his face) why he had thrown those two soldiers down the stairs.

He replied, "Because they weren't Paratroopers!"

"Oh, I see," I said. I went about picking out a girl to dance with. The next day I told everybody about what had happened the night before.

About a week later, we were preparing for a "General Inspection," which meant all of our personal equipment had to be cleaned, shined, and laid out on our bunks so that the General's staff could look at it and say whether we were fit for duty. I cleaned and shined everything I had. I laid my gear out on my bunk and went to the latrine to take a leak. When I got back, my canteen and eating utensils were gone. "Hey," I said, "did anybody see somebody take my stuff?" Nobody said a mumbling word! Now that was really strange, knowing nobody had been out of the area and nobody had seen anything.

I figured they were playing a joke on me of some kind and decided to walk through the barracks looking for my gear. My initials and last four numbers had to be on everything I owned that was Army-issued. I got to the last bed on the opposite side of the barracks and saw my gear on Willie B.'s bunk. "Hey, Willie B., this is my gear," I said.

HOG HEAD glared at me with his beady eyes and said, "Yours how you F--- with it. Now get the F--- away from my bed!" The whole barracks was looking at me. I could have heard a rat piss on cotton at that moment. I was shaken and had a flashback of those two soldiers lying at the bottom of the stairs. I wondered, *What do I do now? If I try to take my stuff, he will kill me for sure.* I looked around the room for some kind of movement. Nobody moved or said anything! I retreated.

I went back to my bunk and silently started to cry, tears rolling down my face. If I let him get away with this, he would be taking other possessions of mine. How could I stop this wrong with no help from anybody? Everybody was scared to death of this guy, especially me!

The tears finally stopped, and my mind began working overtime. I was scared to death, but I knew I had to nip this thing in the bud or he would be taking my money next.

HOG HEAD was sitting on his bunk with his back to me. He seemed certain that I was not going to try anything! *I got it!* I said to myself. I took my entrenching tool (a folding shovel used to dig a foxhole) and fixed it in the "chopping" position. I then took my steel helmet by the strap and stood up. "Willie B.!" I yelled. I got the whole barrack looking at ME. When he turned around and looked at me, I threw the steel helmet at him. I was giving him time to duck, and duck he did! *Great!* I said to myself. *Doing this will give me time to get to him with the shovel.* The expression on his face when I got to him with my shovel was priceless. He was down on one knee and in no position to defend himself. He had time only to raise his arm to cover his big head. (I almost broke out in laughter but had to keep up my ANGRY tirade.)

Now there was movement in the ranks. Two guys from my Squad grabbed me (thinking I was going to follow through with the threat) and dragged me into the cadre room. Sergeant Smitty told me I had to get a hold of myself, but I was so impressed with my performance that I paid little attention to what he was saying. I told Smitty I was ready to go back outside and finish the job! When I got to my bunk, the first thing I noticed was that my eating utensils and canteen were back on my bed. Yippee! My ploy had worked, and nobody had gotten hurt.

A few days later, HOG HEAD walked up to me and said (with a benevolent look), "Duball, will you go to town with me tonight?" I was stunned! I thought, *He is going to get me in town and kill me, and nobody will ever know what happened to me!* I nervously asked him why he wanted me to go. He said, "Because everybody else is scared of me but you. You got guts!"

The Army had just passed a regulation that nobody was to go off the Base alone anymore because of the Korean War. I had been ignoring the regulation because I traveled better and faster when I was alone. But with HOG HEAD at my side. who was going to mess with me? I said, "Sure, let's go." We became a team.

A month or so later, the First Sergeant called a formation and told everybody to take their shot records out for inspection. I had lost my shot record, which meant that I had to go to the Dispensary and get twelve needles stuck in my arms—six in each arm. HOG HEAD had lost his too, so the two of us were pitched together again. We were the only two who had lost their records out of two hundred men.

We arrived at the Dispensary and were directed to a room where two attendants were waiting for us. Willie B. politely allowed me to go first. Each attendant had a tray of twelve hypodermic-looking needles. The first attendant was an extremely effeminate Black guy with a high-pitched voice. The second attendant was a White guy who seemed to be straight. I walked past the little Black guy, stopped at the White guy, and started rolling up my sleeves. That meant HOG HEAD had to take the gay guy (smile).

My attendant was sticking me in my arm when we suddenly heard a loud KABOOM! It was immediately followed by BA-LAAM! I had a flashback to those soldiers falling down those stairs. It was the *same sound*! *The first sound* came from the guy being thrown down on his back, and the *second sound* came from his *"feet"* hitting the floor!

Oh no, I said to myself, *the gay guy must have said something out of the way, and Willie B. threw him out!* I couldn't get myself to turn around and simply pretended to not notice. Just then there was a tap on my shoulder, and it was the Black gay guy. He looked at me and said (in a sweet, mellow tone), *"Who is your friend?"*

I looked around in complete surprise! Where was HOG HEAD? He then pointed with his needle to the floor behind me? Willie B. Harris was flat on his back and was OUT COLD with his mouth wide open. (I was in shock!!) Did the attendant do this to my friend?

The attendant asked, "What do we do with him?"

I said, "Give him his shots while he is still unconscious and then bring me a basin of water." The sweet little guy got down on the floor and hummed a song as he went about administering his shots on his hands and knees. When he was finished, he brought the basin of water. I said, "Give me the water, and you all leave the room for a minute." They agreed and left the room.

Willie B. was still out cold, so I threw the water in his face and slapped him around a little. He came to, looked around the empty room, and said, "Let's get out of here before they come back!"

I said, "OK, let's go."

When we got outside, I said to him, "They gave you your needles, so you don't have to worry now."

He shouted, "You mean to say they shot an unconscious man?" (He was upset!)

"Once I saw that you had only fainted, I figured it was best for you because you wouldn't feel a thing," I said.

He looked at me with amazement but said not a word. He then broke into a smile and said, "Duball, you CRAZY maaan!" We were like Moses and Aaron after that. All of a sudden, he didn't look so ugly anymore.

The intimidating "General-Purpose" Bag.

CHAPTER 8

The "General-Purpose" Bag

We had to make a practice jump with full field gear. That meant practically everything we owned had to be tied to our parachute harnesses. As luck would have it, Sergeant Smith walked up to me and said, "You will be jumping with a "'GP' [General-Purpose] Bag" on this jump!"

"Hey, wait a minute," I said. "Corporal Lester was sent to a special training school to learn how to handle that kind of heavy equipment jumping! I wasn't sent to any school for this."

Sergeant Smith got up in my face and whispered to me in a low tone of voice that Corporal Lester was afraid to handle this equipment. He said, "The last two times Corporal Lester jumped with this equipment, he cut it loose from his 'chute and we lost all of our radio equipment. The next time he jumped, he did the same thing, only this time he released the bag that had our fifty-caliber machine gun, two bazookas, and our field phones in it! We cannot afford to have this guy throwing away anymore of our crucial equipment. I know you did not get the training for it, but we are talking about human lives that will need this equipment. OK, Duball, can we count on you?"

I swallowed really hard and said, "Sure thing, Sarge!"

Sergeant Smith said, "Allow me to introduce the GP Bag, which will be attached to your parachute, adding approximately seventy-five to a hundred pounds to your overall weight. So we take your body weight of a hundred and twenty pounds [I was very skinny] and add eighty pounds of personal equipment and the thirty-pound parachute. A one-hundred-and-twenty-pound man now weighs more than twice his weight, so that's like having another guy hanging on your 'chute with you."

I had to be lifted into the plane because I could not climb up the ladder to get into the plane. I also was supplied with fifty feet of half-inch nylon rope that was attached to me so I could lower this monster of a bag away from me and not collide with it upon impact with the ground. The Sergeant came over to check my equipment. He looked at my reserve 'chute and said to me, "DuVall, you need to turn this reserve 'chute in and get a reserve that does not have these 'butterfly wings' on those clamps."

"Why is that, Sarge? I asked.

"Because that GP Bag you got to jump with can bump up against your reserve 'chute clamps, and the 'chute will pop right off! They are on the same D ring together. You don't want to lose your reserve 'chute, do you?"

"OK, Sarge." Back to the truck I went with the reserve 'chute. The Sergeant issuing the 'chutes said he was all out of the type 'chute I needed and that maybe I could trade with somebody. "OK, I'll try that," I said.

But NOBODY wanted to trade 'chutes with me. I called the Sergeant over to see if he would trade, but he had butterfly clips too. I was just about to resign myself to the fact that I might lose my reserve 'chute because of the GP Bag when I noticed three Chaplains sitting quietly under the wing of our plane. One was a Jewish Rabbi, the other was a White Presbyterian, and the third Chaplain was a Black Baptist Minister. I decided to approach the brother Minister first with my story since he was nearest to me. I also noticed his reserve had no butterfly wings, so I started explaining the situation and said that I was hoping he would exchange 'chutes. That man looked at me as if I was Satan himself and said, "No way!" I then went to the White Minister, and he was less emphatic, but with a scornful look on his face, he shook his head no! I then turned to the Rabbi, and the same thing happened. He looked at me as if I was out of my mind.

I stood there for a minute looking at the three "men of the cloth" and saw stark fear in their eyes. I said to them, "If anything goes wrong with me up there, you are the ones who will have to explain to the Almighty why you didn't try to help me. (They just sat there and gave me a look that you would not believe.) I said, "So just to show all of you how much I believe in God and how I know He will protect me, I will jump with this reserve and I know I need not fear."

They loaded me into the plane. It was a C-46 Cargo, a twin-engine plane with no doors on it. I wobbled to my position and sat down next to the door of the plane so that when it came time for me to go, I could just roll out of my seat and fall out the door. But when the time came for me to exit, I could not get up! Two men had to pull me up and help me to the door. I stood at the door of the plane until I felt a tap on the leg, the signal to jump. I leaped out and tried to assume some kind of proper body position, but all I could do was follow the GP Bag and pray for the opening shock. In my head I counted, "One thousand, two thousand, three thou—" WHAM, PING! The 'chute opened, but what had made that PING noise? I realized the reserve 'chute had popped off one D ring and was hanging by the other. I was able to grab the reserve 'chute and reattach it to the D ring. I looked up at my canopy; it was beautiful.

I then went about looking around me and under me. Nobody was near me, so I began lowering the GP Bag with the fifty-foot rope until it reached its full length. I prepared myself for a rough landing, but it was not bad at all. A heavy ground wind was blowing that reinflated the parachutes and dragged a lot of the guys around on the ground, and they were having a tough time trying to recover. Those ground winds could really cause injuries. But lucky for me, that GP Bag was like an anchor, so I just lay there until I was ready to get up.

I hopped into a truck for the ride home, and who did I see in the truck but the three Chaplains I had spoken to earlier. They did not want to make eye contact with me. But I did manage to say aloud, "See, God loves me too!" Nobody said a mumbling word, and it was that way all the way back to camp. They never looked up at me. Was I the invisible evil spirit? The three of them just sat there like crows on a fence. At least I ruined their trip, as I knew they wouldn't dare act as if they were having a jolly good time in front of me.

Because of my GP Bag performances, I was promoted to Corporal, was reassigned as Squad Leader in my Platoon, and was made a "GP Bag Specialist." (OH BOY, just what I needed.)

CHAPTER 9

Nicodemus, the Black Paratrooper (1950 to 1952)

The Black soldiers were given a secret code name so that they could identify themselves when they were in the field or in enemy territory. The secret code name was "Nicodemus." Nicodemus was one of the few Jews who spoke up on Jesus's behalf at his trial under Pontius Pilot's rule as Governor of Jerusalem. He was also at Jesus's side when they took him down to bury him.

While I was participating in a field exercise one day, the Radio Operator I was assigned to had to answer the call of nature and asked me to answer any call that might come across the radio.

I said OK, and he took off. All of a sudden, this voice came across the radio: "'Niggerdemus One, this is Easy Fox. How do you read me, Niggerdemus? Niggerdemus, we need your help. Are you there, Niggerdemus?"

The Sergeant reappeared and shouted to me, "Don't you hear that call for help, DuVall?"

I said, "I hear somebody who can't seem to say that code word correctly! If he was in need of help, he should be able to pronounce that name as it should be pronounced. Otherwise, I see this call as a security risk!"

The Black Sergeant looked at me and said, "My job is to answer the call for help no matter how he says the word!" The Black soldier also said he could have me "shot" for negligence of duty!

I copped a plea by saying I was sorry, but deep down inside of me, I could not forget the sound of that White boy's voice as he articulated that word. Even after this incident, the Eighty-Second did not change the code name, despite the fact that the custom was to change the code name every thirty days or so for the sake of security.

My buddy, Owenby, and me on bivouac.

Thomas DuVall standing in the door of an airplane, ready to jump.

CHAPTER 10

The Black Paratrooper

The Black Paratroopers were of a different cut than their counterparts, the ordinary soldiers or "ground-pounders," as they were referred to by the Black Paratroopers. They were also referred to as "straight legs" because the ordinary soldiers were not allowed to wear jump boots with their uniforms, so their pants could not be bloused over their highly spit-shined Corcoran Paratrooper Boots (the Stacy Adams of military footwear!).

The Paratrooper boots were made with a clunky rubber heel that didn't sit well with us Black Paratroopers, so we took our boots to the shoe repairman and had him remove those clunky rubber heels and replace them with a thinner, leather heel, which made the toe of the boot look like it was pointing skyward. When we marched down the street, our heels sounded like one BIG TOCK! This sound made all the wives of the White Officers swoon as we passed in review.

The Black Paratrooper also altered the U.S. Army uniform to give it a little more spiff and pizzazz. He folded the collar of his shirt under and tied his tie in a nice Windsor knot to keep up with the "Billy Eckstine" tradition.

As Black Paratroopers we had to get up at 4:00 a.m. and stand in formation by 5:30. We would be loaded into trucks and taken to a parade field in the White area of Fort Bragg. There we had to stand in formation from 9:30 to 10:00 a.m., when the White Paratroopers would start to show up and stand in formation from 11:00 a.m. to noon. Then the band would show up to play music, and we would all march in review past a grandstand where all the Commanding Officers would stand with their wives.

It would take about forty-five more minutes before we would get a chance to move our legs to try to march. Since we had been standing in the same spot since 5:00 a.m., we really had to struggle with our legs to get the blood moving again. And it was incredible how many White soldiers would be lying on the ground by then. They didn't seem to be able to stand in the noonday sun for long. When the parade ended on any given Saturday, the Black Paratroopers were the only group who would finish the parade with the same number of men they started out with!

I asked the Company Commander one day, "Why do we Blacks have to get up so much earlier and stand so much longer than the White Troopers have to?

He said, "Because we have a reputation for being late for everything, and I am determined to dispense with that stigma. *'WE'* will always be there when the Whites *arrive!*"

As we stood watching a Division mass jump on a drop zone area at Fort Bragg, a friend once said to me, "I can tell whether the plane is dropping White or Black Paratroopers!"

I said, "How can you tell?"

He said, "When the White Troopers exit the plane, they don't seem to be able to exit in a rhythmic manner. They have gaps and hesitations in their streams. When the Black Troopers exit the plane, they exit the plane with one smooth move—'swoosh'—and they are all out in one unbroken stream!"

I said, "Yeah, you are right!!"

As Black Paratroopers, we had our own dictionary of words that sounded the same but had a different meaning, such as:

Apple: a woman's buttocks

Phat girl: plenty of hip, ass, and titty

Ghost the scene: to disappear, to leave

Short: car, ride

Tee shirt: a White guy

Scratch: money

Split: leave the scene

Spook: Black guy

S'blib: Black guy

Shoe, soul, bro, or home: a Black guy

Wheels, rubbers, or ride: car

Cop some ZZZs: to get some sleep

New vine: new suit of clothing

The Black Paratroopers of the Communication Platoon of Headquarters Company, Third Battalion, 505th Airborne Infantry Regiment, Eighty-Second Airborne Division, at Fort Bragg, North Carolina, had a mascot. His name was Cyrano de Bergerac.

Cyrano de Bergerac was a soldier's soldier, a swashbuckler, and a poet of great acclaim. He fell in love with Roxanne, the girlfriend of his best friend, Christian de Neuvillette. Christian was able to get Cyrano to write love letters to Roxanne, whom Cyrano loved secretly.

Roxanne wanted to hear all the sweet things Christian had written to her while he was away on the battlefield. And when he was home on leave, she wanted to hear him rhapsodize. Christian de Neuvillette was very handsome but had no gift for words. He could not tell Roxanne that the words Cyrano had written in love letters to her were not his own words. And Cyrano, with his heart breaking from the pain he felt, vowed to keep it a secret.

Christian died from wounds he received in battle. If Cyrano had only come forward, he could have had Roxanne's love, as she was in love with the *soul of the writer*! Badly wounded from being on the battlefield, Cyrano finally told her it was his words she loved; then he died. She was in double pain from both deaths.

A soldier in our Platoon decided he would use some of Cyrano's suave finesse with dialogue and style in his letters to his girl back home in Philly. He especially liked the line, "Roxanne, Roxanne, your name rings like a bell in my heart!" All he did was change the name to the name of his girlfriend, and lo and behold, it worked. The girl fell for it hook, line, and sinker. She was now in love with this "poor, lonely soldier" aaaalllll the way down there in Fort Bragg, North Carolina.

He began writing such letters to multiple girls. Two of them happened to meet to talk of their love letters, only to discover identical words and phrases. They wrote back that they wanted something a little more original than that and said that they too had now seen the movie!

I was *OK* with Cyrano, but I passed on the letter writing. However, phrases like, "Send me Giants" (meaning "Bring it on!") stuck with us. Cyrano was an anti-disciplinarian, which we respected, so we could easily relate to him and his traits and habits. When one of the guys could recite a poem from Cyrano or a Cyrano statement that was apropos for that moment, he was crowned *"CYRANO"* for a day!

One bright, sunny fall day, an announcement went out to all companies of the 505th Airborne Infantry Regiment that they were going on a ninety-day maneuver operation and would be operating out of San Saba, down near Brownsville, Texas. San Saba was near the Mexican border. We figured we were all going to jump out of a plane when we flew over the town, but that was not the case. The First and Second Battalions were flying down. The Third Battalion (a.k.a. "The Black Bat") was being trucked down by an Army Convoy traveling at thirty-five miles per hour (Army regulations) for over two thousand miles. It took us two weeks and 520 piss calls to get there. We all also had sore behinds from sitting on those hard wooden truck benches for fourteen days. However, I enjoyed the camaraderie and got to see North Carolina, South Carolina, Alabama, Louisiana, Tennessee, Mississippi, New Mexico, and Texas by looking over my shoulder in the back of the truck.

We once stopped by the roadside because we thought we had reached a body of water. We all grabbed our soap and towels and headed for the water. We soon found out that it was a man-made lake, as the owner had gotten wind of it and had come out to take pictures of all of the naked Black bodies. (There were about three hundred of us running around buck naked.) He must not have called the police, though before we knew it, a crowd of White people had gathered, and they ALL had cameras. They stayed until we were done, and then they left too.

It took us about a week to get to Texas and another week of traveling through Texas to get to Southern Texas. Texas is the only place I've been where you can travel all day, go to bed, wake up, travel all day, go to bed, wake up, and still be in Texas. (Gracious sakes!) And there was nothing to really see except a lot of sheep shit and cow dung! (Boy oh boy!)

We went through one town that looked just like the ghost towns in the movies. They gave us leave to go into town, so we got dressed up and went to this ghost town. We saw an old tavern with swinging doors and decided to go in. Though there were only four of us Black Paratroopers, I think we outnumbered the population.

We walked through the swinging doors and could not believe our eyes! It was just like in the cowboy movies, with the bar rail and foot-rest, spittoons, and a young maiden who approached our table. (We were just waiting for the movie cameras to roll!) She asked us what we would have. We immediately said, "Four beers, please, and a shot of rye."

She looked at us with amazement and said, "We don't serve alcoholic beverages here!"

"Why not?" we asked.

"It's against Texas law to serve alcoholic beverages. This is a dry state," she said.

We couldn't believe we were in a real Western tavern but could not get whiskey! So one of the soldiers asked, "Where were all those cowboys drinking that we saw in the movies?"

"What can you serve?" we asked.

"We have plenty of Coca-Cola and orange drink."

"Listen, where can we get some whiskey to drink?" we asked.

She called the proprietor, and he said he was going to call the Sheriff. That's when we got nervous. The Sheriff came; he was a big Black guy with what looked like the biggest, whitest, ten-gallon cowboy hat I had ever seen. He asked us what kind and how many, so we told him a fifth of scotch and a fifth of rum. "Wait right here," he said.

We stood there a little while, and he came back with nothing in his hands. He stopped at our table, took his hat off, and revealed two fifths of whiskey in his hat. We gave him the money and went back into the tavern. The proprietor told us that we would have to keep it out of sight by pouring our drinks from under the table.

When we ran out of whiskey, we went looking for the Sheriff. We found him, but he was going off duty. He took us to the Post Office and said to the guy at the stamp window, "Give them what they want when they want it, OK?" The guy agreed, and the Sheriff said, "This is how we do it down here!" We thanked him and went back to the tavern. That's the way it *was* all the way to San Saba, Texas.

Part of the reason it took so long to get from Fort Bragg, North Carolina, to San Saba, Texas, was that the Army traveled only eight hours a day, so we had to stop and pitch tent, prepare a meal, and sleep out in the woods on the outskirts of town. In the morning we would get up, have breakfast, break camp, load up the trucks, and start out for another eight hours of driving. Then we again had to offload trucks, pitch tents, dig sumps for latrines, and so on before bedding down for the night. It was a fourteen-day routine and did not include showers.

The First and Second Battalions had gotten there within hours because they had been flown down to San Saba ahead of us. They had made several exhibition parachute jumps with disastrous results. The White Battalions had been underestimating the Texas ground winds, and many of the men had been injured. The injuries mostly included broken ankles, arms, and legs, from what I could tell as the man chosen to run back and forth to deliver and pick up mail and messages to be delivered to Headquarters Third Battalion.

I reported what I saw to the Company Commander (Captain Cain from New York City), and he suggested we rise early, have a light breakfast, and jump early because the sun made the winds stronger as it got higher in the sky. Were the White Paratroopers trying to please the midday crowds? That seemed to be the case, so the Third Battalion decided to truck everybody to the airport the night before the jump and sleep under the wings of the planes. We arose at around 5:00 a.m., suited up, had breakfast, and waited for the pilots to show up. When they arrived around 9:00 a.m. to rev up their planes, they were surprised to see us with our 'chutes on, ready to jump. They said our request was most unusual because the other outfits had not been showing up until 11:00 a.m. Our Commanding Officer told them there had been a change due to scheduling and that we had to be back at our stations by noon. The White pilots begrudgingly drank their coffee and started up the engines.

By the time eleven o'clock came around, we were already jumping. We had no casualties—not one! We picked up our 'chutes, marched back to our trucks, and were back at our base camp in time for lunch and a noonday nap. We received no comment from officials at the

Regimental Headquarters, but they managed to punish us by not making it possible for us to reach the Greyhound and Trailway buses for transportation to the nearest town (San Antonio) on weekend passes. The only way we got to see San Antonio was by hitching a ride. A few rundown pickup trucks stopped by the Black Troop area one weekend and gave us a lift to a town for some recreation.

The local people got wind of our plight. They banded together and threw a big party at one of their ranch houses for us. These people looked like people of mixed blood; they were Black and Indian people who lived side by side on the open ranges. They were all ranch helpers and sharecroppers, I think, because their dwellings were all rather dilapidated and in dire need of repair. But they were doing their damndest to make us feel like human beings, and we deeply appreciated their efforts, especially since they had so little themselves.

We were all standing around in the yard talking about where we were from when a lady came to the door and rang a dinner bell. There must have been about thirty of us, and with the family members and neighbors there, we must have totaled about forty or fifty people. When we got inside, we saw all this prepared food that they must have been up all night the night before preparing, and we were hungry. They all stepped back to allow us to go first. We all stepped up, and the floor began to creak. The creaking got louder and louder. I looked around at the host and neighbors for a reaction. They were greatly concerned, as the floor had begun to sag in the middle!

We stood holding our drinks and food in our hands. Suddenly the floor began moving downward to the basement. We didn't know how deep the basement was and whether we would all break our legs when we hit the bottom. Luckily we fell only about three to four feet to the ground floor, so the party went on. We offered to come back the next week to help them build another floor for their house, but they would not have it. They said that they would fix it themselves and that we should not worry. God bless those good people!

CHAPTER 11

The Second Year with the Eighty-Second (Early 1952)

I was into my second year at Fort Bragg, and it had been interesting, to say the least. I was told to report to the Company Clerk, Corporal Kent. He was a short, stocky guy with a tough, affected sound to his voice. "Corporal DuVall, I have orders on you," he said.

"Orders?" I said. "Orders to do what?"

He said, "You have been assigned to the Twenty-Fourth Infantry as a cadreman [a non-parachute, black outfit made up of young draftees to be trained for duty in Korea]. Your duties will be to render Army Basic Training [Boot Camp] to new draftees. You will prepare them to be sent to Korea for frontline duty.

"Korea, where is that?" I said.

"You don't need to know where it is. Just prepare them for their trip."

I was taken to another section of the "Smoke Bomb Area" (where all of us Black soldiers lived). When I got out of the jeep, all the Black soldiers started saluting me. I said, "You don't have to salute me; I am a Noncommissioned Officer. You only salute Commissioned Officers who have bars on their shoulders."

"YES, SIR!" they said.

"You don't say 'sir' to me either. I am 'Corporal' DuVall; that's all."

"Yes, sir!" was their reply.

This was a learning experience for me too. Some of the guys had never seen running water before. I had to go behind them and turn the water faucets off in the morning. I finally got everybody together and held a meeting in the latrine on the proper way to use a sink.

Several weeks went by, and some of the guys were still saluting me and calling me "sir." A White Officer witnessed this one day and called me into his office for an explanation. I told him I had been trying to put a stop to it and maybe it would help if he could say something about it to them. He looked at me with disdain and said, "Don't let me catch you doing it again!" I couldn't believe my ears. Hadn't he listened to what I'd said? Anyway, whenever the brothers saluted me, I would return the salute and say, "You don't need to salute me!" They could not accept the fact that I was not an Officer.

One day I was finalizing things in my Platoon and preparing for the great graduation day for the new Black Troops of the Twenty-Fourth Infantry (who would soon be famous for their heroic performance in Korea). One of the inductees walked up to me and in a very flirty, ladylike manner said, "Corporal DuVall, I bet I will make Sergeant before you will!" The guy had been in the Army for two months, so I couldn't believe what he'd said. *What is he up to,* I said to myself. *Is he just letting me know he is gay?* I passed it off as loose talk.

Graduation was over, so I headed back to my regular outfit. When I arrived back at the barracks, I found I didn't know anybody in the place. Guys were approaching me and asking me my name. I asked them where my outfit was, and they said, "Oh, those guys were all shipped out to the One Hundred and Eighty-Seventh in Korea." Wow, all my buddies were gone! I still cannot describe how bad I felt. It was like coming home to my family and finding someone else living in my house! I was an orphan now.

Payday came, and there was no pay for me, as my records had not caught up with my moving around. I had to hitch a ride down to the White Troops' area to talk to someone in Payroll. When I finally reached my destination and walked into the office. A Staff Sergeant stepped up to me and said, "I am Staff Sergeant Williams. May I help you?" The voice was familiar to my ears, but I could not place it. Then with great delight and a big broad smile, he said, "Ohhh, it's you, my favorite Corporal!" Then he said, ever so sweetly, "SEE, I told you I would make Sergeant before you would!" I looked and saw that he did not have three stripes, but *five* stripes on his arm—three up and two rockers! "What can I do for my favorite Corporal?" he asked.

I told him my story. Still smiling, he said, "Don't you worry one bit. I will have a check cut for you and send it to your Commanding Officer post haste, OK! Now you come back to see me OK?"

"OK," I said and left. When I got outside, I had to find a place to sit for a minute and ponder what I had just witnessed. I returned to my barrack and found out the Company Clerk had been looking for me. Corporal Kent told me he had orders for me to report to the Eighty-Second Signal Company on the Main Post. I was being transferred to a White outfit. I told him I preferred to stay where I was.

Corporal Kent said to me, "You go where your orders send you. You don't have a choice in this matter, so go pack your things. You are no longer in the Infantry." I said I wanted to speak to the Company Commander.

I went to see the Company Commander, Captain Cain, and he said, "President Harry S. Truman said we must integrate the Armed Forces. I selected you because you would set a good example for the Black soldier."

I told him I was not interested in being a Jackie Robinson. I enjoyed being with my own. But he said, "This is the Army, and you go where you are told."

"Yes, sir," I said! I saluted, did an about-face, and walked out.

It was about this same time that my sister, Jeanne, wrote me a letter saying she had bumped into Rosita Phifer (the girl from St. Vincent de Paul) and that she would send me her address. I did write her, and we did hook up in DC.

CHAPTER 12

Integration in the Ranks (Mid-1952)

It was 1952, and I was being sent to an all-White outfit to serve out my third year in the Army. I arrived at my new home and was escorted to the place where I would sleep for the next twelve months. There were eight other guys (all White) in the Squad, and I was the ranking man, so they made me the Squad Leader. The guys were all older than I was; some were in their late twenties and early thirties. I was only eighteen years old. Right away I felt dissension. I saw malevolence in their eyes. But it was my first day, so they said not a word.

The next day I was given orders to take my Squad to the parade field and drill them. I called my Squad to attention, and this one White guy decided he had to get me straight. He said, "I'm not taking any orders from the likes of you, and you had better be very careful because you don't want me to get my 'IRISH' up!"

So I said to him, "You had better do as I say because you don't want to get my 'NIGGER' up!" For the next twelve months, he did not give me a bit of trouble. (Blacks must have had a BAD reputation where he was from!)

The injustices became even more evident as time went on. I found myself involved in many a fistfight. It was a horrible experience. It was UNBELIEVABLE! When the White guys argued with each other, they would refer to each other as a "Black" son of a bitch or a "BLACK" bastard? I had never seen the likes of it. It seemed that if you wanted to make a White guy really angry, all you had to do was call him BLACK. (Lord, have mercy!)

I once lost my cool and addressed the Platoon as you SOBs, and boy oh boy, things really got out of hand then. They immediately surrounded me, and the most muscle-bound man in the group stepped forward. That's all I remember. The next thing I knew, I was in the latrine and they were throwing water on me, trying to bring me around. I looked in the mirror and saw the biggest fat lip I had ever seen. They had to take me to the hospital to get stitches in my mouth. The lesson I learned was that it was more acceptable for a Black to call someone an MF. Just don't call a White an SOB. If you do, make sure that there is a wall or a door against your back or that you've got a fast horse!

The Black soldiers in the area found out about the assault on me and begged me to press charges against the Private who'd put my lights out. I could not get myself to do that, mainly because I felt I had been wrong to address those soldiers out of their name as I did. So I blamed myself for that.

CHAPTER 13

Having Fun on Route 301 (Circa Late Summer 1952)

When things had settled down somewhat, a few of the White soldiers asked me if I would be interested in taking a trip somewhere with them (I can't remember where right now). I was surprised they had asked, so I said OK. I wanted to see how going to a White town with a car full of White soldiers would work out. We left on a Saturday afternoon at around 4:00 p.m.

I cannot recall what town we were in, but I do remember it was along Route 301 North. We decided to make a stop, and I had to find a restroom. I went inside this roadside restaurant to use the restroom, and the guy behind the counter yelled, "Hey you, where you think you goin'?" I looked at him and pointed to the restroom. He yelled back,

"The Hell you are. You goin' to that Colored place about ten more miles down the road, that's where you goin'!"

The place got quiet. They all looked at me to see what I was going to do, so I decided to walk back out the way I had come in. When I got outside, the White guys could see I was not happy and wanted to know what had happened in there, so I told them. Surprisingly all five of the White guys I was with wanted to go back inside to teach those civilians what the U.S. Paratroopers had to say about it. I wouldn't have it, so one White soldier said, "If DuVall can't go to the restroom inside, we are all going to go to the restroom outside on the grass!"

The other three White soldiers yelled, "Yeah! Let's piss on his grass." They all pulled out their peckers and proceeded to urinate on the grass in front of the shop in broad daylight. Then the soldiers looked over their shoulders and yelled, "Come on, DuVall, we are doing this for you, man. Come on, take your joint out and piss. We stopped for you to do this, so come on!" I could not get myself to pull my pecker out of my pants to save my life.

When they were done, we got back in the car and hauled ass out of there, periodically looking back for the Fuzz! Then the silence was broken by me saying, "If you see that Colored place down the road about ten miles, would you please stop for me to go to the restroom and get a sandwich?" The driver said, "You had your chance back there, DuVall. Now you want us to stop again, with the cops on our tail?"

We laughed and did end up stopping at the Colored Joint, where we bought chicken, potato salad, collards, and so on. The food was so good that whenever we saw a sign that said "Colored Only," we automatically stopped and tanked up on gas, food, drink, camaraderie, music, and big smiles. This went on all the way up 301 and all the way back to Fort Bragg, North Carolina, circa 1952. God bless Shroeder, Como, Owenby, Nungesser, and Kovack. They were good Troopers!

CHAPTER 14

From Being Ski Trooper to Being Discharged (Circa 1952 to 1953)

The Army decided I needed more training, and this time they wanted me to be a Ski Trooper. They sent me to Camp Drum, New York, for training in winter survival. I had to drive a jeep from Fort Bragg, North Carolina, to Camp Drum, New York, up near Niagara Falls, a distance of about two thousand miles, it seemed. I did not have a driver's license, nor did I know how to drive. I informed them that I did not know how to drive, figuring that would get me out of it. The Sergeant looked at me and said, "We'll teach you!" And that they did!

I tried three times to pass the driving test and failed three times. The Captain looked at me and said, "DuVall, fail this test one more time and your ass is going to jail!" I said, "Yes, sir" and passed the test. They gave me the jeep, and off we went to Camp Drum. It took us about a month to get there.

The Army gave me these skis and a set of three waxes—yellow wax, black wax, and red wax. Each colored wax had a special area under the skis that it had to be applied to. I applied the waxes, and they sent me out there one day to learn how to stop, how to maneuver, and most of all, how TO FALL! I worked on the falling part most.

I was out there all day and half the night. After a particularly bad fall, I lost one of my skis. The thing came off and kept going. I had to walk back to camp, which took me all night. I got back to camp frozen stiff and tired as hell of walking. I turned in my one ski and told them I was not coming back. They wanted to know about the other ski. I told them it was still going, as far as I knew. I then went to bed.

Looking for a place to hide out from skiing for a while, I went to the dayroom and heard some kind of swinging music. It was mambo music coming out of the dayroom. I could not believe my ears. I went inside to see what was jumping off and saw this brother dancing like crazy by himself! I found out that his name was Roland Cave and he was from Washington, DC. "Hey man, I'm from DC too!" I said. He danced like a real professional, and I was taken aback by the drumbeats and rhythm solos. I wanted to find some conga drums and join in on the music. I made up my mind then and there that it was the first thing I was going to do when I got my discharge. In the meantime I spent a lot of time and money running back and forth to New York to pick up Rosita and spend time at the Palladium (the home of the mambo!).

When I got back to Fort Bragg, I had about six more months left there. The day came for me to be discharged, and they did not even mention reenlistment to me. They cheated me out of the opportunity to say "no thanks," but I was just glad to be out of there.

I arrived at the Fayetteville, North Carolina, train station to find out there was going to be a four-hour layover. I didn't know what was I going to do for four hours in the town that had thrown me in jail the first hour I was there back in 1950.

I was a veteran now and still had to drink my water from the "COLORED" fountain. Of course, the "Colored" fountain was not working, and a fat ass White cop was stationed nearby to see to it that I did not break the rule.

I sat down in the COLORED section of the station to think for a while. Another just-discharged Paratrooper soon entered the station. He was an Oriental fellow who had a certain air of independence about him. We caught each other's eye and saw we were from the same outfit, but we did not know each other. We started talking and found out we were both going to Washington, DC.

He said his name was Chung and pointed out that we had time to take in a movie. I told Chung I was not going to pay for a ticket and sit in the balcony of a Jim Crow movie house with a Discharge in my hand. He said, "Balcony! We are going to sit down in the Orchestra!"

I laughed and said he was kidding. He looked at me in a stern way and said, "Come on, you and I are going to the movies together." He was not smiling, so I said, "OK, let's go!"

We walked up to the theater. He bought his ticket first, and then I put my money in the window. The woman in the box was not sure what to do, so she sold me a ticket with a long stare. I stared back and picked up my ticket. Chung and I swaggered in and picked our seats square in the middle of the theater. The theater was full of White Paratroopers. They pretended not to see us. I was a little nervous but was not going to show it.

Then the inevitable happened. I had to go to the restroom. I told Chung I had to go take a leak. He paused for a minute and said, "I better go with you." This guy sounded like Bruce Lee when he said that. I was impressed with his tenacity. He was a little guy but was stouthearted. His face was stern and set.

We hit the men's room, and the place was empty. As we were standing at the urinals, the restroom filled up immediately with White Paratroopers pretending they had to go too. We both noticed their behavior but did not bat an eyelash. (I felt so proud of this little Asian man standing by my side.) I felt no fear of the enemy, even though the odds were at least ten to one in that little room. We stood at the urinals until we were done, swaggered over to the sinks, washed our hands in a deliberate manner, turned slowly, and dried our hands. He slowly reached for the door and allowed me to exit FIRST. He followed me out, and we went back to our seats (Orchestra Center) and enjoyed the rest of the movie.

We left there and went back to the train station. We picked up our bags and went to board the train. We were near the front of the train, which was where the car they allowed the "nigras" to ride in was. It was placed right behind the locomotive because that car would take the most impact if there was a head-on collision. Hence, most of the dead and injured would be in that car.

I gave the conductor my ticket and was about to board the train. The conductor said to my friend Chung, "I can't let you on here; you will have to go down to the other end."

Chung said, "I want to sit with my friend, and I refuse to do otherwise."

The conductor said, "You will go to the back, or you will not get on this train!"

I said, "Chung, this is not China. I am thankful to have met you, but the law is the law." I shook his hand and said good-bye. "Maybe I'll see you in DC," I said. He said OK, and we boarded the train.

About twenty minutes into the trip, a soldier plopped himself down next to me. It was CHUNG! I asked, "Hey, man, what are you doing here?"

He said, "Nobody is going to tell me where to or where not to sit. This is supposed to be a free country, and we are free, right?"

I said, "Right on!"

About an hour or so later, all the sisters in the coach were reaching under their seats and pulling out baskets of food. Now the whole coach was abuzz, and the smell of fried chicken was everywhere. We had never seen so much food. They broke their necks giving us plates of golden brown fried chicken, potato salad, coleslaw, homemade biscuits, sweet potato pie, lemonade, bread pudding, candied yams, chocolate cake, peaches, and licorice sticks.

Chung was completely BLOWN AWAY. He was no longer Chinese; he even looked Colored now. He would never be the same, and neither would I. We weren't even asked if we wanted to eat. They just fed us and fed us and fed us. Boy oh boy, my people, my people—God bless us all. As we were about to leave, all the women gave Chung a big kiss.

We pulled into Union Station, Washington, DC, and I grabbed my bag. Chung rose, we embraced, and he got back on the train for Boston. That was the last I saw of Trooper Charlie Chung, bless his soul.

"African Holiday," a touring revue at the Apollo Theater, featuring these performers: Alvin Ailey, Beebee Capps, Zebede Collins, Joe Commodore, Afida Derby, Akwasiba Derby, Curtis James, Tommy Johnson, Peggy Kirkpatrick, Baba Moses Miannes, Mickey Newby, Delores Parker, Brock Peters, Mike Quashie, and Helena Walker.

CHAPTER 15

Back on the Block and Hangin' Out (May 9, 1953)

I arrived back at the house, and my family was glad to see me. Monday morning came, and I hit the street to look for a job. I was filling out applications to beat the band. There were plenty of jobs for veterans available, though I found out those jobs were for White veterans.

About a month later, I got called for a job at the Federal Trade Commission on Seventh and Pennsylvania Avenue NW, DC, as a Mailroom Clerk for $49 a week. The work environment included all the Racism of a modern nightmare.

They sent me across the street to get some kind of classification card I had to have. (It may have been a Social Security Insurance card.) They had a space there for race, so I put Black. The woman called out my name, and I proceeded to the front desk. She was a Black woman and wanted to know why I had put "Black" down. She looked at me and sarcastically said, "You ain't Black!" She tried desperately to erase my choice.

I asked her what I was, and she replied, "You are 'Colored.'"

I said, "Well what color am I?"

She glared at me and kept erasing. She wrote "col." and said, "Now that's what you are!" She then handed the card to me.

"Lady, where I just came from, 'col.' is the abbreviation for "colonel!" I said.

Shortly thereafter I ran into my friend Roland Cave, the mambo dancer I had run into up at Camp Drum! He told me he was trying to start having mambo sessions in DC. He wondered if I would be interested in working with him. I said sure, and we met every Saturday evening at the Cairo Hotel, the Dunbar Hotel, and the Capital Caravan Hall.

Roland Cave taught me how to dance and how to play the mambo beat on the conga drums. This was my introduction to playing drums, and the rest was history. Thank you, Roland Cave!

I was a conga-drumming, mambo-dancing, Afro-Jazz, Afro-Cuban NUT! I had met Machito and Graciela, Mongo Santamaria, Candido, Willie Bobo, Arsenio Rodriguez, Tito Rodriguez, Bovain Hunt, etc. If they were on the scene in the late forties and early fifties, I probably knew them. I also knew people like Carnation Charlie, Peanuts, Celia Cruz, Eddie Bonnemere, Joe Loco, Joe Panama, Ray Barretto, and Fats Greene. The list was long.

About a year or so after I was discharged, I decided to marry my childhood sweetheart and just move up to New York because it was getting expensive to go back and forth so much. I had fallen in love with New York City while I was in the Army and visiting Rosita and her relatives, plus I missed being able to go to the Savoy Ballroom and the Palladium Ballroom. They always had the top dance bands there. I also believed I could make a better living there.

Rosita and I talked it over and agreed that we would do better if we lived in New York City, so we decided that she would return to her Aunt's place on 128th Street, between Seventh and Lenox Avenue. Then she would find a room for rent for us to stay in until I could find a decent job. Eventually we found an apartment on 127th Street near Lenox Avenue. It was above a storefront Baptist Church. The Pastor and his entourage were constantly complaining to me about hearing the beating of those "diabolical drums" over their heads. I asked them to invite me down to play for the prayer services and pointed out that that way they could enjoy it more. WELL that went over like a fart in Church, so we started looking for another place to live because I did not want to stop drumming.

In the meantime I kept hearing this distant drumming and singing in the neighborhood (New Yorkers sometimes called it the "'hood"). I just had to find out where it was coming from. It had a haunting beat that kept me mesmerized and enchanted! While standing on the southeast corner of 127th Street and Lenox Avenue one day, I saw an elderly Black man standing there. He was wearing a gray gabardine trench coat and a wide-brimmed fedora-looking hat cocked on the side of his head. He was a proud-looking soul. In his hand he carried an Army duffel bag that I could see contained some kind of drum!

I decided to follow the man as he headed for an office building on the corner where I was standing. (I think the name of the building was The Mutual of Omaha Insurance Company.) He went up the steps and entered an auditorium. There were other people waiting for him. When he appeared everybody started taking off their street clothes and donned their leotards and dancing skirts. There were two or three male dancers there. I learned their names: Mickey Newby, Zebede Collins, and a big guy named Joe Commodore. The female dancers there were

Esther Rolle and her cousins, as well as Joan (Akwasiba) and Merle (Afida) Derby.

The leader of this group was a guy named Asadata Dafora. They were mesmerizing! The other Drummers there were Montego Joe and Chief Bey. I couldn't believe all of this was going on within a few hundred feet from my place on 127th Street!

The old man and his two cousins had my undivided attention. I have never heard any drumming like that before! I could not tear myself away. I asked around for the name of the old man. I was told his name was Moses Miannes, but he was called "Machine Gun Moses" by the people in Harlem. They said his hands were so fast when he played that his drum sounded like the rapid fire of a machine gun! He was from Nigeria and was a descendant of the Ijaw people who lived on the delta of the River Niger. It was only natural that he and the men of his tribe were seafarers. He and his cousins had joined the British Merchant Marines. They sailed from Nigeria to England, where Baba (it means "father" in Swahili) Moses fell ill. His two cousins left for America on the next ship out of England. The two cousins decided to jump ship and stay in Harlem.

When Moses was released from the hospital in 1933, he caught the next ship sailing for America and came straight to Harlem in search of his two cousins. Baba Moses had heard so much about Harlem as a boy, and his dream was about to become a reality. He and his two cousins were all hanging out on the corner of 125th Street and Lenox Avenue with no big city skills for work. They were trying to figure out how they were going to find jobs to sustain themselves when a big black Cadillac limousine suddenly pulled up in front of them. The car door opened, and a well-dressed White man smoking a big cigar jumped out of the limo and walked up to them. He said, "Hey, if any of you know of any African-looking men who can beat on some drums, give me a call because I can give them a job." He handed Baba Moses his card. The man was a booking agent! He said he was looking for talent for the Chicago World's Fair of 1933 (which is the year that is on the birth certificate my mother helped me get).

The two cousins were upset at the White man's remarks and wanted to pounce on him, but Baba Moses cooled them out by saying, "Wait, we need the work! So let's find some drums and call him back!"

They set out looking for some hand drums in New York City and could not find a one. One of their neighbors said they knew of a carpenter from Trinidad who lived on 116th Street and could probably help them. They sought him out and found that he *was* familiar with the type of drum Baba Moses described, so he agreed to build the three drums for Moses and his two cousins. Once the shells were completed, they had to find skins for them.

They were told of a slaughterhouse in Brooklyn where the Kosher Rabbis slaughtered their livestock. Baba Moses hopped on the A train and went to Brooklyn in search of this slaughterhouse. He found it and was able to purchase three calf skins that had to be cured and dried before they could be attached to the shells. They bought yards and yards of hemp rope for the lacing. When all was done, they had three fine-looking "Ashiko" Drums. They were the Mother Drum (which was the biggest), the Papa Drum (which was somewhat smaller than the Mother Drum), and the Baby Drum (which was the smallest of the three).

The Ashiko Drum Family was now ready to go to the Chicago World's Fair! While there, Baba Moses and his cousins were approached by Paul Robeson, the famous singer, actor, narrator, and historian, who hired them as part of his traveling entourage. Baba Moses accompanied such notables as Ismay Andrews, Pearl Primus, Alphonse Cimber (Haitian Drummer), Asadata Dafora, Josh White, Canada Lee, William Marshall, Maya Angelou, and many others. He also played in Orson Welles's production of *Macbeth* in London.

Asadata Dafora of Sierra Leone had come to New York City to start his own Troupe and hired Baba Moses and his cousins to be his Drummers. I also met another up-and-coming Drummer doing the same thing I was doing (digging the drumming scene). He too was a recently discharged veteran of the Armed Forces. We started talking, and he said his name was Al Humphrey. (He is now known around town as "Babafemi," and I am still in touch with him.) Getting together with these guys became a weekly event and was my first introduction to real African dancing and drumming. But I had to leave the neighborhood because the Church owned the building in which I rented the room, and my landlord wanted me and my drums out!

Just as those Drummers inspired me, I've been told that I inspired these performers: Doug Carn, Karen Daniels, Juan Gray's Voices Ensemble, Mike Friend, Hanif, Kehende, Yahya, Eric Lewis, Tommy "Matombo" Freeman, Rudy Morales, Steve Nash, Olujami, André Richardson, and others.

Rosita and I found a five-floor walk-up apartment on Amsterdam Avenue for more money and agreed to share the place with her brother and his family. That arrangement did not last long, so we ended up landing a place in the Lincoln Projects at 132nd Street and Madison Avenue. I was back on the East side and was only five short blocks from Baba Moses's place of rehearsal, at 127th and Fifth Avenue. This same building housed the Afro Arts Cultural Center of Harlem, headed by Mr. Simon Bly, Jr., Director and Founder. Two blocks to the West side was where Sidney Poitier and his wife had their corner neighborhood store. Harry Belafonte was also in the 'hood, as were Mike Quashie (the Limbo King), Leon Thomas, Ozzie Davis, Ruby Dee, Lionel Hampton, Sugar Ray, Jackie Robinson (at Chock Full o' Nuts), Max Roach, Paul Partin, and Sydney Brown.

So there I was again, back in the 'hood an' just "*hanging out*!"
HARLEM, U.S.A.

PART III

CHAPTER I

The Office Boy
(Circa 1955 to 1956)

I had been a veteran for almost three years when I finally landed a steady job as an "office boy" through the New York City Catholic Charity Employment Agency, which was down on Twenty-Second Street on the East Side. They sent me to a place called *Atlas Magazines,* then located on Madison Avenue and Sixtieth Street. The company produced exposé magazines on Hollywood movie stars, who would show up at the office from time to time to make their New York City appearance.

The person who interviewed me was a handsome, middle-aged woman named Ms. Augustine. She was the office manager there. During the interview she discovered I was married and had two children. She wanted to know why in the world anyone married with children would want an office boy job. I told her I was a Black ex-GI and could not find work in the field I was trained, which was as a Cryptographer in the military. In civilian life it was an exclusive (no Blacks) field. She said she was impressed with my sense of responsibility and asked me if I could start immediately! I said yes, and she hired me.

Getting this job allowed me to ride the Madison Avenue bus to work, which stopped at Sixtieth and Madison. I stepped off the bus and walked up the steps to work. I felt like I was on a roll. I tried to be the best office boy they had ever seen. I kept that office in Inspector General Condition. Every pencil in that office would always have a fine sharp point. I did everything but scrub the floors and shine the brass!

In the meantime my GI Educational Benefits were about to expire! I had to decide where I was going to school or I would lose my GI benefits. Mama had always tried to encourage me to pursue my Art training, so I figured this was the perfect time to move on it. I started looking for a good Art school that I could enroll in.

I visited all the Art schools in Manhattan and decided I wanted to go to the Art Students League on Fifty-Seventh Street. Unfortunately the U.S. Government would not pay for it, as the league did not have a curriculum designed for Commercial Art and the Government refused to pay for a Fine Art curriculum. My second choice was to attend the Art school on the next block, about a hundred yards west of the Art Students League on Fifty-Seventh Street. It was called the Pan American School of Art in New York City. The Instructors at the Art Students League also taught at the Pan American School of Art from time to time, so I would be getting the better of two worlds—a school with both a Commercial Art curriculum and a Fine Art curriculum.

I liked the place, so I put in an application. They told me that I would have to face a review board and provide some samples of my ability. I would also have to pass a drawing test. For this test they set a large plaster cast statue of *The Thinker* on a table in front of me and asked me to draw it in its entirety, "twelve inches high, in twenty minutes. You will be judged on its accuracy, its completeness, and attention to detail," they said.

I didn't know where to start! I decided to start with the feet and work my way up to the head. That's the way I had done it as a child. Twenty minutes later, I heard, "Time's up!" The Instructor came over to me, looked at the drawing, and said, "Mr. DuVall, we distinctly said it should be twelve inches high!" He measured my drawing and got about seven inches or so. "Would you like to try again?"

"Yes, if you don't mind," I said. This time I had to remember to make it twelve inches high. I threw myself into my drawing. I was pleased that the drawing was looking so much better and was determined that this one would be the *clincher*!

The Instructor looked at the drawing and said, "Mr. DuVall, your drawing is now only six and a half inches. It's getting smaller when I asked you to make it larger!" He looked at me as if I were an alien. He jumped up, took the drawing in his hands, and said, "I'll be right back!"

I was really feeling low in the esteem department now. How could I have done such a thing? I was just about to slink out through the side door when I heard my name being called. "Oh, Mr. DuVall! Mr. DuVall, may I see you for a moment, please?" the Instructor asked.

"Oh, OK! What can I do for you?" I said.

"It's not what you can do for us; it's what we can do for you! Your drawing has been accepted as one of merit by the Director and co-owner, Mr. Nestor Castro. Congratulations!" Mr. Castro came out to greet me with a big smile and said hello with a heavy Spanish accent. My esteem had gone from zero to a hundred in nothing flat! I called the Veterans Administration and gave them the name of the school they should send the check to. To my surprise, they also gave me a stipend to help pay the rent and food.

In September 1956 I started school. I said, "Mama, this one is for you; I promise I won't let you down this time!"

My first course was Anatomy, and I was required to complete a thousand hours. Then it was a thousand hours of Watercolor, a thousand hours of Advertising and Design, and so on. Everything was measured and accredited based on the completion of a thousand hours! I enjoyed every minute.

The Instructors there were from various parts of Europe and South America. The only stateside Instructor we had was Mr. Peterson, who was the Sketch Artist for the famed *Superman* comics. He was an expert in perspective anatomy. I had one Instructor from Bolivia and others from London, Spain, Colombia, Ecuador, and Argentina. The most impressive Instructor I had was Gabriel A. Mayorga, who was from Bolivia. He taught Fine Art and Painting. They were all characters. Helena Castro, Nestor's wife and co-owner, helped operate the school as its Administrative Director; they were from Argentina. The school was housed in the Black Friars Theater building located on Fifty-Seventh Street near Eighth Avenue, one block west of the Art Students League.

My class consisted of about twenty students. About fifteen were White, and four or five were Black. As the year went on, I noticed that there were fewer and fewer White students. *Are they dropping out of school?* I wondered. The next year it was the same thing; we would start out with twenty Whites or so, and by the end of the year, at least half of them would be gone.

I was walking on Thirty-Fourth Street one day and saw one of the White guys I thought was a dropout. "Hey, Charlie! Wait a minute!" I yelled. He saw me and stopped. He had a big grin on his face as I asked him why he had dropped out of school.

He said, "I didn't drop out of school, I was hired from the school by a big ad agency!"

"You mean the school found you a job?" I asked.

He said, "Well these agencies call the school and ask for students to work as apprentices. They train us, and we then become full-time employees!"

"Oh, I see," I said. "So you didn't have to *finish* school?

"That's right! Well so long now, I have to get back to work," he said as he walked away.

When I got to school that day, I went straight to the Administrative Director's office and asked about these apprentice jobs. She had an "Oh, you found out about that" look on her face. She then said to me, "Well, Thomas, these agencies do call from time to time, but I say to you that if you stay in school and graduate, I know you will be able to find a job in your field. There is no segregation in the Art field!"

It was the same old routine: Whites got plucked out of school, but Blacks had to GRADUATE and then *"pray"* somebody would hire them *with* a diploma. If and when they did find work, the guy they thought was a dropout was now their boss and had seniority and tenure. So much for that thought; I had to get back to school.

CHAPTER 2

The Guadalupean

Some months later I was called into Mrs. Augustine's office. One of the men in the IBM department was quitting, and Mrs. Augustine wanted to know if I would be interested in learning how to operate the electrical accounting machines. I said yes, and she said she would send me to an IBM school to learn how to wire the machines to perform the different tasks of the company.

I admired her because she did not have to do what she was doing. I was the only Black in that school—and the only Black in all of New York City at that time, as far as I was told—working as an IBM Electrical Accounting Machine Operator on the first and second generations of today's computers. Not only that, but the company discovered I was attending Art school and decided I might be interested in working part time with the Staff Artists there. I was elated.

Everything was done on an assembly line. The Artists who did the drawings then passed them to another Artist, who took the drawings and inked them in India ink. When the drawings were inked, they were sent to be statted, and then another Artist read the story and added the colors. That's where I came in on the assembly line—I did the coloring of the stats. Then the stats were sent to the printing house in Chicago, where they would be printed and paginated into comic books. The finished product was sent back to us to be delivered to the newsstands and retailers.

During a discussion in the office one day, it came out that the company would never hire Blacks to do the artwork. I then let it out that day that I was a Black man, and their mouths dropped. They suggested that I go along with the assumption and continue to work as a Guadalupean! They even said please! (Wow, they really wanted me to stay!) I stayed and even got to work on some of Stan Lee's *Spider-Man* strips. Stan Lee himself was on the staff there. He had spoken to me on visits to the department but did not know me personally. I did not mind being "DuVall, the Guadalupean" for the sake of it all and the experience I gained.

Atlas Magazines eventually had to close its doors because of a court decision against the comic book industry claiming it was demoralizing the youth. This news came as a big blow to us. All the kids up in Harlem whom I used to give free comics to had to start spending their pennies.

Some of the performers on Olatunji's *Drums of Passion* album
(left to right): Michael Babatunde Olatunji, Akwasiba Derby,
Afida Derby, Thomas "Taiwo" DuVall, Delores Parker,
Helena Walker, Barbara Gordon, Chief Bey,
Beebee Capps, and Helen Haynes.

Michael Babatunde Olatunji (center) clowning around with
Thomas "Taiwo" DuVall, Ralph Dorsey, Ronald "Beans" Whitley,
and Sam Phils.

CHAPTER 3

Michael Babatunde Olatunji

It was also during this period at *Atlas Magazines* (circa 1955 to 1956) that Zsa Zsa Gabor and her mother and sisters had a gift shop at Sixty-First and Madison Avenue. During their lunch hour, spectators would gather to peer through the plate glass window to watch the Gabors at work. From time to time, an African guy who appeared to be a student also would pause there to peer. After peering for a few minutes, we would nod at each other, smile, and walk away.

There was a restaurant around the corner called The Shadow Box, and several times a week, I would see the same African guy there (with his accordion-style briefcase in hand) ordering his lunch. One day we had to share a table, so I introduced myself, and he said his name was Michael Olatunji. We talked as we ate our lunch, and afterward we shook hands, walked by the Gabors, and split back to work.

The next day I saw this guy again at the restaurant. We shared a table, and this time we asked each other questions. He worked for a publications house at Sixty-First and Madison Avenue; I worked for a publications house at Sixtieth and Madison Avenue.

During our lunch hour one day, he told me he was the President of the African Students Union here in America. He said they had asked him to speak at a convention in New York City at the Manhattan Center on Thirty-Fourth and Eighth Avenue. He also said he had told the Students Union he wanted to play his drums as part of his presentation, and they were trying to discourage him from doing so. I asked him why they were trying to discourage him, and he said the students were embarrassed by the idea! Some even said it was "savage" and that he should avoid anything that would make them look "uncivilized." I asked him what *he* wanted to do, and he said if he got his drums in time, he would play them. I asked him where his drums were. He said, "They have not arrived from Africa."

"Well you can borrow mine, if you want to, until they arrive," I said.

He was shocked when I said that. "You play drums?" he asked.

"Yes, I play drums," I said.

He wanted to see these drums of mine, so I took him up to my place in Harlem on 132nd Street and Madison Avenue. I showed him some handmade tack head drums from Cuba. He was surprised and amazed by my knowledge of Yoruba music and wanted to know more about the history of drumming in the Caribbean. He also found out that I spoke some Yoruba (his native tongue) and that I even sang the same traditional hymns. He wanted to know how it could be, and I told him my friends from Cuba, Haiti, Trinidad, and Jamaica had been instrumental in teaching me the fundamentals of their culture. I had appreciated their sharing their culture with me. My grandfather was a Jamaican, so I had always had an interest in things Caribbean.

I told him that he should be proud to know that there were individuals who have tried, against all odds, to keep these things alive here until we could unite with our brethren in the Motherland.

I said, "You have *finally* arrived, so welcome to my house. The circle has now been completed."

Olatunji then asked me if I would do this presentation with him.

"But," I said, "I don't know how you do it; I only know what I know!"

He said, "From what I have heard so far, you don't have to learn anything new. Just play what you know, and it will be just fine!"

I told him it would be an honor and a pleasure to be his assistant. This was the beginning of a long relationship—a rich and rewarding one.

Olatunji eventually got his drums from Africa. They were beautifully hand carved and had been made straight from a tree.

Olatunji called me one day to do a job with him up in Tarrytown, Connecticut, for some rich White folks. We went and played for their private party. The host and guests were all Whites who had put something on their skin that made them look dark-skinned and were all dressed in the finest of African apparel.

We had to catch the Grand Central train back to New York afterward. When we got to New York, we went to the baggage car to claim our drums, which we carried in Army duffel bags. We presented our baggage stubs, and the conductor threw our bags off the train at us.

They hit the ground with a sickening thud! It sounded like two bundles of chopped up firewood. We opened the bags and saw that someone had smashed our drums to bits. We immediately registered a complaint. They claimed that was the way we had given our drums to them, so we took them to court.

The Judge ruled that the Grand Central Railroad had to pay Olatunji for his drums because they were from Africa. However, the Judge ruled that I would not be reimbursed for my drums because my drums were made in Cuba and had no commercial value. That meant I had to shell out more money if I wanted to play drums anymore!

One day while on our lunch hour, Olatunji expressed his desire to quit his job and take his drums on the road. He wanted to know if I would join him.

I said, "What would we be known as—'Mike and Tom,' the African Drummers?"

He laughed and said, "My African name is Babatunde Olatunji. They call me 'Tunji.'"

"Well, my name, 'Thomas,' means 'the first born of twins.' What would the 'first born of twins' be in Yoruba?"

He said, "It would be 'Taiwo.'"

So I said, "Hey, *'Tunji and Taiwo'*—that might work!"

Olatunji eventually did quit his publications job, drop Michael from his name, and present himself as Babatunde Olatunji. I quit my job (at the objection of my wife, Rosita), changed my name to Taiwo DuVall, and hit the road with him.

Olatunji had an agent who was lining him up with universities and colleges to do presentations in which he tried to blend music and dance with political overtones. Tunji was a clever politician; he was a graduate from Morehouse with a degree in Governmental Protocols.

Olatunji rented a station wagon, and we loaded up our luggage and drums and headed for Pittsburg, Pennsylvania. The first stop was Pittsburg University. From there we drove to Ohio and played all the major universities there. We had just finished performing at Kent State University and were on our way to another university when the infamous riots took place there and those students were shot down by National Guardsmen.

Then we drove to Mississippi, Minnesota, Louisiana, Georgia, Alabama, Florida, North Carolina, South Carolina, Virginia, Pennsylvania, and so forth and so on. We had a reputation with the car rental people; they said we made old cars of their best new cars, so they stopped leasing to us. We had to continuously look for new car rental companies to keep going. We finally wore out our car rental connections, and nobody was willing to rent us another car. Tunji had to bite the bullet and buy his own company car. He bought a Buick Roadmaster, and we ran up about five hundred thousand miles on it before it conked out. By that time there were *new* car rental companies to do business with that did not know about our reputation, so we were off and running again.

This time around Tunji had two singers/dancers with him. They were the Derby sisters, Joan (Akwasiba) Derby and Merle (Afida) Derby. They definitely added life and luster to our drumming and singing.

It was at about this time that a few of the Drummers began leaving the Asadata Dafora Company for various reasons. Some went back to Africa, like Baba Moses's cousins and Guy Warren. Montego Joe tried to interest me in working with Baba Moses because his job at HARYUACT (Harlem Youth Action Group) in Harlem was beginning to conflict with his drumming, but I was a bit overwhelmed by the man's drumming and felt too inadequate to face Baba Moses Miannes.

One day there was a knock at my door, and it was Montego Joe! He said he was there to take me to meet Baba Moses. From there he wanted to take me down to the Police headquarters to have me take out a cabaret license so I could work in the New York City nightclubs. (I had been dragging my feet on doing so on my own.)

After working with Baba Moses awhile, I tried to talk him into hooking up with Olatunji, but Baba Moses kept reneging on doing so. He said Tunji was going commercial, so for a long time, I was torn between the two. Then it got to a point where Baba Moses would only use me to accompany him. Julito Collazo was hired by Pete Long (Producer for the Apollo Theater) to work with Baba Moses, and I was thrilled to have Julito there! He was a Master Drummer from Cuba. But Baba Moses was having trouble with Julito being there. Julito asked me to find out why the old man didn't like him, so one day when I was with Baba Moses, I asked him why he was having trouble with Julito. His answer was that Julito was always singing. I said, "That's the way those Cubans are. They sing and drum at the same time!" So Baba Moses said, "Oh, OK." From then on everything was smooth sailing.

It's interesting to note that the big-time producers were always fragmenting our (the Blacks') material. For example, they wanted to present Olatunji at Radio City in New York City, but they only wanted "him," not his material. They had a little spot in the show where they wanted to hear an African drum, so they hired Tunji to play his drums for that spot. I was happy for him!

Columbia Records wanted Olatunji to produce an album, and again they wanted him to do it alone. Tunji asked me if I would help him with this album. It was a first for me, so I agreed. At the end of the first session, which was in an old Church that Columbia Records was converting into a recording studio on the Lower East Side, Tunji turned to me and said, "Taiwo, I want to add a few more Drummers. Can you help me with this?"

I said, "Sure, I have some Drummer friends who I am sure will be interested in doing something like this." I called Montego Joe and Chief Bey, two Drummers I had worked and studied with before I met Tunji.

They showed up, and I introduced my friends to Tunji. He explained to us what he wanted, and we went to work on it. Next he added the female voices—Akwasiba and Afida Derby, Barbara Gordon, Peggy Kirkpatrick, Beebee Capps, Helen Haynes, Delores Parker, Ruby Pryor, Louise Young, and Helena Walker—and the rest is History. We produced the *Drums of Passion* album.

Now comes the Big Boom. We did this with the understanding that most likely we would never be able to collect any royalties for our efforts. They did not even give Olatunji royalties, and it was his material! They said the best they could do for him was to "sell" him so many albums for, say, a third off, and whatever he sold after he paid Columbia for the initial amount, he could keep for himself. That meant Olatunji had to sell his own records in order to get his money back and make a little something for himself. The Drummers got a one-time payment of $300 per session, and there were about two or three sessions. The singers got less than the Drummers.

His next step was to produce the album *More Drums of Passion*. For that album I got Olatunji to hire a few more of my friends to help him, like Chief Bey, Montego Joe, Ray Barretto, Robert (Beans) Whitley, Sabu Caldwell, and Roland DuVall. Things got so busy that I missed out on a year of school (which they allowed me to make up). I was paid up; I just wasn't there.

The next thing I knew, Olatunji was asking me if I had a passport. I told him no, and he told me I needed to take care of that immediately. I said, "Enough said; I'll do it right now. I know I need one."

"We will be going to the West Indies and beyond to perform," he said.

"Straight ahead," I said.

The next day I went to the Immigration Bureau to apply for my passport. The first thing they asked for was my birth certificate. I told them I had no birth certificate. They gave me some forms and a list of things to bring with me, like old school records, affidavits, proof of residences, and so on. I looked at these things and decided I would need to go to Washington, DC, to do some extensive research and find some proof that I was born. I started with the Bureau of Vital Statistics and was told there were no records of my birth on file.

I decided the best place to find my school records, baptismal records, confirmation records, or any other important papers would be St. Vincent de Paul Church. I went there, and the Priest on duty pulled out these old dusty books dated from the 1930s to the 1950s. There were no records of a Thomas Joseph DuVall ever being there as a student—not a Baptism Certificate, not a First Communion Certificate, not a Confirmation Certificate, and not a Graduation

Certificate. (How could this be?) So, I asked him to look up the name Phifer, and he found records of a Rosita Phifer. For Rosita Phifer, he had a birth certificate, school records, a First Communion Certificate, a Confirmation Certificate, and a Marriage Certificate for a Rosita Phifer to a *"Thomas J. DuVall in 1954."*

I then asked him if he had any Lumpkins on file, and he found a *Baptism* Certificate for a Thomas Joseph Lumpkins. Lumpkins was my grandfather's name. "That's impossible," I said. "I can't be my grandfather's son!" My grandfather had two children—William Lumpkins and Constance Lumpkins, who was my mother, I said.

He showed me the Baptism certificate, and it read "Thomas Joseph Lumpkins." My mother was listed as Constance Meekins. *Nobody* in my family had ever heard of anybody named Meekins. I tried to do some research on the name Meekins, and everything came to a dead end!

They had my grandmother listed as Jennie Buchanan. I could relate to that. They had her listed as my "Sponsor."

When I got back to the house I asked Mama to explain to me what was going on. I asked her why she had lied to me about the doctor dying in an automobile accident. She refused to give me an explanation. I begged her to tell me *who* my real father was, but she wouldn't say a word.

Wow, I had come all the way from New York City for nothing! I wondered, *Am I really real, or is this all a bad dream?* Mama was no help. Was she going to go to her grave without telling me who my real father was? I wondered, *Why, why, why is it that my real father is such a big deal that his identity must be kept secret? What kind of mischief is this?* Even today, every time I go to the doctor's office, I'm asked about my father's medical history. I tell them I was never told who he was.

I did eventually get a passport that I used a few times when I went to the West Indies with Olatunji. The two of us traveled to the Virgin Islands, Guadalupe. It was there that I came to realize why people thought I was a Guadalupean. They all looked like me there! I felt right at home.

Olatunji and I had a rough time in Guadalupe because neither he nor I knew a word of French and NOBODY spoke English. We had to point to everything we wanted and nod if things were OK! The worst part was going out to eat. The menus made no sense at all to us. Can you imagine being "starved to death" in a place with plenty of food cooking because you didn't know what to ask for? I was surprised that nobody spoke a word of English, as we were not that far from New York City. We weren't in France! I looked for a word with some romantically culinary sound and saw the word *pullet*. I said, "*Pollo* is Spanish for chicken, and *pullet* sounds enough like chicken to me to go for it, so are you game?" Tunji said yes, so we both ordered *pullet* and dined sufficiently.

We ate chicken all week long. Olatunji finally said, "No more chicken for me. I want something different even if I have to leave it on my plate!" So he pointed to something on the menu, and it turned out to be a lobster dish. He was lucky, but I don't like lobster, so I had more chicken. Our worst fear was ordering a dish that would turn out to be snails! Then I recalled they were called escargot, so we knew to look out for that word!

We also traveled to Bermuda, the Antilles, the Virgin Islands, and Trinidad. Trinidad was the *most* interesting experience for me. We were met at the airport by the Prime Minister himself, Dr. Eric Williams! We were really impressed with the reception they gave us. We were on the front page of the leading newspaper shaking hands with the Prime Minister. We were given the royal treatment there, and I can't say that about any other island. That was in the late '60s, if I remember correctly. It was also in Trinidad that I was to learn something about myself.

The first night of the concert, which was held in Trinidad's Grand Stadium, we were presented by the Prime Minister to the people as the "Ambassadors of Goodwill" from Africa and America. The performance started at around noon, and we had an intermission at about one or two o'clock. During the thirty-minute intermission, I was approached by two well-dressed men who said they wanted me to come with them because they wanted me to meet their leader.

I thought they had confused me with Olatunji, so I said, "I am not the leader here; Olatunji is the leader."

They said they knew who Olatunji was but wanted ME to meet their leader!

I was dumbfounded! "OK, where is he?" I said.

The well-dressed men said, "He will not come here, so we must take you there. We have a limousine waiting!"

So I said, "A 'limousine?' Where do we have to go?"

The well-dressed men said, "It's about a four-hour drive across the island, near Port of Spain."

"But I am on a twenty-minute coffee break, so there is no way I can go with you guys and be able to keep my job here," I replied.

The two well-dressed men said, "They will wait, don't worry."

"Listen," I said, "I am certain you want Olatunji. He is *from* Africa. He is the chief Drummer and leader. I am only his assistant!"

The well-dressed men expressed to me that Olatunji was not the man they wanted because he was not drumming for Shango but I was. (The drumming he was referring to was Baba Moses Miannes's Ashiko Drum that I was using on the tour.) "So come," they said. "We must go now; they will be here when you get back."

I jumped into the limousine and off we went. It was a beautiful scenic drive on the Cross Island Highway. We stopped now and then to get ice cold coconut water. I was the guest of the Government, and the people showed it! They did everything possible to make sure I was content and not wanting for anything.

I noticed that I was seeing less and less sunshine as we went deeper and deeper into the forest land. There was hardly any sunlight filtering through, and it was nice and cool. No one was perspiring, and there was a pleasant breeze. We left the limousine and started out on foot. I felt like I was in a "Garden of Eden." Suddenly I heard drums. We came into a shady grove, and I saw beautiful women—some dancing, some playing, some singing, and some preparing meals. The men were sitting and playing music; some were African, and some were East Indian. I was asked to be seated, so I sat. I felt like I was on another planet! The people even looked different. Then I realized there was a large influx of East Indian and African blends there. The drumming, the singing, and the string instruments sounded just beautiful. I was still waiting to meet this leader they had been talking about.

Now things were beginning to heighten somehow. I saw more women moving about, and the drumming was getting richer in tone. There was food being placed about, and more children were running around and dogs barking. Some of the women were beginning to dance with each other, and some were forming lines and singing chants with call-and-answer themes. I felt like I was on a Hollywood set. I kept looking around for hidden cameras and someone hollering "roll 'em!" But this was *"real"* time, and I was somewhere near Port o' Spain, Trinidad, transfixed! I didn't ever want the moment to stop.

Suddenly the crowd parted, and a man who was about my height and had a similar complexion and flaming red hair and a fierce red beard (my mind flashed back to what Malcolm X may have looked like with a red beard) walked up to me, broke into a great big smile, and said, "Welcome to our village. My name is Mansa Musa, but they call me 'Baba Shango!'" (Shango is the Yoruba god of fire, and red is the deity's color of identity.) *Oh boy, just what we need, another Big Red,* I said to myself. We sat arm in arm and hand in hand. It was as if we were long-lost brothers! He had a gentle way about him and made me feel like we were back in Harlem, hanging out on the block. He presented me with a small drum made from a coconut tree. It was the baby drum. I've lost track of the drum over the years, but I remember the whole experience as if it were yesterday. God bless you, Mansa Musa, wherever you are.

It was time for me to leave. It was now approaching nighttime, and it was a long drive back across the island. We arrived back at the stadium around midnight. I was fit to be tied. How was I going to explain this evening to anybody?

I was taken back stage to the exact spot where I was first approached by the two well-dressed men, and all of a sudden the stadium lights began to come on one at a time until the whole stadium was fully lit. The people started filing back in and filling up the seats, and in no time flat the stadium was once again alive and full of people.

The Prime Minister came out and announced the continuation of part two of the concert. Olatunji came out to say what he had to say, and the drums started playing. I turned and asked someone for the time. They said it was now ten minutes after midnight! Intermission was over, and it was now show time. I went out to do the Ashiko solo one more time before leaving for New York City. I gave thanks to Almighty God for allowing me, a little nobody from America, the opportunity to play the Ashiko Iya Ilu (Mother Drum) that belonged to Baba Miannes in *Trinidad, the "drumming" capital of the World.*

God bless Sam Phils, the Shango Drummer of Trinidad Tobago. He and Alphonse Cimber of Haiti taught me so much about drumming when we were together with Pearl Primus and Percival Borde. I miss you, man, and I still need and want to spend some time with you.

My only regret is never having been able to reach the shores of Africa, especially to meet the Ijaw people of the River Niger, Baba Moses's descendents. I do give thanks to the Almighty for allowing me to do what little I was able to do for the causes of Freedom and Dignity! I have since then had a replica made of Baba Moses's drum for myself and donated his drum to the Shomberg Collection in Harlem for all who wish to view his Ashiko Iya Ilu Drum.

CHAPTER 4

My First Art Job

I answered the ad in *The New York Times* for a Commercial Artist at a Lord and Taylor Department Store Ad Agency. They needed a Designer for towels and bath items. I can't remember the name of the woman in charge of the studio, but she told me the job paid $35 a week. I was then making $75 a week as an IBM Operator but figured Rosita would understand that I was quitting the $75-a-week job for a $35-a-week job so that I could break into the Art field. I felt that if I had a job *working* as an Artist, I would soon be able to double my salary. But she was infuriated with me. She said I was the biggest fool who ever lived. I was determined to prove her wrong.

I showed up for work on the first day, and she put me to work on a design for some towels for the department store. About a week later, she hired a Hungarian guy. We worked together for about a week, and he was constantly complaining about the low pay she was giving him.

He said he couldn't live off what she was paying him, so I eventually asked him what she was paying him. He said, "Only seventy-five dollars a week!" I was shocked. I did not have the nerve to tell him what I was making, so I kept it to myself. But I knew I had to say something to the White woman who'd told me the job started at $35, especially since the Hungarian man's work was not as crisp as mine!

The next day I approached her and told her what I had found out. She looked at me and said, "I am taking a big risk hiring you. You must realize that most of the people who come here to buy our merchandise are from the South. I risk losing my customers if they walk in here and see you sitting there as the Artist!"

I was enraged. I had informed her previously that I had quit a job where I was making $75 a week and had emphasized to her that I was a family man. But I needed the job to launch my career as a Commercial Artist, so I was trying hard to reason with her. I composed myself and replied, "Can't you just hide me in the bathroom? I can understand what you are saying, but I figured seventy-five dollars was a good lateral and starting salary. I don't mind hiding out, I can work with you on that, but you started the Hungarian out with seventy-five dollars, and you know his work is not as fresh as mine. I mean, can't we agree on something so that I won't lose my wife and family?"

She replied, "I am sorry. I cannot do that. It's thirty-five dollars or nothing."

"Then I guess nothing it is! I'll gather my tools now," I said. Now I had no job and a wife and two kids. I couldn't get unemployment compensation because I hadn't been laid off or fired. I had just quit two jobs. (Boy oh boy!)

OK, Lord! It's me again. What do I tell my wife now? I prayed and wondered. There was no answer. I guess the Lord had had enough of me too. I hit the pavements trying to find somebody who would hire a Colored guy. I couldn't use the last two jobs as references, so I was sure I would have to take a job for less money.

Weeks went by, and we were desperate for money. My wife was thoroughly disgusted with me, and I couldn't blame her. A few months later, I went on an interview with a marketing research house down on Twenty-Eighth and Broadway. It was a small firm that needed someone to do statistical surveys for marketers. The job called for a degree in Market Research, which I did not have, as I was an Art school graduate. But I knew how to use the machinery that would give them the results they wanted. I was interviewed by a woman who immediately let me know she was a Hungarian who had come to New York and made a name for herself. She explained how this hired person would also have to do a lot of writing and wanted to see a sample of my handwriting. Luckily Art school had taught me how to do lettering, so I was able to pull that off. She offered me the job at $65 a week, and I took it. It was only a $10 loss from the IBM job. (Thank you, Dear Lord!) In about a year's time, I was back to $75 a week, but by then I needed $100 a week at the bare minimum.

As time went on, they found out I did not have a degree in Market Research. They were shocked and amazed. I told them I was an Art school graduate; they were then even more amazed and befuddled, as my market research results were flawless. They were firing guys with degrees all around me for poor performance. I had also been able to pick up extra money doing portraits of the employees and their relatives. I stayed at that job for about five or six years before becoming restless.

Another point I need to make here is that the companies and affairs I worked for in New York City as a Musician were basically Jewish, and when they gave their affairs, I was always invited to sit with them. I was offered whatever they themselves were eating and drinking. When I found myself working at Christian affairs as a Musician, I would have to sit at a separate table that was distinguished by "not" having a tablecloth on it. When I saw a table with no tablecloth on it, I did not have to ask where I should sit. Not only that, but I was never served what the Whites were served. If they were eating roast beef, I could bet on having cold ham sandwiches and warmed-over coffee. (I swear to God on this one.) I never complained because I wanted to get paid without a hitch. (It's tough being Black in America, but you gotta eat!)

CHAPTER 5

Purple and Yellow: Phase 2

During my last year in Art school, I was in an oil painting class and was laying out my colors on the palette. I recalled my childhood experience with purple and yellow and decided to see if it still had an effect on my stomach, so I squeezed out some purple and reached for the yellow. I opened a tube of *cadmium yellow light*, and before I could squeeze it out of the tube, I started feeling dizzy and nauseous! I put the cap back on the tube at once and said to myself, *This isn't going to work!!* The only way I was able to paint was to remove the purple from the palette, because I needed that yellow. I decided not to use purple at all. Red and blue mixed together did not seem to bother me, so I always "faked" any purple hues when necessary.

I decided to talk to the Instructor about my plight. Surprisingly enough, he was familiar with the problem! My Instructor, Gabriel

Mayorga, a successful New York Artist from Bolivia, South America, asked me if I had heard of a Spanish Painter named Salvador Dali. I had heard of him, so Mayorga suggested I read his autobiography. I did that, and to my amazement, I found out that he had the same problem! For the first time in my life, I felt I was not the only one with this problem. I actually felt somehow "normal" now! As irony would have it, soon after that, the people in Harlem started calling me "the poor man's Dali." They said, "Boy, if you were White, you would be rich! Nobody up here got no money for Art. You need to go downtown!"

Salvador Dali was from a well-to-do family in Spain. I was from a "nobody-in-particular" family and had little or no money! Hence, I was a starving Dali-ite in Harlem! Salvador Dali was quite popular around this time in New York City. He had just won a lawsuit against Macy's Department Store for allowing one of their flunkies to alter his window display design without his consent. He did not say a word to Macy's. He just went over there, threw a brick through the big plate-glass window, and waited for the police to come and arrest him. They did, and that was Macy's death knell. The Judge told Macy's that neither they nor anyone else had the right to alter anybody's artwork!

One day I read that Salvador Dali would soon be at the opening of his show at a gallery down on Fifty-Seventh Street that would be open to the public! I knew he was from Spain, so I figured that if I brushed up on my *Spanish,* I would be able to ask him a few questions. I crammed and crammed. Finally the big day arrived, and I headed downtown to meet and speak to the famous Salvador Dali!

When I got there, there was a queue of people standing in line to speak to the painter, so I took my place on line. About forty-five minutes later, I was nearing my turn. He was an eccentric-looking figure with a long black cape, a diamond-tipped, pearl-handled walking stick, and his well-known waxed handlebar mustachio. When it was my turn, I stepped forward and greeted Mr. Dali in my best Spanish accent. He looked at me in stark confusion. He turned to an Interpreter and said something in French. The Interpreter turned and said (in a heavy French accent), "I am sorry, Mr. Dali no longer speaks Spanish; you must speak to him in French now, if you please."

We three stood there while they waited for me to speak in French. I was dumbfounded! Finally I said, "*Bonjour, mon amis!*" And then I went back uptown to Harlem. Regardless of the fact that I wasn't able to communicate with him, I was happy that I had gotten to meet the Artist, and I am still impressed. I wanted to ask him if he was still having trouble with purple and yellow. Oh well, I guess (we) will be okay!

Taiwo and a little admirer in front of his artwork at
Brooklyn's Fulton Art Fair.

CHAPTER 6

Art on the Move in Harlem (Circa 1957 to 1959)

Simon Bly, the President and Founder of the Afro Arts Cultural Center in Harlem, wanted to start having Annual Outdoor Art Exhibitions in Harlem. He asked me and several other Artists to participate. I cannot remember any of the other Artists' names now except for Mr. Springer, a local Artist who painted in oils. I remember him because he was an older man with plenty to say.

The Harlem outdoor exhibition ran for two years (1958 and 1959) on Fifth Avenue between 125th Street and 124th Street. The turnout was poor on the first day, and the next day it rained. The following week some of the Artists did not return, and the turnout of spectators was lower still. I remember asking Mr. Bly if there was any way possible that we could exhibit around the fence that encircled Mt. Morris Park (located at 124th Street and Fifth Avenue, just across the street). He assured me that that could not happen. He said the Police Department would not issue a permit to use public property. In Brooklyn, however, we all hung our work on the fence around the park. I asked myself, *Do the precincts make their own rules?*

I thought it was a great idea and could just see it: Art Exhibition at Mt. Morris Park! Wow! But it would never be, so we had to hang our work on the fences of neighbors who did not mind. Not all the neighbors had fences or were that sympathetic.

At the end of the exhibit, Mr. Bly presented me with an award, which was a traveling oil paint box fully supplied for my efforts. Mr. Springer told me that he was going back to the Greenwich Village shows, where he knew he could sell something. He invited me along, so I went. Mr. Springer stopped painting and went into the framing business on Thompson Street. I asked him why he had stopped. He told me that people kept asking him if he did framing too, so he decided to say yes, and with that single word, his starving days ended. He made a lot of money.

I had just started painting, so I got involved with some brothers who were operating a gallery called the Soul Gallery, which was located on Bleecker Street in Greenwich Village. We did a lot of portraiture and caricatures there, and after a period of time, I announced my withdrawal. (I was tired of staring at people's faces for portraiture.) They gave me the address of a collective Black artists club on the Lower East Side, so I went there.

The place was very small and poorly lit, but there was a great camaraderie there that I enjoyed. Only two or three guys could paint at a time. Others would sit around and play chess or read aloud until one of the people painting would pack up his or her gear and give someone else a chance at the easel. The club had elected officials and held monthly meetings. Mel Green, Charles Hudson, Ray Sneed, Ernest

Crichlow, and others were affiliates. They would travel from state to state throughout the Southland to give lectures about what they did. I was impressed. On one such trip, there was a terrible car accident, and the president and three staff members were killed. (I regret to admit I cannot remember all of their names now.)

The only survivor, as far as I can remember, was my friend Charles Hudson, who sustained severe head injuries. The accident left him with slurred speech and impaired motor skills. His wife left him because she could not deal with the disfigurement. Poor Hudson was all alone and was hearing voices because of all the brain damage. He would call me all hours of the day and night because I was the only one who was sympathetic about his disfigurement, he said. I loved the guy in spite of himself, and I'm sure he knew it. We had become good friends playing chess while waiting our turn at the easel.

Ironically, after his accident, his painting skills soared! His work actually sparkled. He had a painting of Malcolm X becoming a prominent figure before he was prominent. His brain injury seemed to have made him clairvoyant! It was awesome to me. I tried to tell him how his painting had been heightened in brightness and clarity and how everything seemed to GLOW! He had a way of giving things a glow where there was no glow—sometimes bordering on being incendiary, yet purifying and immaculate. He was seeing colors I know he had not been able to see before his head injury. His colors were now as pure as a snowflake and as warm as an ember!

Charles Hudson called me one day and asked me if he could leave his collection of works with me because the Whites in the area where he was living were trying to wrestle his work from him. I went down and helped him move his stuff into my place. Hudson wanted me to hold his work because I was the only one he could trust, he said. I told him not to worry and that he should just convalesce so he could return. He walked out and flew to Mississippi to stay with his aunt. Some months later, Hudson passed on.

I received a letter from his aunt in Mississippi many months later. She said Hudson had talked of me often, and she wanted me to take his artwork to the Judson Memorial Church at West Fourth and MacDougal Street, situated on New York University's campus at Washington Square in Greenwich Village, for a Memorial Service and Art Exhibit they were having there. I told her I was reluctant to do that because that was the Church Hudson said was trying to bamboozle him out of his work. She totally ignored everything I had to say. She tried to tell me that Hudson was not in his right mind and said that the Church was "only" going to use the work for his Memorial Service and then would return the work to her. I told her if they got their hands on this artwork, they would burn up every piece of it! However, it was her request, and she was his surviving relative, so I followed through.

I do remember that my worst fears came true. I distinctly remember her calling me later to say she had not heard a word from that Church in Greenwich Village. They wouldn't return her calls, she said. They never did get back to her, nor did they ever return my calls. I will always regret having released that work. But she was his relative, and I had had no choice but to reply, I felt. (I pray my friend Hudson forgives me for giving in.)

The Artist club was never the same after all that, and I found myself back uptown. Two other Artists from the club were James Sneed and Melvin Greene, who moved to Mexico and hooked up with Elizabeth Catlett from Howard University. Sometime later I received a phone call from James Sneed. Sneed, now living in Harlem, started talking about reorganization and said he wanted to do an outdoor Art exhibition in Harlem.

Brooklyn's Fulton Art Fair, an annual event held at Fulton and Schenectady Avenue, was the only outdoor Art fair featuring Black Art that I was aware of in the late fifties—1958 to be exact. I was a participant and displayed pieces of my artwork including an oil painting of my Drummer friend, Beans, which I called "The Young Musician."

I had the honor of being set up between my Childhood Heroes, Jacob Lawrence, who was the co-Chairman, and Ernest Crichlow. WOW, what a "gas" that was!

I told Sneed to count me in. He asked me to ask around to see how much support we could find. I did that and was surprised at the response. Artists were coming up from all directions—The Bronx, Queens, and all the other Boroughs.

Taiwo's Studio on Strivers' Row.

CHAPTER 7

The Black Art Movement in Harlem

We put on the exhibit on Seventh Avenue, from 127th Street to about 130th Street. This was in 1964. The turnout was better than expected, and spirits were running high. We found ourselves juggling and jockeying for space.

James Sneed suggested we join him in forming his new organization, which was to be called the Twentieth Century Creators. I liked the idea of an organization but didn't much care for the name "Twentieth Century" for a Black Art group. I would have liked something a bit more ethnic, but I was willing to accept whatever the whole agreed on. "We need a place to meet that is central," Sneed said. There was a pause, so I volunteered my studio, which was at 248 West 139th Street, between

Seventh and Eighth Avenues, known as Strivers' Row. They all said OK and set a time for 8:00 p.m. every first Wednesday of the month.

The first meeting found Raymond (Abdul Rahman) Hall and his wife, Malika, Theo (Abdullah Aziz) Gleaves, Rudy (Baba Kachenga) Irvin, Otto Neals, Gaylord (Hassan) Smith, Harry Drysdale, Perry and Dindga McCannon, G. Falcon Beazer, Bill Howell, Bedford (Ademola Olugebefola) Thomas, Ronald (Okoe) Pyatt, and me. The man with the plan (Sneed) never showed up, so we just made small talk. We eventually said good-night and promised to return on the first Wednesday of the next month. Then we all split the scene.

The following first Wednesday of the next month came, and everybody showed up, but it turned out to be a repeat of the previous meeting. We again agreed to try to meet with Sneed in another month. That Wednesday came, but Sneed did not show up. We decided to try one more time. Some of the Artists came from as far away as Long Island and said they were not coming back for a fourth time.

I decided to go look for Sneed myself. I found him in a store not too far away from my place. "Hey, Sneed, what's up? People have been coming by my place for months now, and nobody has seen hide or hair of you. This is supposed to be 'your' baby!" I said.

"I am the President, and the President doesn't have to be at every meeting," he said.

I asked, "But why didn't you call? You have my number!"

"I've been busy," he said. "Just tell everybody to go on with the meetings, that's all!" (I could not believe my ears.)

I replied, "OK, I will tell them what you said!"

At the next meeting, I told the Artists what James Sneed had said. Everybody started saying at once, "Who does he think he is?"

"We have heard of absentee landlords, but this is ridiculous," someone said.

Malika Rahman said, "We should form our own group, and if Sneed wants to join, he would be welcome, but as a member, not as an absentee President." We all agreed with her. We began searching for a name. Everyone agreed it should be a name that reflected our heritage. I suggested they get Otto Neals to come up with something, since he was the only one studying an African Tongue, Swahili.

Otto Neals suggested the word "*WEUSI*," which means "Black People" in Swahili. We all agreed immediately on the name the "WEUSI ARTISTS." It had a ring to it, and the way it was spelled in Swahili—We-Us-I—was so meaningful. It was 1964, and another era was born. We were now a "Collective."

Weusi Artist Collective of the Nyumba Ya Sanaa Gallery (front row, left to right): Otto Neals, Abdul Rahman, Irving Brady, and Taiwo DuVall; (second row, left to right): G. Falcon Beazer, Milton Martin, and Kay Brown; and (last row, standing): Weusi Founder Rudy Irvin, Okoe Pyatt, Jim Sepyo, Rene Pyatt, and Ademola Olugebefola (Harry Drysdale, Bill Howell, Perry and Dindga McCannon, and James Phillips, not pictured). They paved the way for members Ché Baraka, David Byer-Tyre, Stanwyck Cromwell, Robert Daniels, Ogundipe Fayomi, Rod Ivey, M.L.J. Johnson, Karl McIntosh, Nii Ahene-La, Ed Sherman, and Emmett Wigglesworth.

(Photo by Ed Sherman)

CHAPTER 8

The Winter of 1964 and the Weusi Artists

W e decided to hold an affair to celebrate our newfound movement. We called it the "BLACK BALL!" The sisters decided
to get together to design a cloth that they would all wear to show
their support. Bill Howell came up with a design with the words
"Black Ball" in green and red letters silk-screened onto a nice black
material.

It was held at the Renaissance Ballroom at 137th Street and
Seventh Avenue in November. The door prize was a piece of original Art donated by an Artist in the group. It was a great idea and a
great success! We gave other affairs after that and participated in other
events around the Harlem area.

One Artist in the group approached me after a meeting one Wednesday. He started talking to me about how the Harlem area needed an Artist Gallery we could invite the public to so they could view the works of the Artists who lived in the area. His name was RUDY IRVIN, and he was a disabled war veteran who was on leave from the Bronx Veterans Hospital. He knew I was a war veteran also, so he singled me out to speak in his behalf. "Why me?" I asked.

He said, "I heard you say once that you had been a Paratrooper, so I figured if anybody could help me, it would be you; everyone else sees me as an *'invalid'* first." I didn't know what to say.

Rudy Irvin was a Spunky Spirit. He would arise from his hospital bed, strap his paintings to his crippled body, and head for the outdoor Art Shows in any one of the Boroughs of New York City on foot. He walked on two crutches and had a bad case of cataracts. But Rudy had a dream. He wanted to be an Artist in the worst way, and he wanted me to help him. I said to him that as one veteran to another, I would do his bidding.

At the next meeting, I brought up Rudy's proposal, but it was shot down. I walked with Rudy to the subway. Rudy and I talked some more about keeping the pressure on. He said, "It is nice to give affairs and parties, but we need a 'Home' for our work." So we decided to press on.

A few meetings went by, and some of the Artists started to come around to our side of the fence. They were G. Falcon Beazer, Theo (Abdullah Aziz) Gleaves, Gaylord (Hassan) Smith, Otto Neals, Perry McCannon, and Bill Howell—six Artists out of a collective of about thirty Artists. For two years we beat the pavements of Harlem looking for a "Home" for our work, but nobody wanted to rent a place to a bunch of "struggling" Artists. Then things got worse for me; I quit my job with Solomon Brothers on Wall Street. I had wanted them to hire somebody to help me with tabulating and tallying their accounts and to allow me to work less than twelve- to sixteen-hour days. I lost the fight.

The same day I was fired, I got a call from Rudy Irvin. He said he had found a place! He wanted me to meet him as soon as possible at 240 West 132nd Street to meet the landlady. I told him I was on the way.

I arrived at the address; it was a nice-looking brownstone that had been well kept. I went to the second level and saw Rudy waiting for me. He invited me in and asked, "What do you think?"

"You mean to say this place is going to be our Gallery?" I asked.

He said yes, and I wanted to know how he had done it. He said, "Our Church moved out to a larger place right across the street."

"You mean this place was once your Church?" I asked.

He said yes, and I asked, "Does the landlady know we are a bunch of crazy Artists with no guaranteed income?"

He said, "Yes. She was hesitant because she knew she could get a good price on renting this flat, but because my family members are in good standing in the Church, the Church members were willing to endorse my idea to open a badly needed Art gallery in Harlem. Come on, I will introduce you to Mrs. Shepherd, our new landlady."

She was as sweet as she could be and had no problem saying to me, "I hope you all aren't going to be having any 'wild Artist parties' above my head here. You know that for many years St. Michael's Church was upstairs, and to go from that to heaven knows what may not be what I want over my head."

I said, "Don't worry, Mrs. Shepherd, I will *personally* see to that."

I had $300 in severance pay from the job I had just been fired from. I gave the landlady half and told Rudy I would use the other half to get the things we would need to open house.

Rudy and I were dying for the next group meeting to announce our good fortune. But at that meeting, the reception was rather cool. Perry McCannon had become impatient and left for the West Indies, so it was down to G. Falcon Beazer, Abdullah Aziz, and Rudy Irvin. Otto Neals was still interested but said he could not take on a dues responsibility at the moment. I said to Otto, "I will pay your dues until you can do better." He didn't want me to do that, but I told him I could not see us there without him. And that was final. Abdul Rahman had his own place up in the Bronx and felt he did not need the extra responsibility.

The rent of $150 a month would be split among five guys, which meant we would pay $30 apiece. The supplies we needed would be divided the same way, or we would pay for what we used. We felt that should do it!

The floor was in bad shape, so we decided to paint it. Nobody could decide on a color, so I said, "Let's paint it red."

"RED, Taiwo! Wow, that would get us thrown out of here!" one of the Artists said.

I said, "Not if we do it right!"

Rudy said, "OK, let's do it!"

And red it was—"Chinese Red," at that. It was just what the floor needed to give it a feeling of warmth. They asked me how I had arrived at the color. I told them when I first saw we were on the shady side of the street, I knew we had to come up with something to make us feel some warmth; otherwise, it would feel dank. We all agreed. Of course, we had to tell the landlady, who was wide-eyed and gasped when she saw it. I told her that it was a temporary fix. She bought it. (Bless her soul.)

Shortly after that we got a visit from Percy Sutton, who was running for public office in Harlem and thought it would be a good idea if we became part of his support campaign. We said OK. Then he wanted to know the date of our opening. We said November 1. He suggested we open a month earlier and said he would invite some people for the opening. We told him we were operating on a shoestring and our checks had not yet been received, so our move to open sooner was based on how much money we would have to invest once we received our checks. (I was getting unemployment checks. Rudy was getting a disabled veteran's check. The others didn't have that, and we all had families to feed.) Percy Sutton said, "I am sure you will be able to do it, so let me know your new opening date, and I'll handle the guest list. Our reply to Mr. Sutton was that we would certainly try! He turned and walked out.

We knew when we said it that we did not have the money to open a month earlier to fit his schedule. Rudy said, "What do we do?"

I said, "We push on, and if there is any way we can accommodate him, we will, but he did not offer any financial assistance."

We sent a representative to his meeting to state our predicament and were told he saw this as a lack of interest on our part. He backed out, so we pushed on with what we needed to do and what we had to do it with.

The Nyumba Ya Sanaa Art Gallery opened November 1, 1967, on schedule. We had a wonderful reception, and a lot of people came. It was a well-received event (and there was not a politician in the house). Sun Ra (Herman Blount, a famous jazz pianist who also played the organ) came by and was so impressed with the artwork that he asked if he could take the whole show on the road with him to a Washington, DC, concert. He wanted to use it as a backdrop for his Celestial Orchestra.

We had to have a meeting to decide who would be willing to carry what title. We all agreed that Abdullah Aziz should be the Artistic Director, I should be the Executive Director, and Gaylord (Hassan) Smith would be our Secretary and Historian. Kwame Brathwaite became our Gallery Photographer. The other members would fill in for whoever would not be available.

A week or so later, three sisters walked into the Gallery and identified themselves as students at Stony Brook University (SBU) of the State University of New York. They wanted to know if we would be willing to do an exhibit at SBU for Black History Month. They said the school said that there would be no money involved. I told them the school had the money for such events but might feel the Blacks were not organized enough to warrant spending money on. I then asked her how many Black students were enrolled there. They said there were six, maybe seven, Black girls and no Black males out of an enrollment of two thousand or so. "Wow!" I said. "If there are only six of you, why should they qualify you for any kinds of funds when you can join in on their events? That way the five hundred dollars they could allot to a student function could be spent on a majority, rather than a minority.

"If I were you," I continued, "I would speak to the other sisters and start a Black Students Union. That will allow you to present a charter and a unanimous decision, and you can even get your parents in on it. After all, it is a Black History Project, so they can't turn you down! If they do, we will do the exhibit anyway."

"For free?" the girls said in unison.

"For free," I said (with a hard swallow). They gave me a hug and left in high spirits.

A month or so later, I got a telephone call. It was one of the sisters from SBU; I think her last name was Washington. She started telling me how they had presented themselves to the Administrators, who had agreed to give us the $500 to do the exhibit. She also said, "They tried to worm out of it because none of the schools in America had a Black Students Union." The sisters informed SBU that America's first Black Student Union was now formed and chartered (circa 1967 to 1968).

"Straight ahead," I said.

Sometime later we installed an exhibition at the Countee Cullen Library on 135th Street near Lenox Avenue. We called it *What the Mind Sees, The Hand Does*. The exhibition introduced an experience in painting, photography, and poetry. It was well received, and the *Amsterdam News* did an article on the event. This exhibition ran from February through March of '69.

It was shortly after this exhibit that I got a call from Rudy (Baba Kachenga) Irvin's wife that Rudy was back in the VA Hospital. His kidneys had failed, and he was in bad shape. She said Rudy was asking for me. I felt weak all over and had to sit down. Rudy was only about thirty-two years old! I did not want to go to that hospital, but Rudy was asking for me. He was my buddy and my partner. Everybody else was second.

A few days later, I made my way to the VA Hospital in the Bronx to see Rudy. I got to his room, but the man I saw in the bed was not the Rudy I had remembered. Rudy was a brown-skinned man, and the man in the bed was a dark-skinned man. I stood there silently for a moment. The man in the bed looked at me and said, "Well I finally got my wish, Taiwo!" He had called me by my name, which meant that this man was Rudy. He had lost a lot of weight.

"What do you mean?" I responded.

He said to me, "I always wanted to be as black as tar so I could scare White people to death when they see me!"

I laughed and said, "Me too!"

I then asked Rudy how it had happened. He told me that when he was stationed in Germany with the Army Engineers, they had given him some chemicals to use to purify the water of the Rhine River. This meant that he had to purify the water with the chemicals and then drink the water to prove it was purified. Well the chemicals had not worked on the filth in the Rhine, and he was now dying from the damage it had done to his kidneys.

"But what about your legs and the crutches? How do they come into play here?" I asked. Rudy said that shortly after he had been admitted for the kidney problem, he had fallen out of bed one night and broken his hip.

I left the hospital fit to be tied. I was a basket case! There was no way Rudy was going to be coming back to the Gallery. I felt like a heavy burden had just been put on my shoulders. A few days later, Rudy (Baba Kachenga) Irvin was dead.

His wife asked me to please play my drums for Rudy at his funeral. She said he had always wanted to play drums. I played my heart out.

The Gallery was never the same after that. We fell behind in the rent, and things were really slow.

I separated from Rosita because I found out she had been cheating on me before and throughout our entire marriage. A few months later, she took me to court for non-support. She had gotten used to me handing her a check for almost fifteen years, but now it was hit or miss. The Judge sided with her. He said I was being "irresponsible" by trying such a thing. "Now you close down that Gallery and get yourself a 'real' job, or you will be going to jail," he stated.

I replied, "I could never close down the Gallery."

"You will do what you are told. Now get out of my court," the Judge said.

I brushed past Rosita and her long-time boyfriend (who accompanied her to these court sessions). I was fit to be tied, so back uptown I went, with no intentions of carrying out the Judge's orders. I was still giving her money, but it was not on the same day every week. She had a good job, and her boyfriend had a very good job. They were not hurting, but her point of view was that I was trying to get out of my responsibilities as a husband and father. All I wanted her to do was stop cheating and give me a chance to do something for the community and myself.

I did not close the Gallery, and a few months later I was dragged back to court. But this time I had to enter through the door marked "III." The Non-Support Court had three doors to it. The first door was marked "I" and was for first offenders. The door marked "II" was for second offenders. This was my third time going before the Judge, so I was to enter through door III, which everybody in Harlem *knew* was the door of no return. (This meant I was going to jail.)

I packed some personal items, like underwear and toothpaste, in a gym bag. Then I went out and bought myself a roll of canvas, filled my paint box with paint and brushes, and gave my assistant Abdullah Aziz what money I had. (I kept thirty-five cents for subway fare to the courthouse.) I figured that when I got out of jail, I would have completed some work to show and sell.

I arrived at the courthouse on time. I got to door III, and the place was full of people. The Guard told me I couldn't enter with all of my equipment, so I explained that the bag held my personal things, which I was taking to jail with me. The Judge looked up at the door and said, "What's all the racket back there?" It was the same Judge who had told me to close that Gallery. He looked up and saw me and couldn't believe his eyes. He shouted, "Sergeant of Arms, throw that man out of my Court!"

"But, Your Honor," I said, "I'm the man you have to send to jail today."

"Throw him OUT of here immediately," he said.

The Officer jumped to my side and said, "All right, let's go!"

I wasn't sure what to do next. I hadn't brought carfare to get back uptown. I sat down on the courthouse steps to think for a minute. That Judge had recognized me from before, I am sure. The way he had looked at me made me feel that somehow he was sympathetic. I knew that sometimes I had to look beyond what a person said.

I decided I would walk back to the subway and talk to the man in the token booth to see if he would let me go through the gate. Sometimes they'd let someone do that if he or she didn't look like a hoodlum or a bum. I went to the subway and saw that the guy in the booth was a Black guy, which was just my luck, as the Blacks had a reputation for not wanting to help one of their own. When I had asked for similar favors in the past, the Whites always said, "Sure, go ahead." But Blacks rarely would. *Well, here goes,* I thought. I approached the booth and explained to the man how I had left home without sufficient funds by mistake. I said I would be pleased if he would let me through the gate.

He looked at me as if I was crazy and said, "Stand aside, or I will call the law!"

I said, "Would you please call the law?" (I was sure they would help.)

He said, "MOVE ON!"

"OK, thank you," I replied.

I went back outside and saw a White cop standing there. I told the cop what had just happened to me, and he said, "Come on, I'll get you in." He took me back to the place I had just left and said, "Go ahead in, and have a nice day."

I thanked the Officer and said, "And the same to you, sir. Thank you." I was back uptown in no time flat and back at the Gallery.

NOBODY believed I had gone through door III and was thrown out! They were telling me that I was Harlem's "First Door III Reject."

I eventually got a divorce from Rosita and lived alone in my studio. I went to work for Ms. Pearl Primus and her husband, Percival Borde, as their Drummer. There I met Vivian Lewis, a dancer in Pearl's Company. I asked her out to dinner one day, and the next thing I knew, we were tight. We were perfect for each other, they all said. We eventually married and had two lovely children, my son, Talib, and my daughter, Shakirah.

CHAPTER 9

Cooperate or Perish

We were still behind in rent for the Gallery. After Rudy Irvin died, another Artist, Harry Drysdale, also died. That meant two dues payers now could not be counted on. Abdullah Aziz and I were unemployed, and business was slow. Mrs. Shepherd was looking for her rent.

I looked around the room and saw a lot of artwork that belonged to Artists in the Movement who did not pay Gallery dues. I talked to the other Artists in the Gallery and suggested that we confront the Weusi members whose work we had been carrying around with us and ask them to please become dues-paying members of the Gallery. There were about twenty other Artists who were not Gallery members but kept their work in the Gallery. If they chipped in $5 a week, that would take care of the rent. The response was not enthusiastic.

I began looking for a part-time job operating IBM office machines again. I eventually found a part-time job working downtown. Some of my so-called friends got on my case because I had gone back to work for the "White man." One so-called friend attempted to choke me with the necktie I had to wear to get the job I needed to defray the cost of my mission, which was to keep that Gallery open. I had to keep my composure, so I loosened my tie to keep from passing out and kept walking.

The part-time job petered out, so I was in dire straits again. It was at about this time that G. Falcon Beazer, another Gallery partner, was found dead. His wife called me and gave me the details. Shortly thereafter, my friend and partner, Bill Howell, was found comatose on a street corner, rushed to a hospital, and pronounced dead. That left Abdullah Aziz and me. Otto lived in Brooklyn, so we didn't see him very often. Aziz was not employed, so that left everything squarely on my shoulders.

I called an emergency meeting of the Weusi Artist Body and asked them to please reconsider being part of the Gallery as a cooperative, rather than as a privately owned venture. I reminded them of Rudy Irvin's (hereafter to be referred to as "Baba Kachenga," which means "Father who returns to build") dream, which was to have a house for our Art. "Let us not lose this establishment," I said.

They all finally agreed. Gaylord (Hassan) Smith was the first to step forward. Ronald (Okoe) Pyatt was next, and then the number of members became thirteen. Ademola Olugebefola and Abdul Rahman were the only ones holding back on joining. They both said they had their own projects but would make themselves available when needed. I suggested we meet the first Thursday of each month to discuss future projects.

In the meantime I found myself talking to Babatunde Olatunji about whether or not he had an opening for a Drummer.

"As a matter of fact, I do," he said. "Can you go on the road for a few weeks?"

I said yes, thanked him, and started packing a bag and repairing my drum. It meant leaving the Gallery in the hands of others, but I figured we were all adults and all family men, so management was part of our daily existence. The tour with Olatunji ended with the schools closing for the summer, so I was unemployed again.

"The Young Musician" Oil Painting. © Taiwo DuVall

CHAPTER 10

The River Niger

My trumpet-playing friend, Jothan Callins of Alabama, kept bugging me about meeting him downtown to see this new play that was Off-Broadway called *The River Niger*.

He kept saying, "I know you must know this guy because he is about your age and he is from DC. His name is Joseph A. Walker."

I said, "Maybe, I know several Joseph A. Walkers. The Editor for the *Muhammed Speaks Newspaper* is named Joseph A. Walker and is now known as Idris Muhammed, the Journalist. He is in DC now. The other Joseph A. Walker was at Dunbar. As a matter of fact, I knew *two* Joseph A. Walkers at Dunbar High in DC."

I eventually agreed to go and met him on the corner of Forty-Eighth and Eighth Avenue, across the street from the theater. He had me walk in with him so that I would not have to pay admission.

I enjoyed the play very much but had not yet met the Author. After the show Joe Walker came out and spoke to the audience. I could not believe my eyes. It was the Joe I had gone to school with. I'd had no idea he was a Writer. I knew he had a flair for the English language from our school days, but not in my wildest dreams had I ever thought I would see this guy in New York City as a Playwright. He was also working with the Negro Ensemble at that time.

Joe and I immediately started talking about our school days at St. Cyprian's and at Dunbar High. We also talked about the fact that the last time I had seen him in DC was when we were both teaching Mambo Dancing. We had bumped into each other at a dance party in a school hall, and I had told him that I was leaving for New York. (That was the summer of 1954.)

As we talked, we found out we each liked playing conga drums! From then on I was playing congas and Ashiko Drums in all of his productions. He also asked me what I was doing in New York. I told him I had an Art Studio in Harlem on 139th Street and Seventh Avenue.

"An Art Studio?" he said. "What do you do there?"

I said, "I am the owner and operator."

His whole attitude changed, and he said, "You can draw?"

"I try!" I said.

"I've got to see this!" he said.

So I said, "Come on up when you can. I'm there most of the time."

When he did come by, his mind was blown. He just kept walking around the place with his mouth wide open. "Thomas, I never saw you draw *anything* in school!" he exclaimed.

"I know," I said. "They told me when I entered the fifth grade that I was not to be caught drawing *anything* at *any* time during the school year again. So I had no choice but to comply."

While he was there, he bought a $1,000 oil painting of mine called "The Young Musician." He then told me about his studies in drawing and painting, and the rest was History.

We were tight friends until his death in 2003. **God bless his soul.**

CHAPTER 11

The Lingua Franca

It was summertime in New York City in the mid-1960s, and things were a bit slow for young Black Jazz Musicians at the moment. Then the phone rang one morning, and it was Jothan Callins, the trumpet player friend of mine from the Lionel Hampton Band. He said he was getting a group together to play a circuit tour in his hometown of Birmingham, Alabama, and wanted to know if I would be interested in joining him as the Conga Drummer.

I said OK. He said, "Good. I'll call 'Smitty' Smith to play Trap Drums, Cecil McBee to play Bass, Hamiet Bluiett to be on the Saxophone, and Ron Burton on the Keyboard."

The following week we were off to Birmingham! We had gotten as far as South Carolina when we discovered that we had run out of crackers for the baloney and cheese sandwiches we had been surviving off of. We decided that we'd have to make a stop to replenish our supplies.

We finally came upon a little general store. Jothan pulled the car over, and we passed the hat around for the guys to "chip in" to buy some crackers for our bologna. Then I jumped out. As I walked up to the store, I saw a very old Black man who was all bent over and sitting on a box, resting on his cane. He looked up at me, and I smiled, said hello, and walked inside. Two large, White, farmer-type dudes were talking to the clerk behind the counter. When they saw me, they stopped talking.

I walked up to the counter and said, "Hi! I would like to buy a box of your saltine crackers, please."

The store clerk looked at me, squinted his eyes, and said, "Wha' chu' say?"

I repeated, "I would like to buy a box of saltine crackers, please."

There was a pause, and before I knew it, the White guys grabbed me under the armpits, lifted me up off the floor, carried me to the door, and *threw me out*!

I picked myself up and brushed myself off. I was in a state of total confusion. The old Black man hobbled over to me and said, "Boy, what in th' world did you say in there to get those folks all riled up like that?"

So I said, "I don't know. All I said was I would like to buy a box of saltine crackers!"

The old man looked at me and said, "You go back in there, and you tell them you want a box of 'soda biscuits!'"

I hesitated because I did not want to go back in there, but he said, "GO ON!"

"OK, if you say so!" I went back into the store.

The two White guys saw me reenter the store and could not believe their eyes. I walked right between the two of them and straight up to the counter. The guy behind the counter didn't know whether to sh-- or go blind! I looked the clerk straight in the eye and said, "Sir, I would like to buy a box of your 'soda biscuits.'"

The store clerk looked at me, broke out into a big blushing smile, and said, "SURE THING, SIR! Here, take two!"

I said, "No, one is enough."

He said, "Go 'head, take it. It's on me!"

"WOW! Thank you, sir!" I handed him his money, but he would not take it!

He asked me, "Y'all from 'round here?"

"No, sir, just passing through!"

"Keep your money, and stop by here on your way back through, OK?"

"Sure thing, my friend, and y'all have a nice day!" We all shook hands, and I walked out.

I stepped outside and saw that the old man was waiting for me to catch his eye. I looked over at him with a big smile on my face and gave him the "RIGHT-ON" sign. He responded in kind!

When I got back to the van, the guys all wanted to know what the HELL was going on, why those guys had thrown me out, and what had taken me so long. After I told them the whole story, they wanted to go back in there and tear the place apart. I asked them if they had seen the old man talking to me as I was getting up, and they said yes. "Well," I said, "he told me what I needed to say to get what I wanted. I started to tell him to forget it! But he was only trying to help me, and I felt pain for this old man and the things he must have had to tolerate in his lifetime here. So I said, 'OK! Grandfather, this one is for you! I'll put on a show for you that they won't forget!' On my way out, I let him know that I appreciated what he had done."

It was then that I showed the guys in the band the same amount of money we had "chipped in on" for the crackers. (OOPS! I mean soda biscuits.) I guess that showed how broke we all were.

We had gotten TWO *boxes of biscuits* for *FREE*, which meant we could *really* get down with the *baloney and cheese*. That cooled everybody out!

We moved on down the road.

(You've got to know *what* to say and what *not* to say!)

The mural depicting an African village scene.

CHAPTER 12

The Mural
(Circa 1968)

While I was traveling around with Olatunji, he said to me, "Taiwo, we need a backdrop for our traveling company. We need something behind us when we perform so that the people can really get the feeling of being in Africa."

"Yeah, you are right," I said. "That's a good idea; I would just need supplies and tools."

"I'll buy the supplies if you will do the work," he said.

"You've got a deal!" I said.

"What size will it be?" he asked. I said I would make it fifteen feet high and thirty-seven feet long.

Tunji said, "*Great!* Let's do it." He gave me $50 and said, "Will this get you started?"

"I'm on my way to pick up some supplies and material to make a scale model for your approval, and then we will take it from there," I said. I picked up some supplies to make a scale model for Tunji's approval and started laying out a village scene that would extend from West Africa to Egypt. I set up a scale according to the size of a roll of canvas, six feet by sixteen feet. The scale model was two inches to a foot or thirty-two inches high and seventy-two inches long. I laid out the landscape first. Then I gathered my resource materials, pictures, photos, drawings, and other items, and drew in all the characters to be included. The drawing included stilt dancers, masquerade dancers, men, women, and children at work and play, village huts, the Pyramids, the Cloud That Thunders (Victoria Falls), the Nile River, and such animals as elephants, giraffes, and zebras. After everything was laid out, I gathered my watercolors and painted the whole backdrop. It took several weeks to complete, and when it was done, it looked great to me.

I called Olatunji to set up a review date. He said, "Come on over!" I made a beeline for his place, which was the Olatunji Center of African Culture located on 125th Street and Madison Avenue. I was living at 248 West 139th Street (also known as Strivers' Row). It didn't make sense to wait for the slow buses. The subway was halfway between his place and mine, and I didn't have cab fare, so I walked.

When I got there, Olatunji was sitting behind his desk, looking his best. He looked at the scale model and flipped out! "When can you start?" he asked.

"As soon as I can get the money for canvas and supplies," I said.

He pulled out his checkbook, wrote me a check for $250, and gave me the keys to his station wagon to pick up the supplies. I went straight downtown and bought six rolls of canvas and enough paint to cover them. The next day I went to the Center to measure the height of the wall I was going to use to hang the canvas from. The wall was fifteen feet high and forty feet long. It was long enough but was a foot short on the height. Olatunji wanted to know how I was going to hang up the canvasses on the wall. I said, "We need to place two-by-fours along the wall, up against the ceiling, and then anchor them to the wall."

Olatunji's eyes widened, "That won't hurt the wall?"

"Naaah!" I said. "We can use them as a molding so that when we are not traveling with the mural, it can hang in the Center. That way all who come here can see it.

His eyes lit up. "Yeah, that's a good idea," he said. He called in a carpenter and had it done. (I loved this man.) Tunji had a head for grandness.

All I had to do was figure out how to hang the canvasses so that they would meet properly from end to end. I went out and bought fourteen poles that were one inch in diameter and came in eight-foot lengths. I cut twenty inches off two poles. The other twelve poles were cut to six-foot lengths. The idea was to tack the first canvas with the poles that were six feet, four inches, and allow the poles to extend four inches beyond the canvas. Then I "offset" the remaining poles on the six canvasses by four inches to the right and tacked them to the canvasses. I had to insert each offset part into the next roll of canvas at its ends (like connectors) so that the canvasses would be snug next to each other and would not have to be pinned together. I then put two big screw eyes into each of the mounted two-by-fours and two large hooks on the top poles and hung them up like drapery panels.

I was now ready to lay out my drawing. Standing atop my fifteen-foot ladder, I started laying out my gridlines twelve inches apart. That took all day. Then the music jobs started coming in, which took me away from the mural. I was running behind schedule. Olatunji wanted a progress report. I told him it seemed I would have to burn some midnight oil. He arranged with the building owner to issue me a key so that I could come in at night to work.

The following night I reached the Center around midnight with the intention of working until sunrise. About two hours in, I heard all this noise downstairs on the street and went over to see if somebody was in trouble! I looked out the window and saw this guy standing at the corner of 125th and Madison Avenue, yelling at the top of his lungs, and throwing cans and garbage into the middle of the intersection. I tried to listen to what it was he was saying, but he was completely incoherent. I figured it was some drunk who was pissed off at the world and taking it out on passing cars.

I went over to my radio, turned my music up to drown him out, and went back to work. Another hour or so later, my friend was still yelling. I went over to the window. Lo and behold, the intersection was full of debris. It was like a war zone out there. Cars were blowing their horns, swerving, and careening into objects in the street! I stood there in sheer disbelief.

Suddenly a patrol car showed up, and the two officers got out and started a conversation with this guy. They talked for a long while. The guy didn't budge; as a matter of fact, he excused himself from the conversation to throw another box in front of an oncoming car. Then he went back to the cops and stood there, looking up and down the street for the next trespasser. I was glued to the window. They were back and forth with the talk. Then the two cops got into their car and drove off. My friend ran over and picked up a big, dirty old box and threw it at the police car!

I went back to work. About an hour or so later, I heard this fool still carrying on. (Was I in the twilight zone?) I went to the window and saw the intersection was almost *impossible* to pass. There was no way a car was going to get through there without hitting or running over something—or rather *some* things! *Why didn't the cops take him away? Later for them, I've got work to do,* I thought. I turned the radio up louder. Coltrane was on, blowing his heart out! Then they put the Monk on. Wow, this place was ALIVE! The noise outside and the music inside were a wild cacophony of sounds, and watching this almost life-sized mural come alive before my eyes was sending me into a spin; the real and the unreal were all moving simultaneously and congruently. I was drunk on the *"audiovisuals"* of the moment.

The dawn was breaking, and the sun was not yet over the horizon. I started to clean up. I looked back at the project and saw that I had gotten a lot done. I would be back later that night.

When I got down to the street, everything was as quiet as a mouse. The only noise I heard was me trying to lock the door. I turned around and saw not one piece of trash in that intersection. Who had cleaned up the street? Then I saw "him" standing there. He was a scrounger. He looked at me and nodded his head. I nodded back.

I turned and headed down 125th Street toward Seventh Avenue. It was then that I noticed the boxes upon boxes of trash tied up in neat bundles and placed along the curb. There must have been ten or fifteen bundles and boxes there. Who had cleaned up the streets? How did this happen? I had heard no street sweepers pass. I also hadn't seen or heard any sanitation men out, and they would not have taken the time to tie everything in *bundles* before throwing it on the truck. The guy was out of his gourd. Nobody else could have done it but him.

At midnight the next day, I was back at the Center. I let myself in and started to work. About an hour later, my friend was back, yelling as loud as he possibly could and throwing boxes into the street. The neat bundles were no longer lining the sidewalk, which meant he was recycling his trash. I had my radio turned up so he could have himself a ball. He carried on all night long, and I worked all night long.

The dawn was now beginning to break on the horizon. The minute I stopped working to clean up, I noticed a calm outside the window. I finished cleaning up and was down the steps and out the door. To my surprise, the streets were as clean as a whistle. I nodded at my friend, and he nodded back. I started down the street and glanced at the trash neatly tied and bundled up along the sidewalk. This time there were more boxes and bundles than the night before. There must have been at least thirty or forty bundles, all neatly tied and placed on the sidewalk.

On my third night at the Center, I was upstairs trying to create something nice, and my man downstairs was trying to create mayhem! It was about half past midnight, and I was hard at work, though *my friend* down on the street was working harder than I was. I had my radio blasting, and he was yelling as loud as he could and throwing trash into the street like a man possessed. I didn't know where the police were. They never returned.

Morning came, and I started cleaning up to go home. Again there was silence in the street. I got downstairs, locked the door, and found the streets were as clean as a whistle! I nodded to my friend, he nodded at me, and I headed home. I glanced at the trash all along the sidewalk. It now took up about half the length of the block, and a block in New York is at least a football field long. That means there were about fifty yards of trash out there. Where would the madness end?

I made it a point to start asking around about this "mystery man" situation. Nobody seemed to know what I was talking about. But people couldn't deny the amount of trash they found in front of their stores in the morning when they opened their shops for business!

I had been going there for a month, and the guy was still yelling and throwing trash at the passing cars. Cars blew their horns as they swerved to avoid flying garbage. This went on all night long, and the bundles of neatly tied trash had now reached Fifth Avenue. From Madison Avenue to Fifth Avenue is at least a hundred yards.

Another month passed, and my mystery friend was still yelling and screaming at the top of his voice and throwing garbage at passing cars. The trash was not only from corner to corner now, but it was six feet tall. I couldn't see over the top of the trash pile. There it sat, all neat and well packaged. I had asked everybody in the area about this guy, but nobody knew anything. New York was the kind of city where nobody seemed to notice anybody. It seemed that as long as you were not running around naked, you could just about go unnoticed, no matter how weird you might look or be.

The situation was beginning to bug me, as I couldn't seem to have a peaceful night. It had been eight weeks now, and this guy had not given me a minute's peace. What had I done to this guy? And how did he know to clean up when I cleaned up so that we could say good-bye to each other? He couldn't see me from the ground level, yet when I hit the street, he was ready to split too! I didn't always leave at the same time. I had been measuring his progress of trash accumulation, and on the nights I was not at the Center, there were no *new* bundles added to the pile. It was bothering the heck out of me! How did he know when I wouldn't be there?

I was in my shop talking to my assistant, Ronald (Okoe) Pyatt, about this madness, and he said, "Taiwo, don't you know who that is?"

"Say what?" I said.

"Taiwo, this man is a neighbor of yours. He used to live three doors from you on One Hundred and Thirty-Second Street," he told me.

"You are kidding," I said.

Pyatt then said to me, "Listen, remember when you were working on Wall Street and you used to leave every morning going to work with your attaché case, the three-button suits with your Italian shoes, and your snap-brim Hamburg hat with the bow in the back?"

"Oh yeah," I replied, "but what has that got to do with anything?"

"Well that guy used to step out of his doorway after you passed and be dressed the same way you were dressed. He would walk well behind you and imitate every move you made. He was even your size."

"F'real?" I said. (Just then I had a flashback. This guy and I were eye to eye. That means we were definitely the same size.) "Hey, man, that's scary to me," I said.

"He wanted to be just like you!" Pyatt said.

"Why me?" I asked.

"Because he did not have the job you had."

424 | Thomas J. DuVall

"What was his job?" I asked.

"He worked for the New York Sanitation Department. He was a garbage collector," Pyatt said. "He wanted to be something better than that. You were his alter ego!"

"Hey, man, those sanitation guys were making more money than I was on Wall Street. I tried to get a job there myself," I said.

"Yeah, but you will never get him to believe that. Man, when you stepped out to go to your job, the whole neighborhood used to watch you walk by."

"F'real?" I said.

"You were as clean as a whistle."

"Wow, I had no idea!" So this guy had flipped out. Considering his energy level, I wondered if I had a maniac on my hands. Maybe he was harmless. I finally understood why everything was so neat and tidy at the end of his tirade. But what was bothering me still was the fact that this dude was a stalker! He knew my every move. How did a guy stay in the shadow of somebody's life like that? I had heard of cases where these kinds of people would all of a sudden step out of the shadows, and if you repelled them, they ended up attacking you out of frustration. Was this an upcoming scenario? Jesus, I hoped not. But Pyatt was saying he had had years of practice, as I had been living in the area for years. And I didn't know this guy from Adam.

Another four weeks went by, and it was the same routine. Then I discovered something interesting; there was never any glass in his trash. I never heard any glass breaking. Now I must tell you, I lived in Harlem for the best part of thirty years and heard glass being broken at any time of the day, any day of the year. And if you spent a day in Harlem, you would know what I mean. But this man did not handle any glass. The trash he threw would never cause a flat tire. So how crazy was my friend? And what had he said to those cops that they allowed him to do this?

The trash was so high now that he couldn't pile it any higher, so he had turned the corner and was now working his way up Fifth Avenue toward 126th Street. This was unprecedented in the annals of Harlem Trash. The trash was taking on a sandbagging look, as if we were in London in World War I.

People could no longer jaywalk. Ahmad Jamal and his wife, Dakota Staton, had a little gift shop that we would frequent directly across from Olatunji's place. We had to walk to the end of the block where he had allowed a footpath for the public to cross the street and then walk back to the shop. Where was he finding all that trash? Surely the neighborhood couldn't be that trashy from day to day. I had seen many a trash pickup on trash day but had never seen such an impressive acquisition. And I did not have a camera.

We were into our ninth week of madness and mayhem at 125th and Madison Avenue in the summer of 1968. The mural was progressing well in spite of the madness going on. I had only three panels to go. I also came up with a brilliant idea.

Since the last two panels had a lot of animals on them, I decided to get my friend, Abdullah Aziz, to paint the animals in his own unassuming, unique style. I figured we could meet in the middle and join the two styles together. Abdullah had his doubts about two Artists with distinctly different styles working on the same canvas, but when he started, he could see how interesting it would be. And it was beautiful.

I was into my eleventh week and was doing the finishing touches. The Center had been watching the development of this project, and the people there could no longer believe their eyes; neither could I. We had painted a village scene that was sixteen feet high and thirty-seven feet long. Everybody was in on the finish. Olatunji had a fiberglass case made so that we could travel with it.

August was winding down, and I found myself scrambling to get something ready for our Annual Harlem Outdoor Art Exhibit, which was to be held on St. Nicholas Avenue and 135th Street. All of a sudden, it hit me that I should put the mural on display there! I made a dash over to see Tunji about it, and he was a little reluctant. I said it would also help advertise the Center.

Tunji said, "How will it stand?"

I said, "I have an idea for a rigging that will allow it to stand on its own."

Olatunji said OK. He did not doubt I could do it. I made it a point not to tell anybody else until I was ready to do it.

I spent the rest of the day with paper and pencil in hand. I had to figure out what I needed. I knew I needed sixteen eight-foot-long four-by-fours, five hundred feet of rope, sixty-eight half-inch steel bolts, sixteen pulleys, a saw, a drill, and a wrench. I also needed a dolly to transport everything. I sat down and drew up a scale model of the structure that would allow a sixteen-foot by thirty-seven-foot mural to stand alone.

Using a scale of one inch to a foot, I laid out my four-by-fours. I rabbeted the four-by-fours on each end to create interlocking sections. I drilled two evenly spaced holes for the half-inch steel bolts that would interlock for the center beam. Then I did the same for the base beams. After the framework was assembled, I placed heavy-duty screw eyes onto the supporting vertical beams and tied a guide line to each vertical support so that the mural could be hoisted into position and tied down to a stake.

The stumper was how to lift and mount each panel into place. There was nothing to lean a ladder against out there, and no trees were near the area. It took me several days before I got an idea. I was pulling up the venetian blinds to open the window, and it hit me: I could use the venetian blind principle. In other words, I could lift the canvas by the two hooks screwed into the one-inch poles that the canvas was mounted on. Yeah, that was it!

Now that the kinks had been worked out on paper, I was more willing to buy the lumber. I made a dolly and was off to the lumberyard.

The guy at the lumberyard wanted to know if I had heard anything that everyone else should know about. I asked him what he meant.

He said to me, "Well, you come in here buying all this lumber and rope and pulleys. I figured you must be building an ARK! So maybe you got a message from God or something we should know about." I cracked up, but he was serious too! That was when I picked up his "Jewish manner." I told him what my intentions were, and he felt better. He even gave me a discount and wished me luck!

The days to follow saw me focused on not making any mistakes in cutting the wood, as I had no more money to pay for mistakes; one mistake, and I was a goner. I went over my scale drawing repeatedly. Believe it or not, I found a few things that could have caused an abortion. I was up late that night finalizing things to the smallest detail.

I woke up that morning, checked my schematics, and started sawing wood. By nightfall everything was ready. I called a meeting of the Gallery Artists and told them what I wanted to do and that I would need the help of about eight guys.

They all looked at each other without speaking. Abdul Rahman was the first to break the silence. "Taiwo, there are no trees in that area, so how are you going to hang it up?" he asked.

"My dear brother, this mural will stand on its own! We won't need any trees," I said. I could see doubt on their faces.

Ademola said, "But that's a public park. Won't you need a permit?"

"I have already acquired a permit from the 135th Street Police Precinct."

"Do they know what your intentions are, Taiwo?"

I pulled out a multimedia badge I had been issued once for a distant job that I had kept just for a time such as this. I also had a yellow jacket to go with the yellow and white pearl badge so that they would think I was a TV network person or something. My plan raised even more eyebrows, but I was confident I could successfully pull it off.

"Just meet me here at nine a.m. Saturday morning to help me move this stuff over to the park," I said.

"OK!" everybody answered, and we closed down and went home.

Saturday morning came, and a lovely morning it was. Everything was just fine and dandy. I got up, cleaned up, and waited for the gang to show up. Nine o'clock came, ten o'clock came, and then eleven o'clock came, and finally I couldn't wait any longer. I started loading up the beams on the dolly placed on the sidewalk. I thought they might show up while I was loading. Once I completed the loading, I was surprised no one had shown up. I paused for a moment to reflect. What had I gotten myself into this time? What if I pushed all this stuff over to 135th and St. Nicholas Avenue and couldn't get it up? I would be the laughing stock of Harlem! All the problems were solved on paper, so had it been impractical to think it would not work in actuality?

"'We shall see,' said the blind man as he stumbled down a blind alley" (an expression that my mother would always say). People were stopping and staring as if to say, *"Where in the world is he going?"* I was pushing a little overloaded dolly from 132nd and Seventh Avenue to 135th and St. Nicholas Avenue, a distance of about five blocks. I finally arrived at the site to see that I was the only one out there. I also noticed something else. There were a few bundles of neatly tied trash tied to the fence the Artists would be hanging their work on. I got a shudder up my spine. Was it the work of my alter ego? How had he *known* I was going to be out there? Only Olatunji and the Weusi Artists knew of my plans. Then, again, maybe it was a coincidence. I tried to put it out of my head.

It was now afternoon, and I was looking around for anybody. I saw a couple of winos sleeping it off. I woke them and promised to pay them if they could give me a hand. They jumped to their feet and pitched right in. They realized what it was they were doing, and I saw a long-needed look of pride on their faces. It was not the money. As a matter of fact, some of them wouldn't take the money. Thanks to a few winos and a couple of junkies, we were in the homestretch before the first Weusi Artist showed up. It was a site to behold. People were pulling over in their cars and tying up traffic to look at what was going on—f'real!

Most of the Artists had made it to the park, but not before two or three o'clock. I said, "The show was supposed to start at noon, not four in the evening!"

"Taiwo, we promise you, tomorrow before noon we shall all be here." That was all right, as long as they got to the park by noon or so. I could see on their faces that they were ashamed of themselves for doubting that I could pull off this project.

The next day came, and to my amazement everybody was present and ready to do their part, including the winos and junkies. And I gave everybody something to do. We all showed up with our kids, and they played around in front of the mural as we erected the structure. It was like a fairground there! Then we got the conga drums out and started to play and dance.

A short time later, a car careened over to the curb, and this Black man jumped out with a pad and pencil in his hand. Yelling at the top of his voice, he said, "Who did this magnificent piece of Art."

So I said, "I did, sir."

He then said that he was a reporter for the *Amsterdam News* and that this would make a nice human-interest article for the newspaper. The whole time he spoke, he was writing.

He asked me how long the mural had taken me. I said, "Ninety days, sometimes working night and day."

He abruptly stopped writing, looked at me, and said, "Ninety days!" He then immediately, in a fit of anger, started tearing up the paper he was writing on and said in a very scornful manner, "There ain't no story in this! You should have said at least *five years*. Good-bye!" He jumped back in the car and sped off down the avenue. Wasn't honesty supposed to be the best policy?

My mind reverted to those nasty-looking bundles of trash I'd seen on the fence. I went over to that spot and saw even more bundles than before. It was *him*! My heart sank a little.

Abdul Rahman approached and asked me, "What am I gonna do about this guy? We can't allow him to put up all that trash around our artwork." I told him I was skeptical about a confrontation with the guy.

Abdul said, "Well, I ain't afraid of this guy!" He pulled down the first box of trash, and all this money and about a dozen loose potatoes started falling out of the box. We were shocked and amazed. What was in the next box? Abdul broke it open and found some old clothes and a toothbrush. All the other bundles were sheer trash that had been tied up in bundles or wrapped in old newspapers. Abdul pulled all of it down and threw it in the cans on the street for the city to take away. We put the two boxes with the money, potatoes, and clothes items on the side of the fence. The money meant he would be returning with more trash, for sure. My immediate concern was that this guy could think it was me who had destroyed his treasures. My other question was how he was getting this trash from 125th and Madison Avenue all the way over to 135th and St. Nicholas Avenue, a distance of fifteen good city blocks!

Our mystery man did come back, but while the city slept, he did not leave more trash on the fence, and I certainly hoped he got his belongings. That was the end of that saga. He was never seen again.

That night we took the mural down, and I returned it to the Center and hung it in the main hall.

Some of the colleges where the mural has been seen are Kent State, Ohio State, Cincinnati, Cleveland, Hampton Halls, University of Michigan, University of Pittsburgh, Morehouse, Tallahassee,

Talladega, University of Orlando, Bowie State, University of Pennsylvania, Rutgers, Boston, North Carolina, and more. The list is long. In the fall of 1973, the Wesleyan University Alumni Association in Middletown, Connecticut, asked us to put on a Weusi Artist Exhibit in their Fine Arts Building. The mural was part of that exhibit. The mural has traveled to many colleges, universities, and theaters across the land as the official backdrop for the Olatunji Drummers and Dancers Company (1968 to 1974).

Taiwo DuVall's cover design for the book he illustrated,
The Adventures of Fathead, Smallhead and Squarehead,
by Sonia Sanchez.

CHAPTER 13

The Big Mistake (Circa 1973 to 1974)

In 1972 I got a job as a Staff Assistant at Third Press in New York City. I was still running the Gallery at night. The Third Press had me working on many artistic projects, one of which was the Sonia Sanchez book, *The Adventures of Fathead, Smallhead and Squarehead*. They eventually laid me off because the workload had significantly decreased.

In order for me to go on the road again with Olatunji, I had to find someone to handle the banking matters. I wanted to leave the financial responsibilities to Abdullah Aziz, but he was unable to handle the affairs at this time, so I had to turn to Mr. Morris (a Harlem Hospital administrator). Morris was looking for a way to be useful in the Gallery. He gleefully said he would do it, which meant I could hit the road and try to bring in some badly needed funds.

A few weeks later, I was back at the Gallery and ready to take my place at the helm. I saw that some of the bills had not yet been paid, so I made out a few withdrawal slips and went to Freedom Bank to pay the bills. The bank lines were long and slow. I finally got up to the cashier, and she said to me right away that I would have to see the Bank President because my name was not on the account that I wished to make a withdrawal from. I went to see the Bank President, and he said to me, "Your name is no longer on this account, Mr. DuVall. This account is in the name of Mr. Ademola Olugebefola as President and Mr. Albert Morris as Vice President. They are the only people allowed to withdraw money from this account."

I had to get Mr. Morris's name off the account. I eventually caught up with him and asked him if he would make an appointment with me and the bank so that I could reinstate myself with the account. Morris shook his head and said, "No, I can't do that!"

"What do you mean?" I said.

"I am now Vice President and I plan to stay Vice President," he said.

I found Ademola and explained to him what had just happened to me. He insisted that he was President now and that neither he nor Morris would have me reinstated to the Gallery account!

I went back to the bank, and the Bank President told me I had made a drastic and fatal mistake. He showed me the application I had filled out to open up the account. Where it said to fill in the name and title of the applicant, I had written, "Thomas J. DuVall, Executive Director."

"Mr. DuVall," he said, "you should have written, 'Thomas DuVall, President.' Sorry, Mr. DuVall, there is nothing we can do to help you. All the money in this account has to be handled by the President, and you listed yourself as the Executive Director."

I was dead in the water. I begged Ademola and Mr. Morris to undo what they had done, but they refused. That night I found myself on my knees on the Gallery floor. I begged for forgiveness from my dear friend Rudy (Baba Kachenga) Irvin for having allowed this hallowed Church/Gallery to slip through my fingers like that. The pain in my chest had me doubled over in agony. I begged God to take me up to His place.

I knew things would not be right anymore. The landlady was after me for the rent for the Gallery space, and I was unable to hand her the rent that was now way overdue. Creditors were calling for the money I owed for supplies that had been ordered. The situation got worse financially, my marriage to Vivian was on the rocks because of it, and we had two children, plus the two children from my former marriage, to support. Her family asked me to leave their premises, so I had no place to sleep. The only place I had to lay my head was on the Gallery floor, where my name was on the lease as an "occupant."

I was lying on the floor one night, and the phone rang. It was my mother. She said, "Son, I know you are sleeping on the floor up there. Why can't you pack up your stuff and bring yourself on down here? At least you will have a bed to sleep on!"

"Who told you I was sleeping on the floor?"

"Never mind who told me. I know," she said. "Plus I could really use your help." Possession was 99 percent of the law, I had been told, so if I left the Gallery, I would lose it. I didn't know how to make myself President, but my name was still on the lease of this Gallery space, which meant I was still responsible for the rent.

"The doctors are giving me six months to live," Mama said.

I said, "OK, Mom, give me a week or so, and I will be there." I started packing as much as I could carry. About two weeks later, I was on my way back to the DC-Maryland area. I felt like I had lost my heart and my soul. But mothers have a way of nursing you back to health.

God bless Mama. Because of her, I am here to tell my story.

Mama and one of her brother's daughters, Jeanne.

CHAPTER 14

The End of My Life as a New York City Artist

In 1974 my twenty-four-year love affair with New York City came to an abrupt end. When I left New York, there was about $2,000 in the Gallery bank account that I could not touch because I had not made myself President. I asked the bank who was withdrawing the money from the account. The bank said that Ademola had made himself President on the account, so he was withdrawing the money. I don't know what he did with the money, but the money never reached the landlady, who never received a dime for the rent.

My heart became heavier with every report I got from friends about the latest moves by the absconders involved. A year went by, and no rent had been paid, so the landlady put a lock on the door.

Not only did the money disappear, but so did the artwork that I had left behind.

I left New York with all of my belongings, took the Greyhound Bus to Washington, DC, and caught a cab to Hyattsville, Maryland. I found my mother alone in the house and bedridden. I asked her where my brother Herbert was, and she said, "Herbert heard you were coming, so he packed up his bags and moved out." I asked her how she was getting her meals. She said she was depending on her friends for support. They ensured that she got her meals and that her bills were paid.

I called Herbert, and he told me about a job opening at Vitro Laboratories for an Artist/Illustrator position. I went there to apply for the job. They hired me as a Technical Illustrator, and I started working almost immediately. The pay was not big bucks, but it was steady work.

After working for a few months, I decided to send for my wife, Vivian, and our two kids. After months of begging and pleading, I persuaded Vivian to bring the children down. I just knew things would get better. Herbert helped me find a place to live across the street from where I was working so that I could walk to work.

Vivian, the children, and I lived for about six months in the Georgian Woods Apartments on Georgia Avenue in Wheaton, Maryland. We had a garden apartment and had a lot of problems with management not following through on repairing flood damage the property sustained on rainy days because of improper sewage drains. We also experienced constant rent increases.

Two gay men moved in over our heads, and every evening after work, they would change into their high-heeled shoes and dance and stomp around the apartment. The noise interrupted our TV frequencies, so we could not even enjoy our evenings at home. They also had a shortwave ham radio that would actually knock out our TV to the point where we could not even turn it on or off! I finally went up to speak to them and begged them not to carry on like that. They just looked at me like I was crazy, and the noise continued.

I knew that the rules of the establishment were that the tenants had to lay carpeting in their place to prevent the overhead noises of their feet from disturbing the tenants under them. Shortwave radios were a breach of contract, and violators risked being evicted. The management ignored my complaints.

When I could not take it any longer, I went back up there and banged on the door so hard they thought I was the police. They came to the door, and I told them if I had to come up there one more time I was going to "kick their asses black and blue." And I dared them to try me! I then turned and walked away. Things were quieter after that.

I had to run out to the store one day, and on the way back home, I had to go through the intersection of Georgia Avenue and University Boulevard in Wheaton, Maryland, where I saw all of these people lying in the street in the rain. There were at least nine people lying there on the ground, and from what I could see (traveling at twenty-five miles an hour), they were Black people. Other people were just standing around. I knew I had just passed through a movie set shooting a scene for some TV show, so I kept going.

When I got home a few minutes later, I turned on the news and saw that some White guy had been standing on that corner with an Army 45-calibre pistol. He had been shooting Black people in the head as they passed through the intersection! A White policeman arrived on the scene and had to shoot the man point-blank in the head because he would not lay down his gun. The Blacks deemed him a hero and a fine cop. I yelled out to Vivian that I had come very close to being shot to death. She said, "Good thing you are light-skinned. He probably thought you were White!"

Shortly after that we had to move from the Georgian Woods Apartments to Mama's house, because the rent was forever going up and up every few months. It was just about then when Vivian hit me with her plan to take the children and live in Atlanta. She said she no longer wanted to be in Maryland. I had $400 in the bank, and she said she'd take it. I said, "If you want to leave and take the money, then so be it." Mama said I would be a fool if I let her have it!

I then found out something that upset my mother and disgusted me. Mama told me that Vivian had not allowed my children to see her—their own grandmother. My mother was still bedridden upstairs, so she never got to see the kids. I hadn't known about it because I was at work during the day. I was dumbfounded. A few days later, I came home from work and asked Mama where Vivian and the children were. She said, "Son, they're gone." I never got a chance to say good-bye to my children.

I was flat broke again, and Mama was upset with me. I told Mama, "My children will know what happened here one day."

Mama did not die in six months as the doctors had predicted; she survived for another two and a half years. Mama's condition worsened, and I had her admitted to Prince George's County Hospital. I begged Mama one more time to please tell me who my real father was. She would not respond. She died that night, taking the secret of my father's identity to her grave.

She had lived long enough to completely diminish my hopes of returning to New York and trying to regain some of my losses. My career in Harlem had been completely dashed, as had my hopes for discovering my father's identity.

I had made the mistake of taking my name off the deed of the house when I was traveling as a Musician so that Mama and my ex-wife, Rosita, could sell the house and divide the money between them. As luck would have it, Mama died before the house could be sold. Since my name was no longer on the deed of the house, Rosita decided to have me evicted from the house three days after Mama died so she could rent the house out and create some revenue for her bank account. She did this before I could even get Mama's body to a funeral home. I had to get a lawyer to rescind Rosita's eviction notice. The lawyer said that I had a right to be in the house because her claim was not binding, so I stayed there as long as I could pay the note.

As fate would have it, I was waiting for $6,000 from my mother's Government insurance to pay the bills because I had been made the Executor of her estate. My stepfather, Steve, had fled to Boston to live out his life as an alcoholic. He took with him the $6,000 worth of insurance money the Government said I was not entitled to because Steve had married Mama and the Government did not recognize a son as a recipient if the husband was still alive, alcoholic or not. I was left with no money to pay the bills Mama had incurred before she died. The only thing the Government paid for was Mama's funeral. I did not have the money, because most of my paycheck was going to my children, who had been taken to Georgia to live with Vivian's sister.

Luckily I still had the job at Vitro Laboratories. It wasn't a high-paying job, but the money was steady. I was able to stay afloat, but there was no money for movies or dining out.

CHAPTER 15

Li, Chung, and Hsai

About a year after my mother died, a man named Don Hsia became my supervisor at work. He had less training and seniority than I had. Don was a good friend of mine. He was the third Oriental in my life whom I respected. The three who left an impression on me were Li, Chung, and Hsia.

The first, Jim Li, was a good friend I had while in New York City. We were in Art school together. He was from China and was extremely polite and courteous. He was different from the second, my friend Chung, the Paratrooper, who was a bit more assertive. Li would never have volunteered a suggestion or an opinion, as Chung had. (Do you remember the movie theater incident in the North Carolina train station?) Li was more laid back. He would allow me to lead into something and then would chime in. Li was well educated and held several degrees and a Ph.D. He was in Art school to learn drawing so that he could illustrate his research in medicine.

He and I ran into his parents one day down in Chinatown. His parents started talking to him, and their English was terrible; it was really a mess. Then Li started talking to them in the same broken English, complete with mispronunciations, verb disagreements, dangling participles, and so on. I was amazed.

After his parents said good-bye to us and had turned the corner, I turned to Li, smiled, and said, "You are a man of degrees, and I just listened to you 'kill' the king's English. I did not find that to be American! Americans don't speak to their parents in broken English!"

He said to me, "I know, but out of love and respect for my parents, I talk to them in the same manner in which they talk to me. That way they feel smart too! It is our tradition."

"Wow, that's beautiful! Yeah, we could definitely use a little of that around here!" I said.

As I mentioned earlier, the third was Don Hsia, who had come on board at Vitro Laboratories a few years after me and was an unassuming kind of guy with a low gaze. Even though I had seniority on the job, they made him my supervisor. He approached me one day and said he was apologizing for what they had done. He had told the powers that be that I was the one with the seniority and the know-how, but the powers that be said they could not undo what they had done. Nonetheless, whenever I entered the room, he would immediately rise from his chair and offer me his seat! I told him I appreciated what he was doing but that he need not do it.

He answered, "I was taught to respect my peers, and I could not and would not turn my back on my home training." He demanded I take his seat until I had to leave. The White supervisors and co-workers were furious at this exchange of seats, but it did not deter Hsia from doing what he was trained to do. I had great respect for this little big man from China.

After the Whites would leave the room, he would say to me, "Tom, you need to go to CHINA to live. If you go to China, they will make you a PRIEST! There you won't have to live like this. Over there we have great respect for our Artists and our Elders! Promise me you will go see for yourself!"

I smiled and said, "OK, I promise!" (God bless these Chinamen!)

Thomas and Bunnie on their first date at an art exhibit in
Alexandria, Virginia.

CHAPTER 16

Long Live My Eighty-Second Airborne Buddies and My Wife, Hortense DuVall

After Mama died, I found it easier to sue Vitro for racial prejudice, and that's when things really got peculiar for me. I did win the case, but I lost the War. Most of the Blacks on the job would not give me the time of day after the case was won.

Shortly after that I met a young lady on the job, Hortense E. Dines ("Bunnie"), who was as sweet as she could be and was well liked. She told me about her son, Eric, from a previous marriage, and how she was looking for a place to live with him. She wanted to move from her mother's house, so she asked me if I knew where a room was for rent.

I told her that she could have one of the rooms in my mother's house and that I would not charge her rent. She could then save her money for a down payment on her own place. However, I didn't know how long I myself would be in the house, which was in litigation because I had removed my name from the deed of the house. My stepdaughter, Maria, and her husband, James Pitt, moved back into the house. They decided that they weren't going to pay Rosita rent because they wanted to use their money to get their own place.

I did not have the money to cover my expenses, so I missed a house payment. Three days later, Rosita served me with an eviction notice, and the lawyer said he could no longer help me. I told Bunnie that the other shoe had finally dropped. Rosita would not change her mind. She said she wanted me out of my mother's house! Bunnie pleaded with her on the telephone to change her mind, but Rosita was adamant and wanted me out of there. I then advised Bunnie to find a decent place as soon as possible for herself and her son.

Bunnie then asked me what I was going to do. I said, "I don't know. I was going to go to the Veterans Administration to get a room in the Old Soldier's Home." I went to the Old Soldier's Home, and they told me there was a long waiting list.

"I don't know what I'm going to do yet," I told Bunnie, "but don't worry about me."

Bunnie said that she would not desert me. We drove around for days looking for a place to live and finally found ourselves in southern Maryland. Bunnie said, "There's a sign that says 'New Homes.'"

I said, "We don't have enough money for an old home, so how are we going to get a new home?"

"Let's just go look at them."

As we drove up to the only home that had not been sold on Jennifer Court—a model home centered in the middle of the cul-de-sac—we saw three men standing outside. The White fellow was talking to two Black fellows about his experiences as a Paratrooper. I overheard the conversation and asked him what outfit he had been a Paratrooper in. "The Eighty-Second," he said.

"I was in the Eighty-Second too," I said.

"What outfit in the Eighty-Second?"

"The Five Hundred and Fifth, Third Battalion," I said.

He knew once I gave that information that I had been in *the* all-Black Paratrooper outfit, the Triple Nickel. "Oh, man, you guys caught hell up there! I feel so bad about that. What brings you here?" he asked.

I said, "Well, we are homeless and need a house to live in."

"Hell, you can have this house. I can at least do that for you."

"I don't have any money," I said.

He said, "Don't worry. After all the hell you guys went through in the Eighty-Second, you can have this house, and I can make the arrangements."

"We don't have any money," I said again.

"You don't need any money. You deserve this house, so don't worry about the money. Are you all married?"

We said no, so he said, "If you're going to move in, I want you all to be married, OK?"

I was hesitant, but Bunnie said, "Sure, that would work out fine."

I said, "Do we have to be married just to get a house?"

"Yes," he replied.

This novice builder, Mr. Slaysman, a rich young man whose father was bankrolling his construction business, had built the three houses on the cul-de-sac. He said if we got married and made a down payment on the house, he'd pay the closing costs. Bunnie and I loved each other, so we got married, paid the down payment, and stayed in a local hotel (across the street from Andrews Air Force Base) for three months until the house was ready for us to move in. Although our nerves were often frayed in that hotel room, we were not paying to stay there, thanks to Mr. Slaysman's generosity. And we were close enough to where the house was being built to check on its progress regularly, so we persevered. We soon had a place that we could call home, despite all that had happened to deprive me of a way to get on with my life.

Moving into that *new* house marked the end of my New York City era and the beginning of my new life and my wife's self-discovery. Now that's another story…

Thomas, Daddy, and Herbert.

Uplifting, joyous "Slammin'" Acrylics and Oil Mural.
© Taiwo DuVall

This mural was part of the Artcurian art exhibit,
"Artists Speaking for the Spirits."

(Photo by Christopher Wilson)

31710280R00260

Made in the USA
Lexington, KY
22 April 2014